Sketches from a Quaker's Moscow Journal

Patricia Cockrell

Published by New Generation Publishing in 2021

Copyright © Patricia Cockrell 2021

Drawings by Michael Munday – http://michaelmunday.art

First Edition

The author asserts the moral right under the Copyright, Designs and Patents Act 1988 to be identified as the author of this work.

All Rights reserved. No part of this publication may be reproduced, stored in a retrieval system or transmitted, in any form or by any means without the prior consent of the author, nor be otherwise circulated in any form of binding or cover other than that which it is published and without a similar condition being imposed on the subsequent purchaser.

ISBN   978-1-80031-028-5

www.newgeneration-publishing.com

New Generation Publishing

This book is dedicated to my family and to all the fellow travellers who shared this path and those who supported us, especially my many Russian friends who taught me so much and enriched my life.

Contents

INTRODUCTION 1
THE BACKGROUND 5
THE JOURNAL 9
1992/3 21
1994 35
1995 57
1996 91
A HOLIDAY WITH THREE TANYAS 93
1997 101
1998 131
1999 163
2000 191
2001 217
2002 231
2003 251
2005 THE WAR REQUIEM 265
AND FINALLY - THE NIZHNY NOVGOROD
HOSPICE 271

INTRODUCTION

Born a long time ago in Australia, educated mainly in England but also in France, Germany and Russia, Patricia married a fellow student, both having graduated in Russian with German. They spent a post-grad year in Moscow, then taught Russian in Exeter, Roger at the University, and Patricia at two schools, for more than 25 years, with time out to have two children and to go to Canada for an exchange year with a professor of Russian at Toronto University.

For 20 years, Patricia wrote letters to presidents and prime ministers trying to launch a school exchange programme with the Soviet Union. Eventually, with *perestroika*, the time was right: Mrs Thatcher and Mr Gorbachev responded, and in 1988 she was invited by the British government to organise the first official school exchange with the Soviet Union.

After her mother died in a hospice in Tiverton, Devon in 1991, Patricia wrote to John Major asking for money to set up a hospice in our twin city in Russia. Charity Know How was looking for a project in Russia: grants were available, visits and trainings were arranged, and an abandoned isolation hospital near Yaroslavl was converted into a small hospice - the third hospice in Russia.

NOTES

A word about Quakers
Members of the Religious Society of Friends are known as Quakers or Friends (with capital F). A clerk will normally be appointed for a term of three years in a leadership role, and local groups of Friends may have a meeting house, but Quaker meetings can take place anywhere. Friends Centres

or Friends Houses (without apostrophe) would normally be the hub of Quaker work in that country, usually including offices for meetings, administration, networking and project management.

Abbreviations

CO – conscientious objection to military service
FHM – Friends House Moscow
IIHA – International Integrated Health Association
QPS – Quaker Peace and Service, my employer for the first year in Moscow
VZHT – Victor Zorza Hospice Trust

Transliteration

I have used a relaxed version of the Library of Congress system avoiding where possible double vowels at the end of words and leaving names like *Tolstoy* in the version that we know, even though this is not strictly correct. The soft sign has not always been indicated.

Names and photographs

I have given full names only where it seems safe to do so. People who might not wish to be identified have first names only or initials; a few names have been changed. I have avoided using photographs of vulnerable people or those who might prefer not to be known as being part of this work.

Currencies

The exchange rate of the ruble fluctuated widely from 4,900 (8 April 1995) to 6, and sudden currency reforms caused havoc. Prices in Russia were often quoted in USD, and dollars were legal tender for a while; euros were also recognised, though Russians preferred dollars; nobody used GBP. In Ukraine rubles gave way temporarily to kupony and then to hryvni, also known as grivny.

Computers

Few people in Russia had computers in the mid-90s and even fewer had mobile phones.

The Journal includes some articles previously published in *Quaker Monthly* and *The Friend* plus some newsletters sent to friends and supporters.

The lovely line drawings are by our neighbour, Michael Munday.

THE BACKGROUND

1. Students and Teachers

Our first married home was a tiny (about 3m x 2.5) room on the 11th floor of Zone V at Moscow State University. Roger and I shared a pod with Victor who, bless his boots, never complained that a cuckoo had moved in - of course I was not meant to be there. Victor's room was the same size, and we shared a loo and shower. Everyone on our floor could use the communal kitchen, and there was a stolovaia - a basic canteen - in the basement, where students could help themselves to the free bread and mustard, and many did. We occasionally had a bowl of soup there with smetana, but Roger could not face the meatballs or the grey frankfurters. We enjoyed the postgraduate student life, the friendships and winter sports. The Lenin Hills were a natural ski slope, basketball courts became ice rinks in the winter, and it was possible to borrow skates, skis and other equipment from the university sports store.

When I was offered a job with Progress Publishers, we acquired a bright spacious room in a shared flat above a row of useful shops on Lomonosovsky Bulvar, two minutes from Universitetskaia metro station. We had access to libraries and a rich cultural life with student rates for all tickets. As foreign students, we had to keep within the limit of 40 km from Moscow, but still, we managed to get as far south as Kiev at lilac blossom time, and as far north as Pskov for the white nights in June.

Roger's studies led to his doctorate and my salary bought occasional luxuries like travel tickets, or a bottle of wine; it also paid for our own phone, though this was probably bugged. Thus it was that I knew Moscow well when a school exchange at last became possible in the age of glasnost, and we were partnered with School 31.

At the schools where I taught Russian there were exchange programmes with France, Germany and Spain, and even the classicists went off to Greece, but it was not possible to take my sixth formers to Russia. I wrote letters for 20 years and was frequently invited to lunch at the Foreign Office to share my vision and air my frustration, and then in 1987 a Mr Slavin rang me from the Soviet Embassy to ask: 'How can we help?'

TV cameras took an interest in this first official school exchange, as did the Times Educational Supplement. The secretary of state for education, Kenneth Baker, visited our school in Moscow and complicated things no end by offending the Russian headmistress and staff with his reading of *The Charge of the Light Brigade* while sitting on a table swinging his legs. I had to apologise for this behaviour and for his choice of poem; worse - he had told them money would be found for their expenses. Money? What money? I checked with the British Embassy: yes, he had said that, but there was none to be found in Moscow. I rang the Foreign Office: 'Where is the money Kenneth Baker offered to School 31?' 'Oh, there's no actual money he just wanted to encourage them.'

2. Twinnings and a Kruzhok

As students in London in the 60s, Roger and I were members of the GB-USSR Association and of the Society for Cultural Relations; we also belonged to the old Pushkin Club run by Mrs Gurevich, as she called herself. As professionals, after our year in Moscow, Roger joined the British Association of Slavonic and East European Studies, and I joined the Association of Teachers of Russian and was inspired by a presentation at an ATR conference to start a Kruzhok (a little circle) in Exeter - something along the lines of the old Pushkin Club.

There was a lot of interest in the Kruzhok which usually met at our house. We were always pleased to have Russian visitors including Dmitry Alexeevich, the pianist, and Sasha Gorodnitsky, who sang to us. They came via the Soviet Embassy, the British Council or the Union of Soviet Writers, which was linked with David Cornwell (John le Carré), who would occasionally ring us and ask if we would like XX, eg Chingiz Aitmatov. A large Kruzhok gathered to meet him, including my students who had read a novel of his for A-level.

Another Kruzhok centred on Sergei Pavlovich Zalygin, the editor of Novy Mir, who had personally taken the bold decision to publish Solzhenitsyn's *One Day in the Life of Ivan Denisovich*. He stayed with us when he came to Exeter for Russian Week.

Sergei Pavlovich was of course very enthusiastic about glasnost, and I believe it was he who inspired us to strengthen our efforts to forge links with Russia and to build an exchange programme for our school and university students.

A report in Pravda about British interest in Russia mentioned Exeter, and Roger and I, together with a few people from other parts of the UK, were invited to the Soviet Embassy to say some words about promoting Russian culture. This was just before the policy of glasnost was adopted and twinning with Russia became a real possibility.

For several months, a group of four or five people had met, often in our house, to write letters to different institutions in the Soviet Union. Several letters went unanswered, but Roger did get replies from Krasnodar and Yaroslavl. We all looked at a map and chose Yaroslavl, partly because it is not too far from Moscow, but also because Yaroslavl seemed to fit with Exeter, and the letter was very friendly and welcoming.

Nikolai Pavlovich Voronin, director of the Yaroslavl Technical Institute, was invited to Exeter to meet with the Russian Department and the Kruzhok. He recommended contacting Tatiana Kasatkina, and when we met her in due course, it became clear that she was the right person to take this forward. Tatiana was devoted to the exchange of university students; she was also in favour of a school exchange and a city twinning link and she became a loyal member of the Exeter-Yaroslavl Twinning Association.

In the 30 years or so of its existence, EYTA has organised many visits and exchanges including groups of teachers, architects, medical personnel and long-distance runners. In 2005, to commemorate the 60th anniversary of the end of World War II, Roger and colleagues organised a huge project whereby Britten's War Requiem was performed in the twin cities of Exeter, Yaroslavl and Hanau with German, British and Russian orchestras and singers, and a Russian soprano, British tenor and German baritone, as intended by Britten.

THE JOURNAL

SCHOOL EXCHANGES

1. Moscow, 1988

In answer to her question, I told the girl at the Aeroflot office in Moscow that we were neither Intourist nor Sputnik, that we had come at the invitation of School 31, and that no guide had been allotted to us. 'Very strange.'

Strange it was. My colleague and I, part VIP tourists, part schoolmarms, together with our troop of icebreakers in the school exchange programme, were hard to pigeonhole. Thus it was that I had to turn up in person to confirm our return flights, something no tourist has to do, and in response to my VIP status they gave me my very own bus.

The driver was fascinated by my Baedeker map of Moscow. Russian maps are deliberately misleading, he told me with violent whole-body laughter. It was done to confuse the Americans, ha ha ha. 'And it must be difficult for you when they change the names of the streets,' I volunteered. More volcanic laughter. 'When a pensioner dies, they daren't label the coffin! Even our past is unpredictable!' Hoots and guffaws caused his

From top – Lenin, PC, headmistress

eyes to shut, but the bus seemed to know where it was going.

We had the best of things and the worst of things. We were meant to be placed in families, but this had not been understood, as it had never been done before. The hotel was awful beyond belief, but they gave us caviar and steak; we were constantly harassed and dragooned into the loathsome bus, but we were given the most expensive tickets for the ballet and circus; we wanted to go to school and wander around GUM or Red Square in our spare time, but we were handed a killer programme which offered free time for two hours on the day after we were due to leave.

Tourists are easy in communist times: they need feeding times, viewing times and a bus with a guide, and Bob's your uncle. In no time they lose the will to make decisions: they cling to their only reality - the frantic programme and the bus. The plan was to bus us back to the hotel for lunch every day, a 45-minute journey each way. On day two at lunchtime, I saw in the eyes of my students the unmistakable signs of group fatigue. In a paralysis of indecision, nobody ate anything. I cancelled all hotel lunches and established that we could make a sandwich from the overabundance of food offered at breakfast. The Russians were horrified, but we now had two hours of absolutely free time every day, and I hoped that hunger would stimulate their vocal chords. I was disappointed that my A-level Russian set was speaking so little Russian. One of the girls asked me for some water. 'I haven't got any.' 'Well, you could ask the waitress.' 'So could you, and remember if a sympathetic native understands...' They knew the criteria for marks at GCSE. They looked doubtfully at the waitress and wondered whether to use the accusative, but lo! within a couple of minutes, a jug of water appeared. Full marks. On day three, I approached the 4th floor dezhurnaia:

'Please allow me to present my sleeping beauties.' 'Beautiful they are.' 'Yes, but **sleeping** is the operative word. They missed breakfast yesterday, almost missed the bus this morning and tomorrow we're going to school for the first time.' Speaking no English, she turned to them: 'At what time should I wake you?' 'Er, how do you say half, well quarter would do. Oh, let's say 7: sem.' 'Khorosho, 7am. Which room?' 'Er, chetverg. Oh no, that's Thursday.' Giggle, giggle, collapse of head girl. 'Chetyresta (400).'

The school was wonderful. This was what we had come for. The spark of life was rekindled as they sang, joined in lessons and played volleyball. As they chatted and giggled in the school canteen, they made arrangements to meet their Russian friends, and the telephone and metro became vital elements of life instead of GCSE exercises or tourist exhibits. Drinks machines quenched thirst, once the instructions were deciphered; shashliks, ice creams and directions all had to be asked for, as I had the only map and lunch was off.

A farewell concert was organised with a good deal of singing and drama. Our rendition of the Mechanicals in Twelfth Night (with Mrs C starring as the Wall, as Stefan put it) was greeted with whoops and cheers, as was the King's Breakfast enacted in Russian.

The Moscow visit was a marvellous experience. Russian lessons are peppered with 'wasn't it funny…' and 'do you remember…', and there is still a glow on their faces, but I will not be satisfied until the Russians have made a return visit.

More than 70 schools have now applied for an exchange with the USSR. We feel privileged to have been able to break the ice.

2. Exeter 1989

After our visit to the USSR, the headmistress and a teacher of English brought 13 pupils of Moscow School 31 to the Maynard School and Exeter School for two weeks in April 1989.

This return visit left us reeling with exhaustion but at the same time charmed. The Russians were constantly perplexed. They were bowled over not only by our houses and gardens, our shops and streets, thatched roofs, cream teas and beaches, but more fundamentally by the very concept of exchange.

They arrived in the last week of our Easter holiday and were distributed among the families, some of whom had come to Heathrow to meet them.

'What is the programme for tomorrow?' 'There isn't one.' 'But what time do we meet tomorrow?' 'We don't meet tomorrow.' How can there be life without a programme?

Halfway through the week, I arranged a trip to London for all hosts and guests – a fun outing, time for a catch-up and for the staff to check up on the young Russians, besides no guest wants to go back to the USSR without seeing Big Ben, Downing

Street and Buckingham Palace. We were not scheduled to meet again as a group until school started at 8.45 on Monday morning.

It seemed to me the three-day respite was an occasion for rejoicing rather than fretting, but no - how would the teachers know what the young people were getting up to?

'Why do we need to know what they're doing? Any problems and they will ring me. No news is good news.' I explained that we have done exchanges with France for 25 years or so and have never lost a child, and that all these families have had at least one foreign exchange teenager living with them already. We ourselves have had five, one way or another, but the anxiety continued, so I suggested ringing each family and speaking to them all.

The young Russians had a wonderful time that week. Many had been walking on Dartmoor, some had been sailing or swimming, some had been to a football match or a disco or a party, but I wondered why they hadn't all come to the barn dance which had been specially arranged for them and for all young foreign visitors and their hosts in the local church hall. Later we discovered that the whole group had been summoned to the state committee at the Ministry of Education before their visit and told to adhere to strict rules of behaviour and not to go out in the evenings unless accompanied by an adult. They were supposed to ring the headmistress to ask her permission for all outings, and they had been told not to tell us about this. Most of the youngsters, mindful of the new buzz words of perestroika, *initiative* and *energy*, quickly adapted to the new circumstances, but these stultifying decrees did create problems for a few of them and for the families who were baffled.

The eight girls and five boys were excellent ambassadors for their country. We shall not quickly forget Ksiusha who delighted us with her dancing, or Lianna, daughter of a Bolshoi opera singer, who sang and danced a captivating Ukrainian love song, or Sonya whose knowledge of English history was staggering and who recited a Shakespeare sonnet with aplomb, or Tanya who was quite the funniest Clara in Pygmalion that I have ever seen. They all won the hearts of many an Exonian with their positive attitude and their sense of enjoyment.

Три Сестры — А.П.Чехова

3.   Chekhov's Three Sisters Twice

   i)   December 1989, London

The Redgraves are playing the *Three Sisters*. That should be good. I filled the minibus in Exeter and drove to London.

This was the worst production of Chekhov I have ever seen anywhere in any language. Irina and Masha were dressed as they must be in white and black, but who was the frump in the pinny, and why was she so attached to her peasant headscarf? Can this be Olga, for heaven's sake, the mainstay of the family, noble, honest, calm?

Even worse was Lynn Redgrave as Masha with masses of orange hair (borrowed from the panto down the road?) and bright red lipstick. Masha, who wears black 'in mourning for her life', looked like a Toulouse Lautrec tart - we expected her at any moment to lift her ample skirts and kick a wild leg. When she came to say goodbye to Vershinin, gleefully whooping and wearing her silly black hat, she looked like the Wicked Witch of the East. Why I wondered has nobody poured a bucket of water over her?

There was no sense of frustrated ambition and no pain at parting from a beloved. Vershinin's departure was a relief all round: a man whose arms are windmills, a man who, having said goodbye forever, forgets to pick up his suitcase which remains absurdly on stage, even as Olga closes the play: 'If only we knew why we live, why we suffer.... If only we knew.'

I had told my A-level Russianists to look out for the non-communication and the pauses - easily overlooked when reading the play. We had talked about the Moscow Art Theatre and Stanislavsky's ideas on the natural school of acting, and we had looked at Chekhov's own attitude towards drama: 'People just eat their dinner, and all the time their happiness is being made or destroyed.' There were no pauses, and the dinner eaters at the Queen's Theatre were all stupidly frozen in mid-bite when Andrei, out of earshot and out of their sight, proposed to Natasha. Yes, this is a pivotal moment in the play, but the sisters at the dining table are unaware. That is the point.

But it was not a total waste of time. It was certainly memorable, and I enjoyed hearing my students talking to the others about Chekhov – mood, character, isolation. And we all managed to do some Christmas shopping.

ii)   February 1990,
       Moscow

Tuesday: School 31 told us they have booked tickets for us for the Bolshoi Ballet, and the Puppet Show, but would we like theatre tickets? If the *Three Sisters* happened to be on, that would be brilliant – it is one of this year's A-level set books.

Thursday: 'Here are your tickets for the *Three Sisters*.' 'Gosh!' Everyone now says 'gosh' at School 31. 'But it is not on at MXAT (Moscow Art Theatre), where I have seen it before, it's at the Contemporary Theatre.' Well, double gosh! The Contemporary believes in aggressive innovation; their productions are the more prized the higher they register on the odd scale.

Yes, it started oddly: the sisters walked on stage and climbed to the top of a rainbow in a wind tunnel. They stood for a moment in the gale while the audience clapped. What were they applauding, the scenery? There wasn't any - just plain white walls and a couple of chairs. The agility of the actresses? Well yes, as rainbows go, this was a touch steep. Perhaps it was the fact that in the present dire circumstances, we had all seen fit to come together on a snowy evening to celebrate something unquantifiable.

'It's brilliant, Mrs C,' that's Zoe shouting at me from the right wing, this being a theatre without aisles. She is not wrong. Six, I'd say, on the odd scale, and brilliant: here is the mystery, the pain and joy, the failure to connect with others, the rage, the impossible or impermanent relationships; here is the heavy sorrow of having to keep going through disappointment; here are the characters who are not quite at home at the centre of their being. 'Life has been strangling us,' says Irina, 'like weeds in a garden.' They wonder whether tis nobler to compromise or fight, then find that they have no energy. Chekhov would surely have loved it.

4. 1991 School Visit, Yaroslavl

Because of financial and other problems, including the shortage of food in Moscow, School 31 cancelled the exchange this year after the headmistress had confirmed the visit and I had arranged our travel and bought the tickets. We were not hugely surprised in view of East Europe's turbulent upheavals, but we were disappointed. The Russianists in the group decided they would go to Russia anyway, the parents agreed to pay for board and lodging, and as this could not be called an exchange, we would call it a trip. I rang my friend Galina Alexandrovna – could she make arrangements for my students to stay in Yaroslavl at Easter? Yes, she could, of course. We were linked with School No.4, and accommodation for all was found in families. We went to Yaroslavl, Exeter's twin city, for a week and we had two days in Moscow.

5. 1992 School Visit plus Musings in a Bania in Yaroslavl

Has anybody ever pommelled and pinched your back, or told you off for using no cosmetics, or invited you to lighten your soul while you eat salt fish? No? Then perhaps you have not sampled a Russian bath house - running water everywhere except in the loos, a strong emphasis on health and exercise, and only one employee under 15 stone. The angry young man who punished my back was thin as a rake and monosyllabic, even monoverbal. 'Da,' he agreed, mercifully, when I said I could take no more, but the psychotherapist made up for it.

'Listen to my voice, release all negative feelings, listen to my voice. You will feel at peace, at one with nature, with the scudding clouds.' Oh dear, another fish bone stuck between my teeth. 'Suck,' hissed my neighbour, 'swallow bones, else.' Oh, I see that is the technique. I was a bit nervous on behalf of my incisors, I mean you could kill someone with this fish - hard as an anvil and wickedly pointed at the far end. 'Listen to my voice, you now feel lighter, your problems are dissolving.' Yes, but I am dying of thirst, having sweated in the sauna, exerted myself with the weights, clamped my lips while in the pool, and now this salt fish. I would love a cup of tea, but will probably have to make do with champagne, this being a celebration hen-party for teachers.

What are we celebrating? Well, the usual thing – survival, togetherness, the ability to laugh and to shut out reality even if only for a couple of hours. Teachers and most professional people have not been paid this month. Pensions have gone up again, but there is a notice in the post office saying that pensions will not be paid because the post office has no money. The psychotherapist left us with our eyes shut, visualising the scudding clouds.

Someone switched on the radio. Funny to hear my own voice on the radio while the pedicurist wielded the varnish. She called her colleagues to witness this: she was holding the foot of a woman who was speaking on the radio! None of us was able to hear what was being said, but once the excitement was over, they asked what it was about.

There had been a celebratory dinner in Yaroslavl: several of the people there have stayed in my house in Exeter, or at least supped at my table. During the dinner, I told my friend Viacheslav, deputy director of the Theatre School (he had given a wonderful lesson on the Queen of Spades to my A-level class in Exeter, acting all the parts), that I wanted to help establish a hospice in Yaroslavl and planned to bring a bunch of school leavers to work in Yaroslavl in July 1993. He introduced me to Sergei, the chairman of the local radio, who was sitting opposite and listening to the conversation. So, I spoke about this on the radio and had many offers of work and accommodation for next summer.

I had written to John Major asking for government money to help set up a hospice in our twin city and had been given a grant to pay for the chief medical officer and two people from the Red Cross to come to look at healthcare in Devon, especially the hospices. If a hospice is what they want, can they help with the groundwork – form a team, identify a suitable building...? They rang me a few days after getting home: they had found the ideal place to establish the third hospice in the former Soviet Union. It is a typically Russian longhouse in Kurba, near Yaroslavl. Built of tree trunks a hundred years ago and in urgent need of repair, it was closed and abandoned some decades ago.

I took my GCSE class to Yaroslavl for half-term and went to meet the local doctor and his colleagues in Kurba to discuss possibilities, to make sure that our support would be welcome, to establish lines of communication, estimate costings, agree on desired outcomes: in a word, to establish a strategy. With the collapse of communist central control, local people have already started to make the building weatherproof, but there is no money for equipment or beds or a water heater or anything. The garden is full of birch trees and dandelions; there is a church in front and a field behind. We went to see the priest – yes, he is very much in favour of renovation and of end of life care. He would encourage his parishioners to volunteer.

'Open your eyes, feel at one with the eternal and enjoy the sense of peace!' The psychotherapist was back. He smiled, thanked us for our attention, took off his white coat and retrieved his shopping bag from the bottom of the fridge.

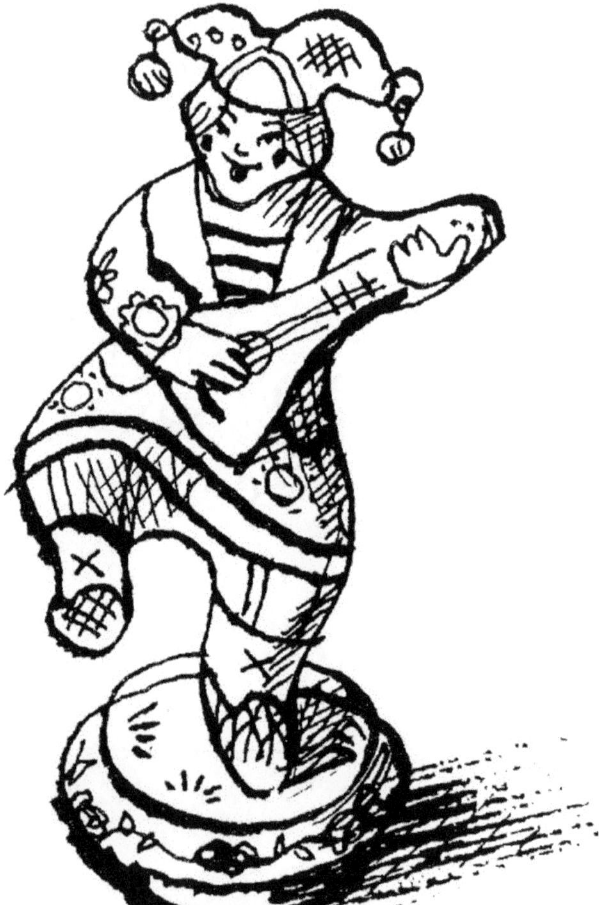

1992/3

Moscow - Yaroslavl

Oh glory, now the tortoise is having a fit - 25 years old and snuffs it when I am in charge! I pursed my lips ready for the kiss of life, but she stopped spluttering and wiped her nose on her sleeves. All gone now. I will buy another cucumber tomorrow, no matter how many hundreds of rubles it costs.

I am sharing a quiet evening with Shusha on the balcony of a Moscow tower block right opposite the Soviet army building, now Russian, I suppose. I don't know about Shusha, but I deserve this calm communion with the setting sun: I saw off the school party at the airport yesterday and have been extremely efficient today. I have seen a lot of people and have managed not to overeat by telling each host that I have already eaten. But this is only one day set against the many when it is impossible to get anything done or to refuse to eat the vast cakes, pancakes and bowls of deliciousness. Such irony - food is so expensive and in such short supply, and yet for a guest there is almost always jam today, never mind tomorrow, and in a country where so much urgently needs to be done, two hours can be taken for lunch and simple things like buying a train ticket can take all morning.

With my GCSE students, I left Yaroslavl yesterday, a beautiful, ancient city on the Volga bursting with hospitality. What a send-off we had! About 40 people gathered with tears, flowers and kisses to wish us farewell on our journey to Moscow.

Exactly a week before that, armed with a fresh rose from the garden, half a man in his own suitcase, some of my students and a colleague, I had set off from Exeter. The rose, the students and the colleague were no trouble at all, but Arthur (arf a man) caused me to be exactly twice over the weight limit. 'What's in there?' 'Not what, who - it's Arthur man, a resusci-dummy, a present from the Exeter Red Cross to the Yaroslavl Red Cross for training purposes. They haven't got one.' He grinned amiably from the x-ray monitor, and they let him through without charging for excess baggage.

Victor Zorza had established two hospices in Russia, this would be the third. When there is nothing more a hospital can do for a patient, s/he is sent home, and the families have to cope as best they can with very little help and no painkillers. Many hospitals have no painkillers either, some have no anaesthetics and some lack the needles and thread with which to sew people up after an operation.

With the help of the Russian Red Cross, we have now identified a suitable building which could be renovated, but there is no chance of local government funding until it can be registered as a health or care facility. Now there's a challenge!

After my appeal on Yaroslavl radio for jobs and accommodation for a group of school leavers next summer, a 95-year-old man took my hand and gazed at me for some moments in silence. 'I'm so glad you're not the enemy.' Well, so am I.

Kurba - Exeter

'So, what are you going to do?' At school, I had told the girls who had come with me to see the potential hospice near Yaroslavl that Dr Valeri had been refused permission by the local authority to renovate the abandoned hospital.

'We are going to go ahead,' I said. I had recently inherited some money from my mother but wasn't sure it would be enough for this task.

'Well, we want to help you.'

Valeri had rung to tell me the result of his application, but I could hear the fight in his voice - his vision would not allow him to accept this decision.

'Let's do it anyway!' I suggested.

'Da, DA. When can you come again?'

'Not until the summer holidays. But can you come to England? I will send an invitation and find money for your fare. It will be a research grant.' England?! He had never been anywhere.

First one school adopted the hospice as a concern and then another, then the local newspaper ran an article, then I got a note from the Cathedral: they want to give us a day's donations. Could I invite the Russian doctor to attend a service at Exeter Cathedral?

He spoke no word of English but recognised his name when it was mentioned from the pulpit: 'And today's collection will be for the hospice near Yaroslavl, our twin city, and we are honoured today to have Dr Valeri among us.' He stood up and bowed.

A small, quiet, modest man of steely determination, he won the hearts of Exonians. Local hospices opened their doors to him, as did the hospital, and he met some of the teachers when he came to a couple of Russian classes. At the end of two days, the whole city was keen to help. How to focus?

Ian Wright, a colleague at Exeter School, suggested a stall at the school's summer fair with placards and pictures, plus a list of needs and a blank sheet for offers of help. At the end of the day, we realised we would need storage space for all the things that were offered including a wooden greenhouse, equipment to set up a dental surgery, a couple of wheelchairs, walking frames, grab sticks, surgical gloves, soap, nurses' uniforms, sheets etc, plus several gallons of paint, which would be delivered from Derby (in the middle of the night, as it turned out). The local quilters offered to make a quilt for each bed, and several people wondered what else they could do to help. Can we come to Yaroslavl? I closed the list at 37 because Russian buses can take 40, but what about the luggage?

I checked with the Russians that what had been offered would be useful and wrote to Lord King, chairman of British Airways: can we bring extra luggage to help establish a hospice in our twin city in Russia?

The phone rang: 'This is Hazardous Cargoes. Has your greenhouse been treated? What kind of paint? What about the acrylic paint you plan to bring for the murals?' A former student, now an artist, had offered to paint some colourful murals at the Yaroslavl School for Children with Little Sight. I rang Miffy in Brighton. Yes, her paint dissolves in water. I gave Hazardous Cargoes the answers to his questions and told him that we planned to bring a few pebbles plus a handful of sand and seashells from the beach to bring a tiny bit of Exmouth for the children. 'Oh,' he said, 'my aunt lived in Exmouth.'

We were given an unlimited luggage allowance and told not to go to check-in but to meet in the basement at Heathrow. So, if we have unlimited luggage, we might as well take more. We contacted local hospitals, chemists, DIY stores and care homes, and the shed at Exeter School filled with boxes.

Now for everything else – visas, tickets, accommodation. My friends, especially my Russian alter-ego, Galina Alexandrovna, set to work straightaway and found families willing to take 37 people for nearly a week; Yaroslavl City put a bus at our disposal, including the trips from and to Sheremetevo airport; they also organised a reception.

'This is my group,' I said to the border guard, who expressed not a flicker of interest. 'We have 35 trolleys. Do you want to know what we have brought?' I had a schedule of what was in each labelled box, and imagined they would open a couple, just to check; they might even make a fuss about some of the donated medications. 'Niet,' he said, practically falling over with boredom.

They had made excellent progress in Kurba: gone were the cobwebs and rotten floorboards; the windows had been replaced, and a shiny new roof meant that what we had brought would be safe and dry. The bus had parked miles away as it was unable to cope with the enormous potholes. Thank heaven for strong volunteers! A band of school-leavers struggled, argued, and eventually built the greenhouse ('Where does this bit go, Mrs C?' 'I haven't a clue.'); others dug the part of the garden which will be used for vegetables, and yes, we had brought seeds, donated by Suttons; another group went to the school to help Miffy with the brilliant murals – she had researched Russian motifs, including the inside of St Basil's Cathedral – and when they finished, they set about cleaning and painting the windows before organising a party for the children. Yes, we had brought balloons and chocolate biscuits. I had some meetings with the health authority to talk about training and publications, there was a good deal of sightseeing and visiting, and links were made with dentists, teachers and nurses.

I was invited back for the opening of the Kurba hospice, but I was afraid too much emphasis would be placed on the intervention from Exeter. I did go later to see it in operation and was appalled to see that they were washing the sheets in the bath, the same bath they were using for the patients. I contacted the British Embassy – have they got any funds? Well, they might have, but first I need to get three quotes, sign a contract with the embassy, buy a washing machine from a recognised outlet in Moscow and transport it to Yaroslavl. This is absurd. I only need about £350. The hospice could buy one locally and get it delivered. 'Can you imagine a hospice without a washing machine?' Eventually they relented, as long as I stuck a Union Jack on it somewhere. I wasn't entirely sure this was a joke.

Valeri had invited the local authority to the opening – the very same people who had refused permission to reclaim the abandoned hospital. They made celebratory speeches in front of the TV cameras, and even agreed at last to mend the road!

Charity Know How wanted to highlight our project at their first conference in London. Would my Russian doctor be willing to come, all expenses paid, and what is his English like? Not a word of English, but I could interpret for him. 'No, you'll be much too busy. It is not about him, it is about the whole process, the partnership: you will both be speaking and answering questions. Can you find an English-speaking senior medical person who knows what you are doing? And can you prepare some info for a noticeboard?'

Yes, the chief oncologist for Yaroslavl Region had taken an interest in our work. He had spoken English to some of the people on the Exeter – Kurba working party. I rang him. Yes, he would come a day or two early so that we could prepare some materials for display. It so happened that he arrived at Heathrow on the same day that I got back from Quaker work in war zones in Yugoslavia, but that is another story. Luckily, Roger was able to meet us, and I slept in the car all the way back to Exeter.

After 25 years, it became clear that I would have to give up my job teaching Russian at two schools and occasionally at Exeter University. I decided to retrain, to make use of the opportunities offered by the new, more open Russia, and to see what door might open next.

Some Research for Keston

<u>Saturday, 24 July</u>: I saw my group of 36 people off at Sheremetevo airport, and then took the trolleybus to the metro for an hour's ride to Tsvetnoi Bulvar, found the Keston flat, not without difficulty, and discovered that I was knee deep in faxes with the answerphone blinking, so I sat on the balcony in the evening sun with a Martini.

I had been asked to do some work for Keston College, the Oxford-based Institute which had been set up for the study of religion in communist countries. The phone rang: please could I rescue a Dutch boy who had turned up in Moscow with nowhere to stay and not a word of Russian? I met him at the Irish shop, and my friend Sergei took him in.

There were eight telephone messages, of which only one required immediate action: I rang Marcus Wheeler at the Daily Telegraph. No reply.

I rang people for whom I had home numbers. D. is away until August; Misha will ring, so will A.; Laurence will come at midday tomorrow; Anita's number was switched to fax, Monika and Karl Heinz asked me to ring on Monday; Zhenia was very eager to talk about all sorts of things. He really needs a portable photocopier, and by the way, did I know today is the last day one can spend notes printed before 1993. The currency reform was announced yesterday afternoon and banks closed immediately. Millions have come to Moscow to try to spend some money. Kiosks are no longer accepting the old currency, and every state shop has a queue of at least 400 cross people. They are buying anything available - 1000 cigarettes, 20 pots of jam, anything. Chaos! I only managed to buy a large jar of golf balls submerged in murky water, which turned out to be bottled peaches.

I arranged meetings or at least conversations with another five people. There is a whiff in the air of something near panic. A synagogue has been stoned and daubed with swastikas. Nobody knows whether Yeltsin has signed the amendment to the Freedom of Conscience Law. Still no reply from Katia. Fr Georgy arranged to meet me at 6pm.

Laurence duly arrived at noon. We had lunch at the flat. The Mennonites are fairly confident that the new amendment, even if it ever does become law, will take some time to implement; they also feel that their work might well fit the parameters of social usefulness.

Nika phoned to invite me to the Christian Resource Centre to meet Sharon and to pick up some material. Laurence and I set off for the CRC in Lomonosovsky Bulvar, which is where I lived in 1965 when I worked for Progress Publishers. The office is spacious and busy. Sharon gave me a lot of reading material and introduced me to Yakov who serves as a lay reader with Fr Gleb Yakunin. Even here nobody knows if the law has been signed.

I went to see Karl Heinz and Monica. Korean Association groups now exist in ten regions of the former Soviet Union and there are five groups in Moscow of 50 to 80 people. They registered with the Ministry of Justice in Moscow last May. The Unification Church is also registered in Armenia, Georgia and Moldova. Members of the church are active in prisons, and orphanages. There is no loud advertising.

Well, that's a relief! There is a good deal of loud proselytising nowadays, especially on the metro steps - mainly American evangelists, but also Ukrainians promising to save the world, a wandering sage who gathers large crowds with a megaphone, and a reincarnation of the Virgin Mary.

I walked up Rozhdestvensky Bulvar to meet Fr Georgy at his church and to collect his autobiography. I waited until

7pm then went home and ate the bottled peaches. What a storm that night, truly Tolstoyan!

<u>Wednesday, 28 July</u>: Slava will ring today at 5pm and will come at 7 to take me to the Muslim Cultural Centre. Fr Georgy rang – he is really sorry about yesterday. He will be at the red house this evening and will wait for me to come after visiting the Muslim Centre.

I had lunch at the flat with Misha R, who then took me to meet Fr Ambrosia, an Old Believer, a modest, quiet man who, contrary to appearances, enjoys a good laugh. He became quite animated discussing the article he had written and looks forward to a time when Old Believers can meet openly in their own church.

Nobody rang at 5pm but at 6 I heard a tap at the door. Yes, Slava would have a cup of coffee and another. Undernourished, nervous, egocentric, he resisted my efforts to feed him, but said he would try the Martini. He did ask my permission to smoke, but when I demurred, he claimed that the presence of an ashtray on the top shelf proved that it was OK to smoke in the flat.

He is interested in making and distributing religious programmes for TV and/or radio: he has a friend but lacks funding; he also wants to open a bank which would function without bribery, and he wants to write his autobiography (he is about 25 years old). 'Are we going to the Muslim Cultural Centre?' I asked. Slava will ring tomorrow. 'Then I'll go and meet Fr Georgy.' Slava came too and suggested going via Natalia. She lives nearby and she may have some cigarettes. Natalia did have some cigarettes, but she was suffering from dental trauma and was trying to meet a deadline. I have a feeling I am reliving a Dostoevsky story involving randomness, unreliability, pain and things not quite hitting the mark.

Fr Georgy was in the red house by the church, and we were invited to join his confirmation class. Slava went home, but I threaded myself through the overcrowded room, hoping perhaps for new insights. I was disappointed as the last hour was devoted to checking that the pupils had done their homework. One after another the neophytes were called upon to recite, with much hesitation and prompting, the Lord's Prayer or the Beatitudes. No doubt the first two hours had been more edifying.

At last, we were released from this tension and from the room where we had been sitting ducks for the mosquitoes. I thought Fr Georgy would hand me his autobiography but no: the 30-yard trip from the red house to the church took about 20 minutes, as so many people were waiting to ambush him with questions. I was told to wait in the church, and Victor would bring the autobiography when he had finished writing it! I waited. Victor felt a bit guilty that I would have to go home by myself in the dark at 10.30. He offered to walk with me to Tsvetnoi Bulvard, though there is not much petty crime in this area as the church's neighbours are the KGB and the mafia. The church, which was returned to the parish 18 months ago, was used as a hostel for the KGB, who destroyed the 16th and 17th century cemetery to build an ugly square building.

I rang Katia and we pencilled in a meeting at 3pm next Wednesday. Rumour has it that Yeltsin has nullified the currency reforms. It is difficult now to trade: the 100 ruble note is the smallest legal tender but prices in the shops are still quoted as they were, for example a wooden bear for my grandchild was marked at 427 rubles, but the only change I was given from a 500 ruble note was a jeton for the metro. Shopping in the market is a lot easier: everything you pick up is 200 rubles, except bananas, and if you quibble, they give you a garlic.

<u>Thursday, 29 July:</u> No, the currency reforms have not been nullified but modified: notes can be used as long as they carry no portrait of Lenin. Heavens!

Only people with passports now have the right to change money, result - misery. Those without passports, for example soldiers, are begging the old women to change their money for them, but the absence of trust gives rise to many a noisy dispute, and in any case not enough new money has been printed. Everyone is looking for someone to blame. Yeltsin is the obvious target.

I met my friends, Vera and Alexei, architects who had come to Exeter on an exchange visit, at Yaroslavski station the following morning. I had bought a water heater for the Yaroslavl Hospice. Valeri brought it in his car to the station, and Vera and Alexei will accompany it on the train to Yaroslavl, where the hospice team will meet it. I called in at the British Embassy, then had a coffee with Marina, with whom the Dutch boy is now staying, and then went to see my friend Megan, a former student at Exeter University. Her friend Viktor, a Ukrainian citizen of Russian nationality, is unable to change money: he has the wrong passport.

Larry Uzzell has left a message on the answerphone. I rang him and arranged to meet tomorrow morning. I rang Rabbi Goldschmidt and left a message.

Saturday, 31 July: Philip rang - can I find Fr Alexander and check his English re a possible invitation to a conference in April in Strasbourg. I rang the number: someone will meet me at Polianka metro in 20 minutes. But I had arranged to meet Larry. 'Come now or not at all. What are you wearing? Glasses?'

The mild acolyte who met me at the station led me on a brisk and puzzling walk, dipping and diving through hedges and under fences to the large white church on Bolshaia Ordynka. He wordlessly indicated that the shadowy figure hovering inside was Fr Alexander, then bowing and walking backwards, he successfully negotiated some tricky ground including a step, a plank of wood and a puddle, looking for all the world as if he were practising for Gilbert and Sullivan.

Fr Alexander, a mild, insubstantial man with a beard to match, seems physically pained by the damage done to his church, but rightly proud of the restoration work. His English is hesitant but yes, he would consider the conference as long as the dates don't conflict with Easter. He is not against the new law: something must be done - all sorts of people are making wild claims. 'Well,' I suggested, 'you could start banning people again, which could be dangerous, because where does it stop, or you could invite me and another 10 foreigners to appear on TV and predict the end of the world night after night in order to foster scepticism.' 'Do you have these people in England?' 'Yes, but they don't flourish.'

Zhenia rang: he'll be an hour late. I waited on the balcony. He is seriously anxious about his car. Mercifully, he has not been able to prepare everything he wanted to give me. He would be interested in organising trips for small groups of tourists, and this could offset some of his expenses. The papers marked with double* have already been sent to Munich, but Zhenia wants Keston to have them too. The information can be used but the source should not be named.

There must be something he can do for me. Well, I have been unable to find Rabbi Goldschmidt. Why not let someone else write the article? Zhenia knows the rector of the Jewish University, for instance. And I am having difficulty making contact with the Muslim Cultural Centre. Zhenia rang Slava to tell him off for being unreliable, but Slava was not at home.

Sunday, 1 August: I wanted to locate Fr A. We had always spoken Russian, but I have a feeling he spoke English to my students at School 31. I thought he might be a better bet for the conference and I wanted to ask his opinion about the new law. I thought someone at his church would give me his phone number, but the church is in very poor shape, and I was told it is not possible to contact him by phone. I got absolutely soaked on my way to the Quaker meeting.

Monday: Misha R will bring the article on Old Believers at 10am, and would Keston like an article on the spiritual problems of the Ingush people? Slava rang: he will arrange something with Muslims. I rang Fr M., another English-speaking Russian Orthodox priest, and spoke to his mother. 'He's in England, or is it France?'

I rang Slava who gave me a number for Shapi K. and told me to expect an important fax; he would ring me immediately after sending the fax. I waited for him to ring, then rang him and was left listening to his hobnail boot dance tune on the phone, while a woman went to find him. He had gone out. I rang Shapi and discovered he was in Syria. Slava rang about an hour later, almost apologised, said he had been ill, sent another fax and offered to find a different senior Muslim for me. He said he would ring again, and can his friend contact me when he comes to England? Will I show him London?

Tuesday: I had breakfast with Megan and went to a BEARR Trust lunch with Evelyn Dobson from the British Embassy. We went to see some mutual Russian friends, then I went home to my farewell tea party. I was given champagne, but would not be able to carry it, so we drank it while consuming Earl Grey tea, waffles and chocolate cake. I rang Larry: can I come and do some photocopying?

Wednesday: Arkady, such a mild and modest person, brought a vast number of photographs, but seeing the look on my face, he quickly calmed me by saying that he would give me only three or four per category. He would accept any terms but of course he has no money. This is a real professional, not a man interested in self-promotion or dollars. Of course, he had no photograph of himself or autobiography, so I took one with what he called my 'soap dish' and jotted a few notes by way of biography.

I had lunch with Andrei Kostin, who was once second secretary at the Soviet Embassy in London and is now a high finance banker. I got to know him when I sent him an article about my school exchange, and he came to see us in Exeter. I had an unconfirmed appointment with Katia at the library at 3pm, but repeated phone calls failed to get any reply. Alexander Sh. came with an article about Muslims and a couple of photographs.

By appointment, I went to see the clinic run by the Seventh Day Adventists: clean, cool people were functioning pleasantly and efficiently inside a pleasant clean, cool building, which was protected by high railings and set back from the road among trees. Patients pay what they can afford for high quality dental treatment. The clinic is largely financed from America. In Russia, Adventists have had two large football stadium rallies, at which many hundreds of people have 'declared themselves for the Lord'. They regularly proselytise on TV and run training programmes.

I faxed my report to Keston, tidied the flat and left for the airport, having given the keys to Liudmila, who helped to carry my extra luggage to the metro station. The frontier guard had never seen a two-visa woman before.

1994

INTRODUCTION TO FRIENDS HOUSE

The Quaker office in Moscow was closed on Stalin's orders in 1931. Almost exactly 60 years later under Gorbachev's policies of perestroika and glasnost, it became possible to think of restarting Quaker work in Russia, and Peter and Roswitha Jarman were appointed to set up an office, not that Quakers had been completely absent in the meantime: there had been deputations, work camps, conferences, visits.

For Quaker involvement in Russia before 1931, see especially Richenda Scott's *Quakers in Russia; Sleigh Ride to Russia* by Griselda Fox Mason; *Constructive Spirit: Quakers in Revolutionary Russia* by David McFadden and Claire Gorfinkel, and Sergei Nikitin's soon to be published *Friends and Comrades*.

Towards the end of 1993 Peter and Roswitha were coming to the end of their contract, and I was appointed to represent Quakers in Moscow, together with Chris Hunter, and to work with others to establish a Friends House in Moscow.

It was a time of hope for the growth of civil society, openness to new ideas and a recognition of the need to seek truth and accept change. There was a thirst for ideas and new publications, for workshops of every kind: authority was being questioned, the old order was giving way to new, and not everyone was pleased. For us it was a fertile time for networking and encouraging the newly emerging non-government organisations - NGOs. Who knew for how long the window of opportunity would be open?

It was -30 when I arrived at Sheremetevo on Thursday, February 10th, 1994 and it took two hours to find my luggage. Valeri had organised a room for me on a sort of B&B basis for as long as I needed it, but I was keen to find a flat. I rang a few numbers, but they were mostly engaged, unobtainable or out of date. Eventually, against local advice, I contacted an agent who offered me a pleasant one-room flat plus kitchen and bathroom, two minutes from Kutuzovskaia metro station. Stalin was fond of Kutuzovski Prospekt, a hugely busy non-stop main road with five or six lanes of traffic both ways, but my two windows looked out onto the pleasant communal garden at the back.

The first few days were given up to a useful handover from Peter and Roswitha. There were lists of names, organisations and contact numbers, plus visits and introductions, cups of tea and lunch with people they had worked with or supported, and then Peter and Roswitha left Russia after a warm send-off.

I stayed at their flat which was still available for another week or so, but, with two rooms plus a small study, it was too big and expensive for me to take on, and my flat was not yet ready, partly because my landlord wanted to be paid in advance in dollars (apparently this was legal at the time).

Most Moscovites sleep on a sofa which has a drawer or box underneath to stow the bedding during the day, so I was grateful for the bed, especially as I became progressively more ill. Resolving not to trudge to the metro through the freezing snow, I cancelled meetings and appointments for a few days. I thought it was flu to be treated with drinks, rest and paracetamol, and yet the increasing and eventually unbearable pain at the side of my left lung made me nervous.

On the night of February 23, Armed Forces Day, I was woken by loud explosions and flashing lights. In a panic of pain and alarm, I wondered if war had been declared but no, these are serious fireworks. There was also the smell of smoke, or was I imagining it? No, the smoke was coming under the door. I rang the British Embassy thinking they would rescue me: 'I'm quite seriously ill and the house is on fire'. 'Would you like to make an appointment with the doctor, 9.30am? 'Yes, thank you, if I'm still alive.' I rang Chris, who said he would come if he could start the van.

Meanwhile I put on boots, hats, scarves, gloves and coats with passport, purse and keys in the pockets, ran a thin scarf under the tap and wound it round my head, covering mouth and nose, and set off down the stairs through the smoke. On the fourth floor I walked past a couple of firemen who were trying to dress a seriously drunk and completely naked man. Yes, they confirmed, he had set fire to his flat. I asked if anyone had been hurt. A fireman had been overcome with smoke, but he is OK. 'Slava Bogu (thank God),' I mumbled. 'Slava Bogu,' said the fireman.

Outside in the snow with my neighbours, I found it hard to stand up and was seriously tempted to sneak into the waiting ambulance and let someone look after me, but where might they take me? How would I let anyone know? No, better to wait for Chris.

The fireman shrugged when I asked if it was safe to go back in the building, so I decided to try to get warm and started the long, slow climb up to the seventh floor, which, mercifully, is not so far in Russia because the first floor is on the ground. It took over 15 minutes to reach the flat, resting after every third or fourth step.

Chris came and made a cup of tea. We got to the embassy in time for my appointment and were told to go straight to the hospital – here is the address. 'It's pneumonia and pleurisy and possibly a collapsed lung. I will ring them to tell them you are coming.'

Chris managed to find the hospital, but they refused to open the gate. He got out and locked horns with the men on duty, and there was a good deal of shouting and arm-waving. It looked like a scene from Laurel and Hardy, but it was too painful to laugh. I wondered if I could walk to the front door, but eventually, still shouting and grumbling, the men gave in and opened the gate. It seems they thought we had brought the post!

I walked in and collapsed. The Russian doctors saved my life with their four-hourly injections, their twice-daily blood tests, their x-rays, massage, and physio. My Russian friends started their usual hunt for needles and antibiotics, but this being the Kremlin hospital, there was no shortage of equipment or medication. The embassy doctor said he was glad I had pulled through! The hospital doctor gave me a severe word about overexertion: did I understand how ill I had been, with only hours left, low oxygen levels and 'awfully awful blood'? Until I could walk the length of the corridor unaided, about 20 metres, I could not go home.

Home? Ah, there's a word. Has Chris managed to pay my Kutuzovski landlord? Yes, and he has the keys. He also has the phone number which is important because it is not usually written on the phone and there are no phone books.

The Moscow Quakers set up a rota to look after me: someone came every morning to prepare kasha with honey or jam, and someone came every evening with food to cook a meal. I had no energy at all for a couple of weeks, so I became a good listener for whoever turned up. Valeri brought my suitcase from the B&B, so I was at last reunited with my clothes.

I had a lot of visitors. They brought lemons, oblepikhovy sok (sea buckthorn juice) which apparently has wonderful restorative properties, as does propolis, a sort of bee glue; they also brought a cassette player and cassettes, some reading material and wonder of wonders - daffodils!

Roger wanted me to go home, but I knew I would not be able to manage the airport as it was not possible to keep upright for long, so he came to Moscow, and we did little trips out into the communal garden.

When I felt strong enough, I rang the Yaroslavl hospice doctors: 'Can I come and be ill with you?' Dr Sasha is married to Dr Natasha and between them they took me on as a project with the full Russian treatment: calf's foot jelly, vitaminny salat with pickled beetroot, plus rest combined with timed exercises including walks, longer each day, along the Volga.

At last, by mid-April, and thanks to all these people who played their part, I was able to look the world in the eye again.

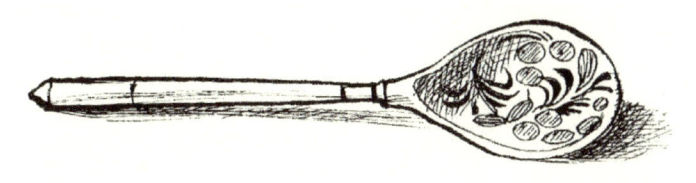

Back from my rehabilitation in Yaroslavl and feeling stronger each day, I was ready to reboot. What assets do I have? My one-room flat with garden views and evening sun (and not too many stairs) is quite central and spacious, very near a metro station and not far from some useful shops, so I normally have food to share; my connections with the outside world are good - my computer and phone/fax work well, though the server is not always reliable; most important of all, I have good friends, meaningful work and realisable plans. Chekhov's *Three Sisters*, who never did reach Moscow, would be green with envy.

It was not hard to get to know the people from the local Quaker group. Different people would come and see me almost every day for nearly three weeks, often bringing provisions, sometimes standing on chairs to clean the lampshades or the windows, and sometimes using my computer to prepare their registration documents. Networking with other groups working on human rights and peacebuilding issues was not difficult either, as they were glad to be able to meet at my flat. A piece of work that can be done while sitting down is organising the visas and accommodation for the meeting of the interim board of the proposed Quaker Centre, and a problem to engage with is that QPS is able to fund this work for one year only. One year will not be enough. Where to find funding? Can the internet help?

I heard from home that an Exeter University student is now working at the EU office in Moscow. I rang her and went to see her. Christine was very helpful. She told me about the European TACIS democracy programme grants and gave me an application form. TACIS was set up to 'prosper the development of harmonious and prosperous links between the EU and the New Independent States', ie Russia and the Republics. Chris and I consulted with local NGOs and filled in the form. QPS in London was not willing to sign the application, but Quaekerhilfe in Germany agreed to sign.

A short walk through a day's log

An email from Lutz[1]: it seems the TACIS application is incomplete. Rang Christine at the European Union office. She is mystified. Will ring Brussels and ring me back.

Tried to fax Hans[2] a distillation of a vision session, which was held at my flat with Chris, Galina, Misha and Tatiana, re views from Moscow on the proposed Friends Centre. I wanted to share it with him, but he answered the phone. Oh dear, it must have woken him up. (Memo - Hans's fax is not an office fax.) Hans says the telex has not arrived for his visa[3]. Does this mean other people have not received theirs either? Will check. May have to send personal invitations. He gave me Hans Ulrich's [4] fax number in Berlin.

Will ring Vladimir Sokolenko, our contact at the Ministry of Internal Affairs, and ask him to authorise more invitations. As a registered foreign journalist, I have the right to invite people to Russia, but I have already been told off for inviting too many.[5]

Inessa rang - can the psychologist peace educators come on Thursday, all six of them at 1pm? (Have I got enough chairs? Maybe I could borrow one from a neighbour?)[6]

Tried to get into email. Cut off several times. Messages from Peter and Walter.

Phone call from Brita - do we want to take part in a gathering of smaller churches? New amendments are being proposed to the 1991 Freedom of Conscience Law which will in effect seek to limit the freedoms of all small churches and worship groups, ie those with fewer than 38,000 members. We have three members plus about 20 regular attenders.[7]

Failed to reach Vladimir by phone. Typed out and faxed personal invitations for everyone coming here for the meeting of the interim board of the proposed Friends Centre. Sent email to Julie in San Francisco offering to fax invitation. Has she got a fax number?[8]

Phone call from France: fax? What fax? Ah, she wants to send me a fax. Vous voulez m'envoyer un fax? Un moment, je err… (how do you say switch on? Would that I had paid more attention at school). She got cut off.

No sign of a fax, though the telephone made one or two weird noises. Christine called from the European Union office: they want an original, ie not faxed, signature from Lutz. Oh dear. Phone Lutz, no reply. Hope we don't miss the deadline with this application for funding.[9]

Tried unsuccessfully to phone Brussels to ask about 1) our TACIS application and 2) the document which the chairman of the Committee of Soldiers' Mothers showed me. The European Union had sent a delegation to investigate conditions in the Russian army and had found these to be appalling. Is that the end of the matter?

A fax came from France – it is Misha's invitation to France Yearly Meeting in August.[10]

Fr M [11] rang - he would like me to translate a letter from German into Russian. Could I come and see him tomorrow?

Sent a message to Alan [12] at QPS about 1) the small churches meeting and 2) the vision of Moscow Friends and Russian board members of the Friends Centre in Moscow.

Irina rang to thank me for the AVP workshop and to make sure she is on the list for the next level.[13]

Went to the bank to change travellers' cheques so that I will be able to pay rent.[14] The bank is closed between 1 and 2pm. Went to Kuznetski Most to find the shop recommended by Fedia where I could buy a map of the

Pamir Mountains for a former student. Most shops are closed between 2 and 3pm; the map shop and many book shops are closed for good. They have given way to trendy gear shops. Back to the bank. Long queues. Must be home by 4 - Masha is coming for a chat before the English group meets.

Six people plus Misha's timid cat, Dinka [15], came for two hours of English and tea and cake. By request, we did obligation words, ought, should, must etc, we then looked for these words in the Quaker list of Advices and Queries and considered why they are not there. It was suggested that we translate A&Q into Russian.[16]

Gave Misha his invitation to France. By 8pm, they had all gone. Sat still for a bit. Had a boiled egg [17], watched TV news.

Svetlana G. rang to invite me to lunch.[18]

Notes:
1. Lutz Caspers signed the application on behalf of Quaekerhilfe.
2. Hans Weening of the Friends World Committee for Consultation, Europe and Middle East Section, was a member of the interim board of the proposed Moscow Friends Centre.
3. Most foreigners coming to Russia need a visa. Before they can apply for these in their own countries, they need a letter of invitation from an authorised person/organisation.
4. Hals Ulrich Tschirner from German Yearly Meeting was a member of the interim board.
5. Vladimir Sokolenko was notoriously hard to find. All invitations had to be authorised by him.

6. This was an important meeting to plan a conference for people interested in peace education.
7. A policy was being developed to make life difficult for small churches and worship groups. I had been invited to join with others to ask for a meeting with the Religious Affairs Committee at the Duma.
8. Julie Harlow of Pacific Yearly Meeting, another interim board member. Apart from those already mentioned, two were expected from Britain, one from Norway and two more from America.
9. Lutz posted a signed back page to Brussels. Our application was successful. It funded the work for another year.
10. Russian Quakers were quite often invited to European or other YMs in an effort to integrate them with the family of Friends.
11. Fr M was a good friend to Quakers in Moscow, but he did not wish this to be known.
12. Alan Pleydell was my line manager at QPS in London. He was also a member of the interim board.
13. Alternatives to Violence Project, a programme devised by Quakers for use in prisons and in the community. Participants start at a basic level; they can then do an advanced workshop, and some will opt for the training for facilitators.
14. This is largely a cash economy. Quakers in foreign parts are paid roughly the same as local professional people: if they cannot afford to buy kiwi fruit, neither can I. As an A-level subject teacher and sixth form tutor, I had a good salary in England. In accepting this appointment, I lost a zero from the unit column, but it was not a problem.
15. Dinka was supposed to help me with uninvited guests: mice had set up home inside my sofa and they were having too much noisy fun at night. Unfortunately, Dinka was afraid of the mice and had to be taken home. A visitor from England brought me

a Quaker mousetrap, so I was able to rehouse the family.
16. We started the following week to translate Advices and Queries into Russian and we published A&Q in Russian – *The Little Red Book* - towards the end of the following year. It took 18 months. *Live adventurously* is one of our advices, and included in the queries is: *Do you keep yourself informed about the effects your style of living is having on the global economy and environment?*
17. A boiled egg was a treat. Eggs were not to be found in the shops, though food was at last more plentiful. People sold all sorts of things on the metro steps including, occasionally, eggs. It was thrilling to find a bag of eggs for sale, though there was no way of knowing how old they were. On the way home you would look forward to cooking your first egg for weeks – boiled, poached, fried? But the first egg was always scrambled because at least one would be broken on the way home.
18. Svetlana Gannushkina became a good friend. Where does she find the courage to battle with the police, the government and with public attitudes while trying to ensure at least minimum support for the many thousands of refugees? Later, when FHM opened, we agreed to let her students use the premises to run a Saturday school for the Chechen refugee children who were being denied access to schools in Moscow.

There is such dislocation in this society as values are turned upside down. While the new rich drive to expensive restaurants in imported cars with darkened windows, beggars, street children and packs of abandoned dogs bear witness to the stresses of poverty. Huge advertisements are appearing in the metro encouraging us to be anxious about hair loss and whiter than white teeth, while at the same time the Moscow health authority has run out of money: only the wealthy can have operations.

Efforts to register the Moscow Friends Meeting (MFM) have not so far met with success. The registration officer took exception to certain parts of the nine-page document including the word 'clerk'. She then went away on holiday and has now moved to a new job. Following advice from a different quarter, I have prepared a shorter version. Let's see if this works! Once registered, the MFM will be able to rent premises, issue invitations, and provide a legal basis for the Friends Centre. Moscow is without doubt a challenging place to be at this time, and I thank heaven every morning for the chance to be here.

NONVIOLENCE – A CONFERENCE FOR TEACHERS

'The bus leaves the Institute of Philosophy at midday.' 'What's the name of the road?' 'I don't know but if you face the Pushkin Museum it's on the left.' We waited an hour for Z. and then left for Zvenigorod without her.

Meanwhile Z. had arrived on the first bus. We all stood about in an untidy heap. Two women were sitting at the registration desk, but we were unable to register because we first had to fill in our names at another desk which was unmanned. Eventually rooms were allotted as were numbered tables in the dining room. We were also put in groups for the group sessions.

R. gave his introductory talk at 5pm followed by a lecture on the ethics of nonviolence. He wanted to introduce the leaders but three were missing: they were probably busy solving logistical problems. Glasnost is all very well, but are there enough sheets?

Russian society, which is only now emerging from dictatorship and strict rules, is perhaps not ready for this experiential learning process in groups where people wrestle with new ideas and try out new skills. There's work to be done. There were some good talks including one on Gandhi introducing the concept of nonviolence which, for many, was a new and startling idea.

A revolt broke out on the third day led by Oksana from a small alternative school. 'This is all very well - playing games in splendid surroundings, but what is it all for? It doesn't help us solve conflicts in our schools. We have real problems. What we want to know is how to solve them nonviolently.' Tanya asked why people had not listened attentively to the previous day's lecture on violence among young people - a statistical analysis of young criminals, as they are called, and violence at home. 'We don't need to know the percentages of A and B,' said Oksana, 'we need to know what to do about it. We haven't got 12% of the population. We have an apathetic and disruptive boy called Petia who has a violent mother. What are we to do?'

It was a bit late now to start discussing expectations of the conference, for example: *if you expect your problems to be solved, you may be disappointed; if you have come with minds open to new ideas and you hope to learn new skills and acquire the confidence to tackle or prevent some conflicts, we hope you will feel encouraged.* In the charged atmosphere of accusation and non-listening, this would not have been heard at this stage.

Sitting together in small groups in the large room, participants were invited to define various concepts: conflict, power, freedom, collaboration, conviction, communication, value, justice, creativity, agreement. These were read out and comments invited, but the noise level prevented meaningful dialogue. As an exercise it had limited success, on the other hand, it did stimulate conversations which were held later in the dining room. The two women at my table were not keen to embrace change: their students had always done well in exams.

'Schools used to be an instrument of the state', we were told in the final session. 'We were preparing Soviet citizens, but now what are we educating children for? Nonviolence is a new concept for us. Discipline can no longer be blind: it needs to find the balance between self-worth and anarchy. How are we preparing our children for the modern world?'

R. had only been told two days before the conference that he had been awarded the Soros grant to make it possible. He must have booked the venue and invited participants in faith. One participant was from Moldova, one from Riga, and there were three from Lithuania, but most were from different parts of Russia. It is good that he did not have to cancel at the last minute.

SEPTEMBER – FATHER ALEXANDER MEN'

A good day we had for it, just the right time of year for such a journey. I am told the weather is always perfect on the anniversary of Fr Alexander Men's death. I went with Grisha and his mother to join the many hundreds of pilgrims who walked together the few kilometres across the fields from the station to his parish church near Pushkino, about an hour from Moscow on the elektrichka.

Sitting on a bench in the sunshine, I enjoyed a quiet moment with Katia. This has been her church for nearly half a century. Fr Alexander was her parish priest - he married two of her children and baptised her grandson. She vividly remembers that Sunday four years ago when the flock had gathered for a service and Fr Alexander did not turn up. Yes, they were alarmed. He had been harassed and threatened by the KGB, but surely those days were over, weren't they?

On the following day they learned that he had been murdered. Who killed him? The police inquiry concluded that the priest had been killed by robbers, even though he owned very little and was not carrying money.

Still more people arrived for the service, young, old, academics, villagers, almost all with flowers - an even number for the dead, an odd number for the living; many brought three or five, some just brought one. To kill a man is to give new life to the spirit.

Not an inch of space in the church; is there room for one more rose on the grave? Fr Alexander's followers now attend the church where Fr Gleb Yakunin, fearless defender of religious rights under communism, served until shortly before he was defrocked last November. Ageing now, he has been at loggerheads with the church leadership since 1965, when he sent an open letter asking the Patriarch to be less subservient to the Soviet authorities. Fr Alexander Borisov manages to maintain the liberal thinking of Fr Alexander Men, but Fr Georgy, another liberal priest, was removed from his popular church in the centre of Moscow, where he too was promoting ideas of tolerance.

We had to be circumspect when we used the basement of a Russian Orthodox Church for our Quaker meetings for worship. The priest was welcoming, but he did not tell his assistant about us, and we had to be careful to whom we gave the address of our meeting place for fear of compromising the priest. We have now been asked to move out for repair work to be done, and it is not clear whether we will be able to move back.

More damage was inflicted on the Church by Khrushchev than by Stalin, whose crude propaganda was easy to fathom. The more subtle tactic of accusations of corruption are used now, though Khrushchev's innuendos and suspicions persist to this day.

The Russian Orthodox Church is rid of a troublesome priest, one who was open to ideas and willing to accept the validity of other denominations and faiths. Fr Alexander emphasised that the individual approach to God might take many paths. While he did not deny the value of Russian Orthodox worship whose traditions have long roots, he promoted individual silent worship and small mutual support groups for worship and the exploration of ideas. Since his death, his books have been published, reprinted and widely read. Quaker Peace and Service in Moscow is taking an active interest in new attempts to amend the Freedom of Conscience Act 1991. Last year's amendments promoted by the Russian government and the Patriarch, and strongly opposed by Fr Gleb Yakunin, finally failed to become law last autumn. There is little doubt that they would have threatened human rights in matters of worship. Life would have been harder if not impossible for small worship groups and non-traditional churches.

REPUBLICAN CHILDREN'S HOSPITAL

It was a party like any other with balloons, cake and small fingers covered in chocolate, and yet it was not like any other party: the doctors had warned us these children, most of whom will probably not reach adulthood, would be reluctant to join in, as they have had very little experience of merriment.

The cystic fibrosis unit in a Moscow hospital, the only one of its kind at present in Russia, was celebrating its first anniversary. A year of many struggles, a year of triumph –

there is now capacity to treat 50 children. Our Friend Roy Ridgway introduced me to the unit some weeks ago, and after we had spent a morning talking to the children, the parents and the doctors, it became clear that our most useful contribution now would be to establish a programme of co-counselling for the parents. The doctors are very sympathetic to the psychological and emotional needs of the parents but have absolutely no time to devote to them. After hearing about the loving care that can now be given to the children, I turned to one of the mothers and asked who looks after her. Never having been asked that question before, she burst into tears.

Roy and Dorothea Ridgway, who established the International Integrated Health Association after their son, Tony, died as a result of cystic fibrosis when he was nearly 30, decided to try to help CF patients in Russia, where the children were condemned to poor health and a short life. Only a few months after their first visit, having experienced frustrations as well as encouragement, they managed to organise training for the hospital staff and a reliable supply of enzymes and antibiotics. That was a year ago.

'The co-counselling is a wonderful idea for next year,' agreed the senior doctor, 'but could you help us celebrate the anniversary? Could you give us a party, and could you take photographs of the children as souvenirs for the parents?' Well of course we could, why not? A bunch of Quakers gathered at the hospital with assorted edibles, musical instruments, games, balloons and face paints, and a fine time was had.

Quaker helpers painted by the children

This has been one small success in a disaster area: a 10-year-old child, one of the street children we keep an eye on, is currently in hospital with suppurating ears. The doctors would like to insert grommets but this can only be done if we can find some on the black market; a woman who urgently needs an operation to remove a growth from the pituitary gland was told to come to the hospital in twelve months' time or pay a million and a half rubles; parents, usually mothers, frequently beg on the metro for money for treatment for their sick children; operations have been cancelled for lack of simple supplies, and doctors are having to supplement their pay by working as house agents or theatre ticket salesman.

Roy and Dorothea are hoping to be able to respond to an urgent plea for help from the children's clinic in Odessa, meanwhile QPS in Moscow will work with them on providing co-counselling training for the families here.

Exercises are more fun if we all join in

COMMITTEE OF SOLDIERS' MOTHERS

Galia, chairman of the Committee of Soldiers' Mothers in Yaroslavl, rang to say she was in Moscow for a few days and would like to come to the Quaker meeting for worship, where is it held and when?

I had met her at a press conference in Moscow on the International Day of the Child (celebrated in Russia on 1 June). We met again in Yaroslavl a few weeks later and talked about her work and mine, our visions and fears, the source of our energy, the horror and waste of mutilated bodies, and the Quaker peace testimony. She invited me to her birthday party. Surprisingly, one of my dance partners was in military uniform. An adviser to the minister of defence, he seemed an unlikely ally in the cause of conscientious objection, but he too is against conscription, or at least he would like young men to be able to refuse to serve in the army as a matter of conscience without a possible prison sentence. He believes a huge army of badly trained and unmotivated conscripts is out of date. He would like to see an end to the twice yearly catch-all draft.

Galia rang again: she wants to bring a few people to my flat to watch the video of her party. I told her I have no video player, but they came anyway, and we enjoyed an impromptu meal in my kitchen with nonstop talk, laughter and tears. Yes, tears. My kitchen is adorned with photos of my family. Particularly touching is a photo of my son bathing his baby daughter. 'We don't allow ourselves to dream of such things. Most of us have only one child and if that child is a boy, the state thinks it has a right to take that one precious child and turn him into a monster or a psychological cripple or a corpse. Many of us will never become grandmothers.'

They told me that more than 30 conscripts a week are sent home in coffins with no explanation. What causes these deaths? The appallingly brutal bullying, the poor health of the undernourished boys, vicious weaponry in the hands of novices, and dangerous dumps of ammunition. There is also a high rate of suicide. The worst jobs, like clearing the debris at Chernobyl, are given to orphan conscripts so that the army will not be bothered by nuisance inquiries from parents.

More talk, argument, laughter, toasts. 'Can I have the carrot recipe?' 'Yes of course.' I got it from Sveta, assistant clerk of Moscow Friends Meeting: grated raw carrots, garlic, walnuts, lemon juice and a little sugar. Then tears again: Galia produced a telegram she had received from the Soldiers' Mothers Committee in Ingushetia: A BATTLE IS BEING PREPARED HERE WITH CHECHNYA. SOLDIERS ARE ARRIVING. TAKE YOUR SONS AWAY. 'We have no wish to send them,' shrieked Galia, 'what right have they to take our boys from Yaroslavl and send them to the Caucasus to kill other mothers' sons or be killed by them?'

I attended two CO court cases this week: two young men were appealing against a previous ruling. Both were claiming their constitutional right not to bear arms; both lost. In another court Alexei, who in a previous hearing had won his case, lost when the state prosecutor appealed against the judge's decision. The Moscow CO conference in October will raise public awareness of these issues. We have been given a European Union grant to work on this and other peacebuilding activities in Moscow. Please continue to keep us in your thoughts and please pray for Chechnya in the Caucasus, where Russian troops are in place.

SMALL CHURCHES AND THE FREEDOM OF CONSCIENCE ACT

In response to our request, Vitaly Savitsky has arranged a meeting to be held on Friday, 16 December at the Duma for representatives of small churches in Russia. There was just enough time for me to acquire a pass.

Lev Levinson, Fr Gleb Yakunin's assistant, came and sat next to me on one side, and then a large man whom I had not met sat on the other side. He introduced himself – Fr Viacheslav Polosin. Wow, the two giants on the issue of religion in the last two years were Polosin and Yakunin, and here I sit between the two arguments: exclusivity, tradition and rightness on one side, and liberal reform, choice and inclusivity on the other. I had read pages of debate between the two. Fr Gleb had offered to come himself to defend the rights of freedom of choice in matters of religion, but people who know a thing or two advised against this - too much passion.

As we waited for more people to turn up, Fr Polosin declared in his not-to-be-ignored voice that a demonstration had taken place that day against the rebuilding of the Cathedral of the Saviour and he wanted to know our opinion of this. Assuming that other people, especially Russians whose budget had been diverted for this purpose, had more right to express an opinion, and also to a certain degree aware of the next day's headline: *Quaker representative angers Patriarch's right-hand man*, I kept quiet. But then he turned his weight on me: 'Patreesha, what do you think?' I said I hesitated to express an opinion as a guest in Russia, but since he has asked me, I told him I do not understand the need for another cathedral in Moscow and, having spent much of my time in Russia with street children, alcoholics, the sick and the dying, I could think of other ways to spend such a large amount of money.

Savitsky: 'The Freedom of Conscience Act of 1990 needs to be reformed because 1) it was enacted by the USSR and not the Russian Federation, 2) the Russian Orthodox Church, feeling itself threatened by all sorts of missionaries and the activities of strange churches, is pressing for amendments, and 3) it is felt that public opinion is demanding that there should be some effort to control religious activities.' He said he was glad to meet us and invited us to present our case at the first hearing which will take place in January. No date has yet been fixed, and we can choose the location - Duma or government buildings; we can also choose the title of the hearing and the form of presentation – slides, a film or a talk; we can also set up an exhibition. Savitski offered to reproduce our materials and to help with projectors.

Quakers decided to organise a leaflet and a wall display; Tatiana offered to deliver a speech.

I spent much of Saturday with Tolstoyans, Dukhobors, Molokans and members of the Baha'i and Roerich groups. The Molokans do not believe they can be a viable group again, exiled as they were in small pockets in inhospitable places and now lacking funds and energy to reassemble; some thousands of Dukhobors were rescued from persecution by Tolstoy working with British Quakers, and they settled in Canada in 1899. Those who remained, escaping from the Abkhaz/Georgian war, moved to a place which seemed fertile, but several of them became ill and died mysteriously; the Tolstoyans, who reject government, are bitterly split; and the Roerich people doubt they could ever come to an agreement on this new law. The Baha'i on the other hand are full of energy.

Most of us here see it as a matter of principle that people should be free to choose, rather than each church presenting its own case. The antipathy towards minority non-traditional churches is based on fear which feeds on ignorance. It seems to me we have a possibly unique chance to dispel some of that ignorance in the Duma in January.

1995

WOMEN IN BLACK RESPONDING TO WAR IN CHECHNYA

In a previous existence, Quakers had sent me to Yugoslavia during the war to find the peace workers and to ask them what support they might need. I learnt some Serbo-Croat from my daughter's textbooks and travelled with my former student, Mara. As all direct links between Croatia and Serbia were blocked, we had to go from Zagreb to Belgrade via Budapest.

The following year when the Archbishop of Canterbury was planning to send a group to talk to the Cardinal in Zagreb and the Patriarch in Belgrade with the aim of organising peace talks or at least a meeting, he realised that the group of bishops, archbishops and other senior clerics was lacking in diversity. They rang Friends House in London and said: 'Have you got a woman?' QPS rang me.

My extraordinarily understanding headmistress asked me to replace myself for the week, which I managed to do with the help of Roger and a couple of his students. We were accommodated at the empty British Embassy in Belgrade, and I was given the ambassador's private rooms with my own front door. The clerics called it my nunnery.

The Cardinal invited us to a lavish lunch with starched white tablecloth, shining cut glass and polished silver cutlery: yes, he would agree to a meeting. The Patriarch received us with a good deal of pomp. He let the men enter the palace chapel but not me. Why not? Because, I was told, the ground is holy. The Bishop of Hereford swept past me, but the Moderator of the Church of Scotland stood with me outside. 'If Patricia can't go in, then neither shall I.' Later he joined me when I stood with the Women in Black as we were sworn at and mocked by passers-by in the centre of Belgrade.

At an anti-war rally in Moscow in early January, anyone with ideas was invited to the microphone. I spoke about Women in Black in Belgrade and gave my telephone number to about 3000 people. The phone rang, and I was invited to a meeting at the Centre for Gender Studies.

I bought 12 metres of black fabric, and three of us made rough tabards to wear over our coats, while another group of women made the long banners WOMEN IN BLACK AGAINST WAR with double stitching on all edges. Often with a TV camera present, we stood for an hour at the back of the Duma, the entrance used by almost all the deputies, and then marched round to the front, led by a Buddhist monk beating a drum. In -30 and in +30 we gathered at noon every Wednesday for a year - Russian women, Chechen, Dagestani, English, German. The discipline is to keep silent and not to engage with abuse. When the woman next to me shouted at a policeman, he came and grabbed the banner which was being firmly held by a line of about 6 women. He tried to tear it but was defeated by the stitching, so he arrested the woman, and we all shuffled up to fill the gap.

At the front of the heavily guarded Duma an irate militiaman foamed at the mouth as he yelled at me, his sweaty face about six inches from mine. It was not a pleasant sight, so I closed my eyes and whispered to the women on both sides of me to close their eyes and pass it on. Faced with a phalanx of calm women, all with our eyes shut, the nonplussed officers went away. When we felt that our point had been made, we took off our tabards and melted into the crowd.

Some years later, I was in St Petersburg when I saw a notice pinned to a tree that said Women in Black were meeting that evening. I joined them. It was a demonstration against domestic violence: WOMEN IN BLACK AGAINST VIOLENCE. I was glad they had repurposed the original message.

SUPPORT FROM INTERNATIONAL WOMEN IN BLACK

Dear Patricia

Thank you so much for your fax. You are right in the thick of it and we send you personally love and our support for what you are doing, as well as to all the women and men who are prepared to take a stand for peace. Thank you for all the information and news that we just do not get over here. I assume it will be okay to circulate this information to women we know, who might be able do something, if not please let us know.

Setting up a Women in Black group seems a really good idea. The power of silence is so strong. It may also be worth copying your messages to Catherine, who has set up a new email network called *Electronic Witches* in Croatia, Serbia, Bosnia and Kosovo, and is very good at passing messages out to other networks.

If you have the time, please pass on a message to Women against the War to say that we are thinking of them and their sisters in Chechnya. We send love and hugs for courage and strength to carry on with what they know is right.

We're thinking too of the mothers of those soldiers we've seen on TV. We've seen coverage of Russian prisoners of war who say that they are better off as prisoners than in the army, and coverage of mothers searching Russian army camps for their sons. If there is anything practical we can do on their behalf please let us know. A message from the WILPF women follows.

With love and the strength that we can share and always for peace, from Di

Dear Patricia

I have sent your note on to Duston Spear - she is with the Women in Black in New York. Are you interested in receiving letters of support from Women in Black around the world, or were you particularly interested in women from Belgrade responding? I was a woman in black in New York in 1993 when we stood in front of the United Nations every Wednesday for one hour. There were moments of great power-inspiring silence. We were also able to reach out to many people on their way home or into the United Nations. Of course, this was not a country where there are difficult tensions due to war: we did not get people spitting on us and calling us traitors to the nation. Please keep me informed on what develops. Perhaps women will choose to write a newsletter and distribute it over email.

Kathryn, Zagreb

Members of Women's International League for Peace and Freedom, British Section, meeting in London on 14 January 1995 send greetings and solidarity to our sisters in Moscow and Grozny. We admire your brave stance in opposing the appalling violence and destruction.

We send our love and join you in working for reconciliation and a peaceful future.

Jean W, coordinator WILPF (Women's International League for Peace and Freedom) British Section.

REFUGEES

There was no Christmas here, nor were there any new year celebrations, in fact most people had lost track of the date. They had set out from Grozny after the bombing started and discovered that they were not welcome anywhere. Owning practically nothing, they arrived in Moscow in search of documentation and status, so that they might prove that they exist, but the Federal Migration Service has had instructions not to register Russian refugees from Chechnya: they have no right to be in Moscow. They were immediately shipped out to the refugee camp.

The camp is 350 kilometres from Moscow. The seven-hour journey includes two train rides, an hour on the bus and an hour's walk from the bus stop in the deep snow. With very little money, inadequate winter clothing, and failing strength, these people are effectively marooned. We, four women from Moscow, who only with great difficulty had discovered the address of the camp, were their first visitors. With tears of rage and despair they told their stories.

One couple, on reaching Moscow after an exhausting journey, was told to go back to Grozny to apply for displaced person status before they can be registered elsewhere; another old and slightly confused couple have a son in Kiev, but because the Ukraine is now a foreign country, they cannot reach him; Tatiana, a doctor, has a daughter in Latvia, but the passport office in Moscow refused her request for a Russian passport, implying that anyone from Chechnya is probably a criminal; Pavel was born in the Ukraine but has

The refugee camp near Tver an hour's walk to the bus stop

lost Ukrainian citizenship: he now belongs nowhere; a pregnant woman is alone and terrified; a blind old man can make neither head nor tail of it all, though he knows he's cold.

Meanwhile the children play riotously and the young men glower. No, they will not go back never, never, and nobody cares, nobody cares. Quaker Peace and Service in Moscow is working with human rights groups and churches, including Baptists and Mennonites, to provide emergency help.

PRESS CONFERENCE, DUMA

Having submitted a list of people who plan to attend the first hearing of the new draft law on religion, I wandered about the Duma looking for people on behalf of Joel McClellan (World Council of Churches) and Gert Weisskirchen (Helsinki Watch), who had rung from Germany asking me to set up meetings for them as they pass through Moscow on their way to Grozny. Fr Gleb would of course be an interesting person for them to talk to, as would Lev Ponomarev, who gave me a direct telephone line to the vice president of Ingushetia, in case that might be helpful for them. It could also be arranged for them to meet some of the other deputies who had been in Grozny with Kovalev.

Sergei Kovalev was at the press conference, having just met with Yeltsin who apparently sat there with his eyes half shut saying nothing. Kovalev had said in an interview televised from the airport that they came back in order to tell the truth about the situation. He was appalled about the diet of lies which was being put out on Russian TV and radio: 'Our democracy is being strangled.'

Lev Ponomarev: 'The ordinary Chechen citizens of Grozny have almost all got a granny or uncle in the villages and have left. The people who are being killed by Russian planes and mortar attacks are mainly Russian citizens who are trapped because they have nowhere else to go. Russians who are injured by Russians are being rescued by Chechen medical teams. Hospitals are in a dreadful state: no medicines, bandages, oxygen.

Irina Dmitrievna from Izvestia: 'Terrible things are said about the Chechens. We must stop this demonisation. I witnessed great kindness and hospitality and felt ashamed to be Russian.'

Anatoly Shabbat: 'Tolstoy was right - it is impossible to control war. War has its own laws. Here is a passport I took from a dead Russian soldier, date of birth 1972; it contains a few dollars and a few rubles and a letter from his mother who is missing him. At least his mother will know now what happened to her son. Most are posted deserted or missing without trace, so that the Russian government does not have to pay a pension.'

Sergei Grigoriants: 'The executive has ignored the Duma. The people have no voice when elected representatives have no power. The president has acted against the will of the people; he has acted against the constitution; he has deliberately deprived our citizens of the right to life. He is supported only by Zhirinovsky and the hard-line communists.'

Speaker from the floor: 'We won in 1991 because we motivated people to come out in large numbers. Let us do the same now, let us rescue our fledgling democracy!'

There were some passionate pro-Yeltsin contributions from the floor, for example: 'I'm proud to have a strong president, proud to be Russian. Everyone knows the Caucasians are criminals.' But these were more often than not shouted down.

FIRST HEARING OF THE LAW ON FREEDOM OF CONSCIENCE AND HUMAN RIGHTS

On 8 January, the day after Orthodox Christmas Day, I went to the Christmas readings organised by the Russian Orthodox Church and the Ministry of Education. The ROC wants to reintroduce, after a gap of more than 70 years, compulsory classes of Zakon Bozhii (God's law); they also want to establish that they are the only people who have a right to teach religion in schools.

My Duma card allowed me to walk in past the huddle of permit seekers at the entrance and to wander around the exhibition and bookstores before going into the conference hall for the first hearing of this new law. The hall was decorated with posters reading: *Holy Russia, Preserve Orthodoxy! Russians, Look to your Heritage!*

Sergei Dvorkin started the proceedings: 'We must protect our children. All sorts of people have turned up in Russia – Buddhists, Krishnaites, all sorts. God knows where they have come from. Let us not frighten each other with tales of how the sects have penetrated our society and our schools. Go to the schools in your areas and ask some questions: who teaches religious education and how did they get in? They are very devious. They offer Saturday clubs for sports or stamps or chess, the children come in and are caught; or they offer free English lessons and then start reading the Bible.'

He read out some testimonies of people who had been rescued: 'They want you to sell your body. They collect money for things like Chernobyl. God knows where the money goes. They offer training sessions and seminars. I am afraid of all training sessions: you cannot know how they will end. Some of these groups are called by weird names like *Meditation Groups*.'

'There is no official record of who is doing what, where. We need you to do the research in your areas. When we have the details, we will publish a black book and force the Ministry of Education to take note.'

Unsurprisingly perhaps, the representatives of small churches were not called upon to contribute.

The law was later adopted as *The Freedom of Conscience and Religious Associations Act.*

TB IN MOSCOW

Are there no preventive measures? 'Yes, but in wartime, with constant stress, poor diet, sleeping in cramped conditions in cold damp cellars for months on end, the immune system cannot cope.' We were talking to the chief surgeon at the chest hospital in Moscow. TB, unlike many conditions in Russia, is treated free, at least in theory, in practice the hospitals cannot afford to buy the necessary drugs or oxygen. Half the patients here are from the North Caucasus. Many are turned away.

Several young men, thin, hunched, some with bandages visible under their pyjama jackets, are exercising in the corridors. Ahmed is not. His father dead, his mother paralysed, one brother missing, possibly in a filtration camp somewhere in Chechnya, and the other, having recently lost an arm, is in a different hospital, Ahmed's chances of amassing the sum essential for the operation he needs are slim indeed. He says quite calmly his fate is in the hands of Allah.

While she looks after her husband, who is no longer able to walk and for whom talking has become an ordeal, Zoia has left her five children in their village ten miles from Grozny in the charge of her 18-year-old daughter. She has had no news of them for some months. Her husband became ill after their house was destroyed in a bombing raid. Is she anxious for the children? Yes, she says, but the village is no longer being bombed. That's the main thing.

Louisa, the very personification of the Cheshire Cat, is sitting cross-legged on her bed. One lung was removed some while ago, and now, after her fifth operation, she can, she proudly shows us, though her grin is the most substantial part of her, not only stand, but walk. In the same ward is 17-year-old Malina who is waiting to have a lung removed, and while she waits, she becomes ever weaker, and the poor hospital diet does nothing to help her to fight the disease. What is she waiting for? A miracle, her mother tells us. She has carefully added up the cost of the drugs which Malina needs both before and after the operation: 4,000,000 rubles, about £580. If this sum could be found reasonably quickly, it might help to rescue one teenager from a story not of her choosing.

Postscript: The money was found within about three days of the publication of this article in the Quaker weekly, *The Friend*. It was conveyed to the hospital and Malina had her operation.

MEETING OF EDUCATORS FOR PEACE AND MUTUAL UNDERSTANDING

The group exists to promote a just, secure and harmonious world through education with a spiritual dimension, concentrating on civic harmony, human rights, cooperation, moral values, nonviolence, and the integrity and unity of nature and society. We aim to promote harmony based on respect.

Our main objectives are to promote:
- respect for the personality of the child, so that he or she will be capable of living in harmony with nature, other people and him/herself
- education for human rights in a world without wars
- education in the spirit of nonviolence in order to establish a peaceful and harmonious global home
- education in the art of global thinking
- education for a peaceful and creative life.

Our tasks are:
- to rewrite textbooks taking out all insults and incitements to violence and intolerant attitudes etc
- to engage in research and publications
- to disseminate our ideas in seminars and conferences
- to collaborate with like-minded international bodies.

Sharing their conviction that educators can do much to reduce inter-ethnic enmity, I was pleased to be able to spend time with this group at meetings, workshops, conferences, and in areas of conflict.

After the AGM, I talked to a deputy minister of education who was at the meeting, and we walked to the metro together rescuing each other from certain perdition on the ice rink which separated the school from the metro. He told me that the Russian Orthodox Church, as part of its campaign to re-establish itself as the supreme church here, is agitating to get into education and to be the only source of religious teaching in schools. Many people are against this. 'Why should Muslims, Buddhists and others be forced to attend such lessons?' He said there would be a meeting the following day at the university to discuss this. Would I like to come?

I told him that I had been to a couple of these meetings and was going to Odessa the next day, he asked if I would take a parcel to his friend in Kiev. He would bring it to the station. He gave me his card: could I please ring him to let him know which train, which carriage?

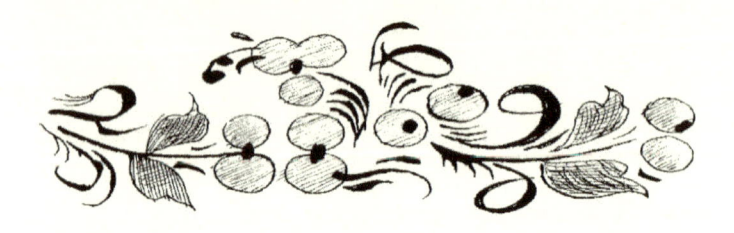

ODESSA – ASSOCIATION FOR VICTIMS OF POLITICAL REPRESSION

The Association for the Victims of Political Repression was established three years ago under the wing of the Odessa branch of Memorial, the human rights organisation which is based in Moscow. Ukraine, unlike Russia and other Republics, does not recognise the needs of these people. As a result of being unable to work for many years because of imprisonment, bad health and bureaucracy, their pensions, which are subject to delay, amount to just over £5/month, which is clearly not enough for subsistence. Most were set free under Khrushchev in the late 1950s, but they were given no residence or employment rights until 1991.

Conditions in Ukraine are very much worse than those in Russia. Although power stations like Chernobyl are still being used, the output of electricity is inadequate, and water is available for only a few hours a day - hot water is a rarity. Inflation leads inevitably to unemployment, the health system is unable to cope with needs, the public transport system is collapsing, but, with impressive spirit and determination, people are coping and continuing to make plans for the future.

Leonid Z., chairman of the charity programme of the Odessa branch of Memorial, gave me a detailed account of the activities of the programme and the costs for the year 1993-4. Together with him and/or with Margarita P., I visited eight of the 130 people who were helped according to need; I also attended the Sunday morning meeting of the nurses, social workers and volunteers.

Although several people on their list have died, the overall number needing help has increased because of the worsening economic situation in Ukraine and the return of the people who were imprisoned under Khrushchev and Brezhnev.

Apart from Leonid, there are three befrienders, four social workers and a nurse. A doctor is on call. The patients are all entitled to free prescriptions, but chemists usually say that the medication is unavailable, as they too are short of money, and they are unwilling to cope with the paperwork involved in reclaiming the costs. The programme relies heavily on gifts of medicines. A small consignment arrived from America while I was there, some of it useful, for example painkillers and laxatives, others seriously out of date or inappropriate, for example pills for the relief of premenstrual tension. Essential medicines have to be bought.

Money is also spent on domestic repairs and on replacing broken glasses, mending hearing aids, a fridge, a cooker and several televisions. Each pensioner receives a grant from the Association which together with their pension allows them to buy just enough food to survive. This grant is increased monthly in an effort to keep pace with the fall in the value of the kupon (Ukrainian currency at the time) and the rise in dollar inflation.

From April 1993 to December 1994, the Association spent $5765. Leonid's ten-page report ends with sincere gratitude and a blessing.

I was impressed with the efficiency and dedication of the team of people in Odessa who provide an essential service for these pensioners, for whom life is bleak indeed. This is not a typical seed-corn funding project for FHM, but I hope we will try to find money to continue to support this programme which concerns itself not only with relief but also with housing problems, pension rights and medical care.

Case studies of the people I visited:

Vera Philipovna (b. 1916) got 12 years for being the daughter of a priest. She is 79 but looks about 90. Her grandfather owned the whole house; she now lives in a small dark room with no access to fresh air. There is a sink and a cooker in the corridor, but to reach the lavatory – a hole in the ground - she must negotiate rickety steps and a hazardous courtyard strewn with bits of metal and fencing. She was released in December 1955 but not rehabilitated until April 1991.

Margarita Grigorievna (b. 1918) was declared to be an enemy of the people in 1951 for no reason that she can imagine. In 1958 she was simply told to leave the camp in Siberia. Villagers helped her to survive the long walk. She too has no lavatory and has to bring water upstairs in a bucket.

Zinaida Leontievna (b. 1919) has retreated from reality which she cannot bear. She has read all her own books and is sad that she is too frail now to get to the library. She got 20 years plus five years' exile because someone had said she had played the piano for the Germans. She has never played the piano and certainly never will: the investigating officer crushed her hands under an ashtray, breaking several bones. Her deformed hand gives her a lot of pain.

Mariana Vasilievna has not been able to cry since 1937 when she cried out all her lifetime's tears. She was head of a research laboratory in Odessa and when told for some reason to go to a certain address, she, suspecting nothing, took her five-year-old daughter. They were put in a car, mother in the front and daughter in the back, and driven to another building. Mariana got out and reached to open the back door, but the car sped off. She never saw Victoria again. She was given eight years.

A sailor, Alexei Alexeevich (b. 1901) got ten years for writing a poem with which he entertained the ship's company at a party. He remembers all his poems by heart and when he had recited this one to me, I asked what it was that so annoyed the authorities. 'Russians are asleep.' In 1991 he was given a new passport and for the years that he spent in prison it was written that he had been in the reserves. 'This is called rehabilitation,' he explained.

Elena Dmitrievna (b. 1911) was an opera singer who happened to be in Romania when war broke out. She was declared to be an enemy of the people and given 20 years. She was released in 1955 and given absolutely nothing - no money, passport, food and nowhere to live. She gradually made her way back to Odessa where she took up residence in a shed. She has been there for 22 years. Leonid is working to have her rehoused.

Anna Edwardovna was arrested for being German. She was severely tortured (permanently crippled) and given ten years plus five years' exile. While in prison she made a pact with another woman that if one of them survived, they would try to find the other's child. Anna's family all perished, but she managed to find and adopt her friend's daughter. Better off than most, Anna now lives in a state of chronic friction with the children of her adopted daughter, who resent having to share their meagre income with an old woman who is no blood relative.

Rosanna Genrikhovna (b. 1909) was arrested in Berlin in 1947 when she was working as a cook for the commandant of the Soviet occupation forces. She has no idea why she was arrested. She was released 24 May 1956 and rehabilitated 17 April 1991.

CONSCIENTIOUS OBJECTION

Yesterday, Pavel was to be tried once more at the regional court for refusing to do his military service. Again, we waited for over an hour for a representative from the military commission.

A TV crew, having been advised by Sergei S. from the Movement against Violence that a conscientious objection trial was due to take place, created quite a diversion in this small courthouse where activity is minimal: occasionally an important piece of paper is urgently transported from one office to another, or a teapot is filled, but on the whole, time passes unremarkably as a few people sit patiently on benches in the corridor.

More out of boredom than duty it seemed, the policeman challenged the TV crew, but he was happy to join in the proceedings, stepping in and out of shot as required. The judge too agreed to be interviewed sticking to matters of fact rather than opinion. The state prosecutor, who was reading a newspaper, was quite willing to share her opinions, but not on camera. She thinks that the previous verdict was correct. The Russian Constitution allows for a person to refuse to bear arms for reasons of conscience, and the fact that there is no organised alternative service is not the fault of the young man. She sighed wearily as we talked about the slow progress of the law on conscientious objection. There was no sense here that this mild beekeeper should be punished.

Pavel first declared himself a CO in December 1993. He was called for trial, but the case was postponed four times. In April 1994, the regional court found in his favour – yes, he had the right to refuse to serve in the army. Some months later he was informed that the military commission had objected to this verdict and had taken the matter to the Supreme Court. A retrial was ordered. The case has been postponed three times because of the absence of a representative from the military commission. Cases are sometimes postponed so often that the young man reaches the age of 27, when he is no longer liable for military service.

I went to several CO court cases as it was thought possible that the presence of a foreigner, and especially one with a journalist's visa, would help to mitigate the aggression often shown to these young men. The judge (usually a woman) would shout: 'Your country has fed you and shod you and schooled you, and you are now refusing to do your duty, refusing to serve your country? You're a disgrace.'

I was glad to be able to support Pavel, a timid young man from a remote village who looked no more than 14. I went with him to more than one court case and we would practise his arguments in the corridor or, as on this day, outside. He knew what he wanted to say, but when shouted at by the judge, he would hunch and look at the floor, his words inaudible.

We practised standing up straight and talking to each other at a bit of a distance using a loud and confident voice, and I encouraged him to believe in his right to refuse to serve in the army.

'Yes,' he said quite loudly, turning to address the trees, 'I do want to serve my country, not by threatening or killing people but by looking after bees to pollinate the crops and to produce honey. I am interested in the ecology of my country. I am not willing to bear arms.'

If nobody turns up from the military commission within ten minutes, the case will be postponed again. Pity!

A PINPRICK OF NONVIOLENCE IN THE CAUCASUS

'Hello, didn't we meet on Mount Elbrus last year?' Thus was I accosted last week on the stairs at the Institute for the Humanities in Vladikavkaz, North Ossetia, by a professor of history, whom I had indeed met last August in the mountains of the Caucasian Republic of Kabardino-Balkaria, or rather at the picnic in the woods at the end of the day. Small world! I had been invited last year to a gathering of the Mountain People, and, on Mount Elbrus (Europe's highest mountain), had swapped visiting cards with people from several Caucasian Republics, including the governor of Kabardino-Balkaria.

This time, four of us, led by Pat Patfoort of the Fireflower Centre for Nonviolence in Belgium, had gone to the Caucasus to run some seminars for young people in conflict management. Not since 1992 has it been possible for Ingush and Ossetian students to study together at the same university, and there is very little dialogue at any level between the two neighbouring peoples - one Christian and one Muslim.

When the Ingush people, having been forced into exile in 1944 by Stalin, were allowed to return in 1957, they found that their houses and property in the Prigorodny region had been taken over by Ossetians.

Claims and arguments, sometimes violent, led to the conflict in 1992 which resulted in casualties and in the expulsion of the Ingush from the region: 70,000 refugees fled from the area and took up residence in railway carriages in Ingushetia, where many still live. They are being encouraged to return to their villages, but in the atmosphere of mistrust born of deep hurt, the violence continues. In a grenade attack last Thursday, two men, one a father of six, were killed. We ran the same two-day seminar twice: for the North Ossetians in Vladikavkaz, and for the Ingush at the newly established University of Nazran.

This was not an attempt to solve the conflict in the area, but rather to examine the roots of violence, the imbalance between people, competition, prejudice, values, bipolar thinking - right versus wrong. How do we ourselves cope with being in a minor position? Is there an attitude or vocabulary which would enable us to relate to people in a balanced way in order to avoid the major/minor struggle? Communication skills were examined and practised, there were role plays, games and laughter.

The method of presentation was new to both groups, but the circle was soon found to be a safe place for discussion. Many positive comments were made, and eight or nine from each group expressed a willingness to meet together with the other group. Among the Ingush there were three Chechen refugees from Grozny.

We were taken from one republic to the other in a car belonging to the temporary administration, as very few drivers from either side will risk entering the other's territory. As we drove along the road, we were told this bit is Ossetian, and this is Ingush, but the geese were equally indignant, the cows indifferent, and the barefoot children looked the same. True most Ingush women had covered their heads, but burdened as they were with heavy buckets, it was clear that they were on the same errand as their Ossetian sisters.

Before she flew home, Pat and I spent two days in Moscow working out a timetable for stage two. The plan is to bring the two groups together for a four or five-day residential workshop in nonviolence in a mutually acceptable place. The last week in August seems appropriate, and Nalchik, the capital of Kabardino-Balkaria, is accessible to all. We should probably be too busy with our portable whiteboards and dry wipe markers, our diagrams, balloons, balls of wool, music for dancing and meditation to fit in a trip to Elbrus, which is perhaps a pity: from a height of several thousand feet the world looks small indeed, small and vulnerable.

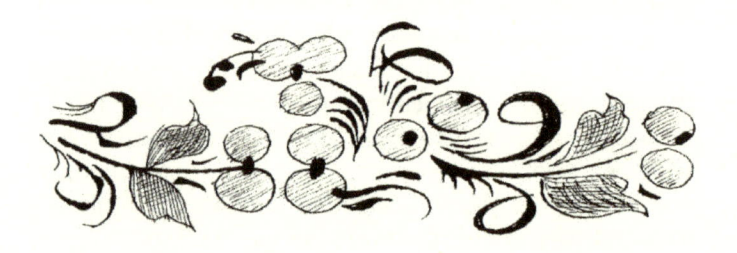

A CAUCASIAN MIRACLE

Do you believe in miracles? I think I do, how else to describe the second stage of our nonviolence work with young people from the neighbouring Caucasian republics of North Ossetia and Ingushetia? We had done the preparation with the two groups separately at the end of June, and they had agreed to meet each other in a neutral place at the end of August.

We gathered in Nalchik, capital of Kabardino-Balkaria – Pat from Belgium, Yana, her interpreter, plus Abi and I - not knowing what on earth would happen next but having faith. Faith had been essential in recent days, as arrangements fell apart: first the person who had said it would be no problem to find a venue was not to be found, Pat's previous interpreter was no longer available, then the local authorities in Nalchik became anxious about the whole undertaking and said we would need the permission of the police. Why? 'Because there might be fights. You don't understand. You are bringing enemies together. Anything might happen. You will have to wait for a fax from the Ministry of Foreign Relations.' We waited several days. The fax arrived as Pat and I were setting off for the airport: 'No, it's not possible to hold the seminar here in our Republic. this is high season in a resort area, and all pensionats and sanatoria are full.' I filed the fax, and we flew to Nalchik.

Raduga is a sanatorium run by friends of friends of my friend, Natasha. What, I wonder, inspired her to ring me about something else with three days to spare and nowhere to hold this workshop? I rang the sanatorium and quickly outlined our plans. 'What? You want to come here? How many?'

We took a taxi from the airport and were greeted by a cat. A woman appeared, then another. 'Hello, I'm Patricia, I rang you from Moscow...' Well, yes, they agreed someone rang, but they didn't really expect us to turn up. Recovering from the shock, they were extremely pleased to see us.

With laughter and cheerful activity, the place came to life as in Sleeping Beauty: rooms were identified, beds were quickly made, and eggs and bread found for our supper. Aslan, the manager, came to join in the celebrations. 'We have had no guests for almost a year. We cannot pay our staff or do any repairs. All holiday venues are suffering now as people can no longer afford holidays.' He was full of apologies for the state of the building and the absence of food, but he exuded good will. We felt confident we could solve all these problems, and so it proved. Would there be any breakfast? Could a cook be found? Would any participants come? Too many questions. We went to bed in faith. I had booked rooms and meals for 22 people; in truth, I had no idea how many would turn up.

Abi and I had constant hot water in our bathroom. The tap could not be mended as it had disappeared, and when the loo was flushed, water spurted out of the side of the cistern. Aslan apologised again, but no, we liked having clean feet, besides for me hot water was something of a luxury, having had none in Moscow for three months; and for Abi who had spent six weeks in Abkhazia, any running water was a treat.

As in a gothic novel, rooms long since abandoned were unlocked for us: rooms to sleep in, a wonderful mirrored room for our seminar, and a splendid attic with dim lighting, comfortable seating and a grand piano which had never been played.

The following day we were thrilled to see the North Ossetians arrive. They were soaking wet but hale and in good voice. We celebrated with tea and cheese and cucumber. They had rung me a few days earlier from Vladikavkaz, saying that they would probably not come, because they were too frightened. We had a conversation, and here they are.

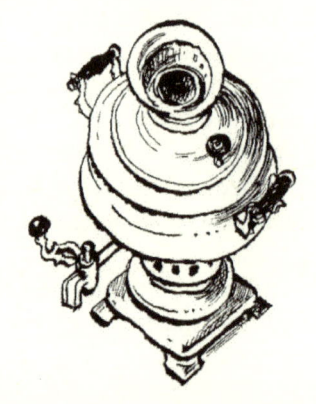

'Patreesha, some more guests!' I went to the front door – hurray, the Ingush have come!

Supper that day was a tense affair of segregated groups, no one knowing what to expect, some perhaps regretting that they had come. The meal was mercifully relieved by the smiles of Luda the excellent cook, whose timekeeping was no better than ours, but whose joy knew no bounds now that she had real people to cook for.

Chris arrived the following morning with another three from Ingushetia. I counted again - extraordinary! Twenty two people (not all the ones we were expecting, but never mind) have gathered in Nalchik for a five-day seminar at the end of August.

We talked of power - unequal power, the power of propaganda and the power of the dispossessed; we discussed nonviolence using quotes from Gandhi, Tolstoy and others; we looked for the possibility of equivalence as opposed to major/minor positions. We sometimes broke into pairs or small circles for affirmation work or problem solving.

Spontaneous cross-national groups began to form: the smokers, the quiet women, the volleyball players, the dancers... A., who had been a student in Vladikavkaz before the 1992 war, was able to ask for news of the friends he had not seen since the day he was forced to flee. The public pressure born of bitter memory and demonisation of the other makes it impossible for them to meet. Many of the young people who had come had withstood bitter opposition from their families.

During the first two days, we played, sang, danced and shared common tasks to build a community spirit; we also practised communication skills – listening, speaking and non-verbal - and explored attitudes and stereotypes. People who had refused to work together earlier in the day found by chance (or was it?) that they met, if only briefly, in the circle dances.

Someone discovered there was a hot spring lake nearby, so we hired a couple of minibuses one evening and luxuriated in the warmth. It was extraordinarily relaxing to lie in the hot mud, gazing at the stars! Towels were urgently handed to whatever mud-coloured body turned up in the dark, no questions asked as to nationality or religion. We apologised to Aslan for the state of the towels, but he was used to this.

The one-to-one controlled pain sharing session was extremely moving as people drew pictures of their burning houses and a refugee camp. This was followed by a fishbowl exercise, where representatives from each group, having consulted with the others, were invited to say whatever was felt to be necessary to the other group. Strict rules were laid down: only the person holding the pen could speak; time was limited, and the listener had to reflect back what he or she had heard before claiming the pen. The space was made as safe as possible with a line across the middle, which all agreed not to cross, and Chris and I were placed at each end of this line, as if to umpire a tennis match. True, I would not have had the strength to prevent a fight, but grandmothers are highly respected in the Caucasus.

For most, this was the first time that they had heard the hurt of the other. The other had always been presented as the bloodthirsty, power hungry, land grabbing public enemy number one. The war in 1992 was the end of life for many and of soul for many more.

'To understand myself I have to understand my parents who returned from exile. In order to understand me, **you** have to understand my parents. What it is like to be labelled *enemy of the people,* to be transported, to return and find someone else living in the house your grandfather built.'

'Yes, no doubt it suits the politicians to create the enemy image in people's consciousness. I have always pictured you as aggressive, untrustworthy, cruel and rich without really thinking about it. Yes, it is necessary to listen to each other.'

Photos were taken, addresses and phone numbers exchanged, and promises made to keep in touch. Two of the women agreed to try to organise a reunion. Much talent was displayed at the final night concert, but truly memorable was the Caucasian dancing performed with such verve and evident enjoyment by T., who had come from Ingushetia with a bit of an aggressive attitude, dancing with A. from North Ossetia, who had been too frightened to come down to supper on that first evening. A miracle or just another triumph of the spirit?

QPS JOURNAL LETTER

I am writing this on the Arktika, the train which leaves Moscow at midnight and reaches the Arctic Circle two days later. I am sharing a sleeping compartment with two children and their father. The children have spent the summer with their grandparents at their dacha in central Russia, storing up vitamins and sunshine against the long months of Arctic winter. All over Russia the trains and planes are full of children returning home: school starts for everyone on 1 September.

The children occasionally call upon me to play noughts and crosses or to mediate a dispute, to sample granny's bread or to plait Alina's fine blonde hair, which has a familiar feel, though it must be more than 20 years since I plaited my daughter's hair, but on the whole, they try to play quietly while auntie Patricia sleeps. I would rather play or chat or read or write - I love these long train journeys - but for some reason my eyelids keep closing. No doubt about it I am dog tired; it has been a stressful fortnight.

I left Chechnya, challenging as ever with its tanks, guns and ruins, this morning; last week I was in Kabardino-Balkaria, and before that in Moscow trying to keep spinning plates in the air. Here on the train, we are protected from the weather, but I know it will be strange to go from +37 to -2 in the same country in a couple of days.

'Don't get off the train, auntie, stay with us!' I had instructions from my friend, Inna, to get off at xx Junction, where she would meet me. It did look a bit daunting in the dying light, but the children gave me an apple and a couple of granny's buns, and their father wrote out their address: I was to be sure to get the next train and find them if nobody met me here. The conductor warned me that the train would only stop for two minutes, and there is no platform, but she had a step ladder.

From the ground, the train looks enormous as it creaks and strains and sets off to Murmansk. I was the only person to get off. True, there is no platform; there is also no station. Nobody, nothing. Am I alone in the darkening world? But then I hear my name. Inna is waving.

Now I am on the return journey to Moscow after a few idyllic days in a dacha at Kandalaksha beside the White Sea. There is no electricity or water, but there is a stream nearby and the light is magical, the air extraordinarily pure, and who needs electricity when we can entertain each other with storytelling and singing? We all slept in the room with the wood-burning stove, and in the morning when you are ready to emerge from your cocoon, everyone closes their eyes while modesty is preserved, everyone except Vasia the cat, who is in such ecstasy now that the stove is lit, his eyes are hardly ever open. We brought tea with us and some chocolate and cheese, but everything else has to be found locally. Prizeworthy potatoes and cabbages are to be found in the garden, masses of berries grow ankle-high in the hills, and the woods are bursting with exotic mushrooms. I learned to distinguish a podberezovik from a podosinovik (fatter stalk), and learned how to prepare a maslionok, a butter mushroom, which surprisingly shares a declension with the young of animals - piglet, kitten, child. I wonder if Roger knows that. He probably does. He knows the dative plural of everything under the sun, though he may not have eaten it or been bitten by it. Mine is the more experiential knowledge - large red swellings on my wrists testify to the presence of miniature carnivorous insects on the blueberry hills.

The main industry in these parts was a huge collective farm which employed 3,000 people, largely in pig rearing, but now that heating subsidies have ceased and transport costs have soared, it is no longer viable to produce pork.

The workers have not been paid for months, and there are now problems of vagrancy, drunkenness and crime. All over the former Soviet Union stressed people are bewildered, lost, unable to take control of their lives - beggars on the metro in Moscow; refugees preferring to remain unregistered for fear of being sent back to the war zones or refugee camps; mothers with very sick children desperately trying to collect money for treatment or an operation as medical services are no longer free; and there are thousands of unemployed people, many of whom were once highly regarded in their field.

Now I am on another train. There is no time to write at home. Only a five-hour journey this time, returning to Moscow from Yaroslavl. Sitting opposite me is a woman in tears. Only with difficulty did she manage to board this train and there is serious doubt that she will be able to change trains in Moscow. Her second grandchild was born recently in Yaroslavl. Like me, she had travelled to be with the family at this exciting time, unlike me she had stayed for two months being a proper granny. In the meantime, a new law has decreed that you cannot buy a train ticket or board a train without showing your passport. She had left hers at home so that her husband could collect her pension. Will she now be able to get home to Briansk?

In Yaroslavl, together with Sergei S. of the Movement against Violence, Galia M. and I talked to the head of the social science department at the university with a view to encouraging a postgraduate study of conscientious objection in Russia; we also looked at the feasibility of setting up an alternative service at the office of the local Committee of Soldiers' Mothers. We collected lists of complaints from parents and soldiers themselves, one of whom was so badly beaten by other conscripts that he now has brain damage.

While in Yaroslavl, I talked with the hospice charity and the health department about the possibility of establishing a centre for day care to underpin the home care hospice work.

In Moscow the Quaker worship group has about 35 regular attenders and there are small groups of interested people in other towns. We are now looking forward to our annual gathering which will take place in a pensionat outside Moscow. My time as Quaker representative will soon come to an end, but a European Union grant will allow me to continue for another year.

CHECHNYA

Friday, 20 October 1995, I flew to Sleptsovskaia from Vnukovo airport with John Shuford, an American Quaker who wanted to see the situation for himself and to do a workshop with students.

'Is it Patricia?' This was Professor B., a teacher of English whom I had met on a previous visit. He seemed not a bit surprised to see me. He walked with us to the bus station where we planned to get the bus to Grozny. The bus now has to go the long way round because the direct road is closed.

I recognised the crossroads where I had arranged to meet Chris at the bank, but the building has been bombed. We looked around in case he had managed to leave me a message in the dust, and John took some photos, but I warned him that we must not be out on the streets as the light fades: I could pass for a Chechen woman with my plastic bag and my headscarf, but tall, healthy-looking John, with his camera round his neck, was clearly foreign.

We walked quickly to the OSCE office to see if Chris was there or had left a message. Russians were encamped outside with plenty of weaponry. Young soldiers who looked about 15 were cooking a desultory meal on a campfire. This is not a healthy place to be as it gets dark. No sign of Chris. Hard to know whether to worry or not – it is impossible to keep to anything like a timetable here.

Where to spend the night? I am told there's a nice family 50 yards down on the left, green gate. The accepted procedure is to pick up a stone from the road and bang on the metal gate. Muslim families will take you in and provide water, something to eat and somewhere to sleep. The family told us they had hidden in the cellar for some weeks and then, stepping over dead bodies, had retreated to a village during the serious bombing of Grozny. The house was filthy and covered in graffiti when they came back, but at least it was still standing. A neighbour said there was a note for Patricia, but it was too dangerous to go and get it. The shooting in the street started at about 10pm. We had access to hot water and a loo, and we were given blankets, tea and the most delicious Isabella grapes.

The plan was to do a short AVP workshop with students, but when we left Moscow the venue had not yet been fixed. There are several places of higher learning in Grozny including two universities, one of which split into three separate sites after the main building was bombed. Where to start? The English Dept, where I knew some people from a previous visit, was very hospitable, so John and I stayed put, and waited for Chris to find us, which he did. The workshop was at the other university.

On Saturday and Sunday, we did listening skills, concentric circles, games; we looked at brute force, evasion, compromise and collaboration, and we examined the iceberg, which has 30% visible differences, 70% invisible similarities. People tend to concentrate on the visible, but we could seek better understanding by good listening, reflecting back what we have heard, and sensitive questioning. Hard to say how useful this was to the students at this time in this culture, but they were keen to engage and to ask questions.

For his safety and ours, John was taken to the airport after the workshop. Chris and I could blend in, find our way around and hop on a bus when necessary, and we knew how to approach the soldiers so that they don't feel threatened (look down and slightly hunch your shoulders); John, with his expectation of timetables, regular meals and running water, was less adaptable. He was also expecting to sleep in the same bed for a couple of nights, whereas for us a bed was a luxury.

We shared the life of the local population for a few days, seeing for ourselves what was going on and listening to their stories. By some miracle, food was produced even when there was no electricity, gas or running water. Salvaged wood was occasionally used to light bath houses so that bread could be baked and omelettes cooked with the remaining heat after ablutions.

There were tales of loss and survival, of grief, generosity and thankfulness: K's nephew's life had been saved by a Russian in the next bed, who fed him for the first few days after his operation to remove a bullet from his lung; several men who had gone missing had been found in a Russian filtration camp; B had spent the whole war hiding in a cellar so that he could look after the cows. He dodged the bombs to make sure they had water, though some of them were killed by shrapnel or shot from helicopters. We ourselves had had to be aware of helicopters: it is astonishing how fast they travel.

People are threatened all the time, not only with guns and bombs but also with the anxiety of losing their jobs, their homes, their right to hospital treatment. The hospitals have no heating and sometimes no water.

We were invited to a meeting of NGOs and elders. What ideas? What about civil disobedience? 'Russia is not England. They would be glad of an excuse to shoot us; besides we are all unemployed anyway, we cannot withhold our labour.'

There's news of shooting at the airport. That is what the helicopters were doing. The airport will be out of action for a few days.

We went to a refugee camp where whole families are in a single room; they have no idea what will happen next. Most of the women are widows and there are quite a few unnaturally silent children. The Russian Ministry of Emergencies is providing basic food and shelter.

How to get out of a besieged village? I was given some bread for sustenance, and I joined a group of women on a permitted shopping expedition. The women talk loudly as we approach the soldiers, apparently including me, though I know very few Chechen words. Most Chechens can speak Russian if they choose to do so. At the first barrier, they ignore us, though one woman is chosen at random for a desultory bag search. At the second barrier the thin, young soldiers are laughing and looking at photos. They take no notice of us at all.

We walk about 2km to the bus stop, then I make my way to the airport. My ticket is out of date, but no one minds, thank heaven. Flights to Moscow are still random. Luckily for me there is a 14.40 flight to Vnukovo.

In Chechnya, I am often reminded of two passages from Tolstoy's *Hadji Murat:* 1) Tsar Nikolai's orders: 'Keep firmly to the system I have laid down – destroy the Chechens' homes and harry them with raids' and 2) 'The village elders gathered in the square and squatted on their heels to discuss the situation. Nobody spoke a word of hatred for the Russians. The emotion felt by every Chechen, old and young alike, was stronger than hatred… a feeling of such disgust, revulsion and bewilderment at the senseless cruelty…'.

FRIENDS HOUSE MOSCOW

January 1st, God willing, will be the start not only of 1996 but also of Friends House Moscow. A gleam in the eye of Russian, British and American Friends has been transformed over the years with much energy and faith into a viable entity. Meetings have been held on the east and west coasts of the USA and in London and Moscow. Eight Yearly Meetings were represented as was the Moscow Quaker group, the Friends World Committee for Consultation and QPS as questions were considered: is FHM desirable? Is it feasible? What is it for? What should it be called? Quaker does not sound too good in Russia - it is the equivalent of 'croak'; 'house' has certain expectations which are not realisable, but it is better than 'centre' partly because we can agree on the spelling. Is Moscow too limiting? What about the rest of Russia? Will the idea be supported by the world family of Friends?

Attention then turned to more detailed questions of structure and programme content, while problems of funding were not forgotten. The interim board was divided into subgroups to work on personnel and legal issues.

Meetings have not always been easy as opinions differed and feelings were manifested, but Quaker process encouraged us to listen to each other. Sometimes a worship-sharing seemed the best way forward, sometimes a period of silence helped us to be aware of another's point of view. Brainstorming techniques were used, and lists drawn up, estimates were established then halved, as the ideal gave way to reality.

The fourth meeting in Moscow took place this week. When the writing on the wall threatened to overwhelm us, we took refuge in the snow, the overworked teapot, and the resident black cat. It seemed that progress was made in inverse proportion to the number of syllables, and we felt that we could indeed go ahead and appoint staff when 11 syllable notions had gradually decreased to one, thus: legally constituted corporation, fiscal accountability, recruitment processes, facilitation, spiritual, Quaker, house. The staff will be accountable to the executive committee which will be accountable to the international governing board.

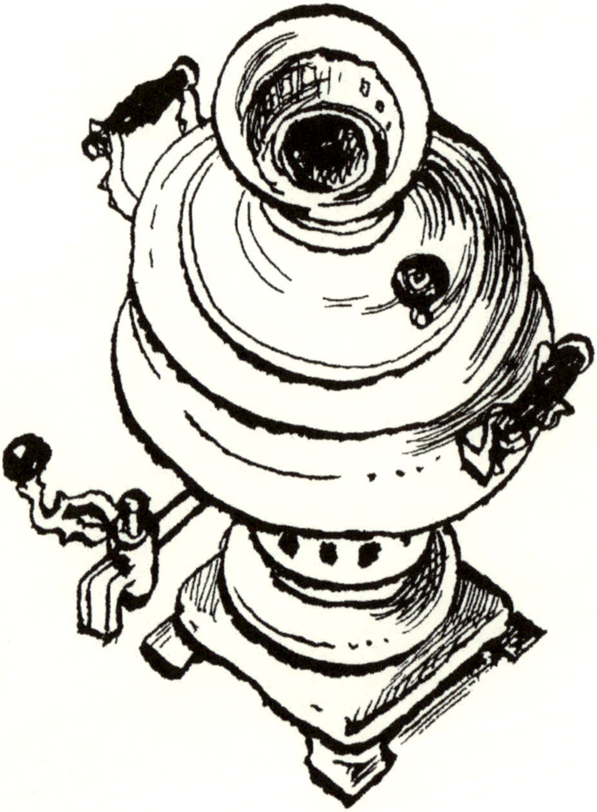

1996

Friends House Moscow Mission Statement:

Friends House Moscow is an initiative of Friends worldwide which seeks to encourage spiritual growth and the development of a civil society based on mutual trust and community cooperation. We aim to provide a stable and visible presence in the face of rapidly changing conditions, as we express the unique faith and practice of the Religious Society of Friends. We put this faith into action by working for social justice based on our fundamental belief in the presence of God in each individual.

Galina and I met the landlady in the metro on 1st January. We paid the first month's rent in exchange for the keys to the flat between the two Arbats. To us it seemed huge – three large rooms plus a spacious entrance hall. There were beds, comfy chairs, sofas, an enormous desk, elaborate lampshades and wallpaper that had once been the latest thing. It could have been a film set for a slightly dishevelled, once grand family. Maybe it was the height of the ceilings that made you wonder if a servant might come and light the samovar.

It will be a good place for all sorts of workshops and gatherings, including the school for Chechen refugee children. It is of course also the office, and we had a budget for a computer, printer and photocopier. I had been appointed clerk of the executive committee, which will meet here four times/year, and luckily for all of us, my fares will be paid by the EU, as I was scheduled to monitor the hospice project in Yaroslavl four times/year. It will be an excellent place for the international board meetings.

I was still involved in trainings, meetings and the line-management of the FHM staff, but my job as Quaker representative had come to an end. Time for a holiday.

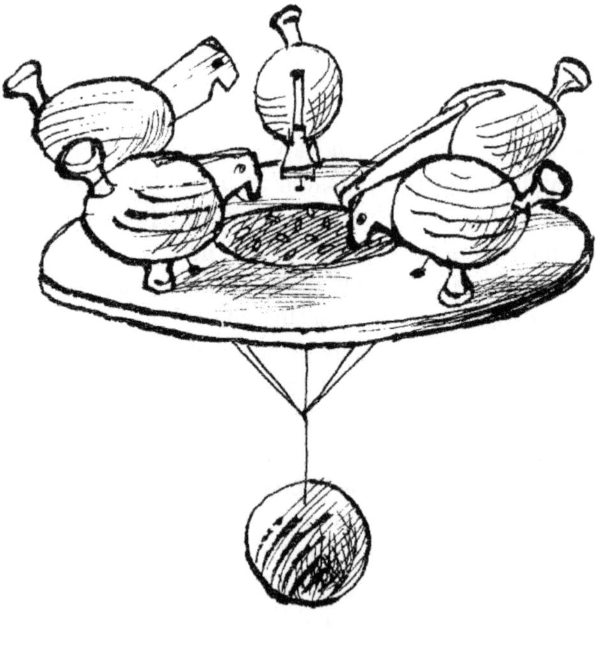

A HOLIDAY WITH THREE TANYAS

My first Tanya: Koktebel, Crimea

The train for Simferopol leaves from Kurski Vokzal at 9.25am, but Tatiana is determined to relocate us all by appealing to the conductor. I am told there is no train to Simferopol but the train to Sevastopol which stops at Simferopol tomorrow afternoon leaves from platform 3. Here is Tatiana with her friend Victor and his wife Nina. The masses of summer holiday travellers, all seeking the warmth of the south, all with large bags, press towards the train as it comes in: there is no hope of changing tickets.

I chug off to the platzkartny carriages and find my shelf buried under boxes, bags and a TV. A gentle inquiry - is that number 11? - earns me an earful from the owner of the boxes. I am invited to share the space opposite by a young mother, but I claim my shelf, and the stuff is eventually redistributed. It is cold in this carriage. There is no heating and no hot water for tea. We are all wearing coats. Like the others, I wrap myself in a blanket. The men find another way to keep warm and by evening most are snoring.

Tatiana ventured along to the cheaper carriages seeking to rescue me by taking me back to her compartment for coffee. She had invited me to share the holiday home in Koktebel on the south coast of the Crimea where she spends every summer, and I had bought a (very cheap) platzkartny (about 40 shelves in an undivided carriage) ticket as there were no kupeiny (4 bunks in a compartment) tickets left. I enjoyed the coffee and conversation but was eager to get back to my carriage where life is somehow more real: a child on potty, a card game, a noisy row, a good deal of eating and drinking, and we all join in the singing when the guitars come out. My immediate neighbours were thrilled when I announced a tea break: I had managed to fill my thermos with kipiatok (boiling water) from an urn further down the train, though, for platzkartny passengers, this is not allowed.

We went to sleep in winter and woke up in summer: the trees are in full leaf and the blossom is glorious; wonderfully, the people on the platforms are in shirtsleeves.

We arrive at Simferopol at 3pm and, afraid of missing the bus, I had to abandon the effort to buy a ticket to Kiev. The bus to Koktebel costs 250,000 kupony and takes 3 hours.

Maria Grigorievna welcomes us at the little wooden house. She charges 10,000 kupony/night each. All facilities are in the garden – a well, a privy and a very efficient washbasin which empties into a bucket which waters the tomatoes. The pogreb (the cool cellar – there is no fridge, in fact there is no electricity) has to be reached backwards down very steep steps then legs first through a hole. It is a bit like a breech birth but worth it, because here are stored the pickled vegetables and bottled fruit which are included in our payment. She also offers to bring eggs from her own chickens and bread every other day.

Tanya washing her hands

The days are hot and the nights cold. We tend to wake at cockcrow and go to bed early. The village is as it was 100 years ago. There are no facilities for tourists though there are a few visitors swimming, walking, chatting. We walked up the hill to the house/museum of Maximilian Voloshin - a beautifully simple house on two floors with panoramic windows facing the sea. We sat on his favourite bench and read from Tatiana's book of his poems. He died in 1932 when he stopped to rest on the walk home from Feodosia and is buried right there under an olive tree. We paid our respects.

We took a taxi to Feodosia so that I could try to buy a ticket from Simferopol to Kiev; I also wanted to find out how to get from here to Yalta where the second Tanya lives, and we planned to visit the Aivasovsky museum but it was temporarily closed.

But the post office was open. I decided to try to ring Tanya at work in Yalta. You order a call from the main desk, pay in advance, then go to a box. My call will be in box 3, but the boxes are not numbered. The call was cut off. Back to the main desk to renegotiate another call. It costs 26,000 kupony but she has no change. Can I pay 24,000? No. I manage to change some money at the bazaar, but the post office woman has gone. Gone where? 'Gone to the market. She has left me in charge, but I can't connect you because I don't know how to do it: she has switched off the main system and left me in charge.' 'Well, if you're in charge... No, never mind.'

I try to check the timetable but the bit I want is torn off. A bus stops right beside me, so I ask the driver. Yes, there is a bus tomorrow morning to Simferopol at 8.25. From there you can get to Yalta. Looking at a map, this makes little sense. Ah well, at least it is progress.

I joined the others eating an ice cream in front of Lenin, and we set off to walk back to Koktebel. No wonder Voloshin died on the way back! 'He died when he stopped to rest. We'll be all right if we don't stop!' Too tired to do much cooking, we enjoyed a boiled egg, some fresh bread and a tomato in the balmy evening in the garden. Maria's neighbour drove me to the bus stop in the morning for 'a lemon', ie a million kupony.

Learning that I am from England, a passenger in a loud voice claims that Russians need to be punished. 'God made all the normal countries, England, Germany etc, and order was created. He then made Russia, and Russians immediately created disorder. Russians cannot be left to get on with it. We need strong leadership. We need to go back to a time when we had strong leadership. We don't need all these priests.'

My neighbour is going to Simferopol to take sewing exams. Her college is closing because there is no money to pay the teachers. She has not finished the course but wants to get a certificate so that she can set up in business. People lack the money to order clothes, but still, she has no other prospect. She tells me how to find the trolleybus which will take me to Yalta. I found the ticket office and a woman eventually came to serve me. It is the wrong window. Yes, there will be a trolleybus but there are no more tickets. There is a two-hour wait for the next one.

I accepted an offer from a driver who will take me to the very door in Yalta for $25. He is a Crimean Tatar. His family, along with all the other Tatars, had been exiled to Kazakhstan by Stalin. When they were allowed to return to the Crimea in 1989, they found it really hard to create communities and reintegrate. Russian families took over their houses while they were away. They are called 'blacks' and face discrimination every day. He is not hopeful for the future. Everyone I spoke to in the Crimea wants to be part of Russia: red flags fly on public buildings, Lenin still stands proudly, and flowers are laid at his feet on public holidays. 'During the referendum there were tanks in Simferopol just to frighten us,' he tells me. 'The capital of Crimea is Simferopol. We refuse to accept Ukrainian time.'

My second Tanya: Yalta, Crimea

Tanya is ten years younger than her sister, my friend in Moscow, Galina. She works at the Wine Research Institute as a translator. To survive the Gorbachev reforms, they had to call it the Institute of the Grape and Grape Products. Many vineyards were lost, but inefficiency or sabotage saved a considerable number.

We walked to the Livadia Palace where Churchill met with Roosevelt and Stalin in 1945. There are splendid views of the sea from the Mediterranean garden. We tried to do a nineteenth century walk along the promenade, but bits of it have been bought up by the 'very rich bandits' and turned into private bathing or drinking areas, so we were forced into grubby back streets with rusty fencing and glimpses of the sea - not exactly *Dama s Sobachkoi* (Lady with the Little Dog), more *Boys from the Black Stuff*. It was a beautiful evening. Tanya is working tomorrow. I might take a boat to Lastochkino Gnezdo, a castle built on a cliff.

I took the bus to the promenade but somehow got lost and fell in with a man who walked me to the sea. His job was to organise holidays. Factories would book the pensionats here for the whole year, so that different groups of workers could enjoy the health-giving fresh air and the sea for a couple of weeks at state expense, but now factories are closed and nobody comes any more.

Today the fog is so dense that the boat is not visible from the beach. I sat on a bench and waited – will it lift? No. Change of plan: I will try to find Chekhov's house.

As advised, I took a trolleybus then the number 8 bus and asked where to find the house. This caused some confusion on the bus as people on their own do not do things like this: it is open for booked guided tours only. Still, I found the house and yes, the note on the gate said ЗАКРЫТ, but I tried it anyway, and it opened into a pleasant garden. There was nobody around to ask, so I wandered in. 'Zhenshchina! (Woman!) Can't you read?' I explained that I am from England, I have waited 30 years to see Chekhov's house, I taught Chekhov plays for many years and could even recite the beginning of *Three Sisters* (which I did). I said he would surely understand, in the spirit of Chekhov, that life is greater than rules. 'Ten minutes only,' he said, pretending to be fierce, then pointed out some interesting features. I stayed for about half an hour. The garden has pleasant shady seating. The large, white, wooden house is set back a bit, and the balcony is now almost completely hidden by trees, no doubt the ones Chekhov planted.

I walked back down the hill and by chance found the trolleybus which would take me to Tanya's workplace. We ate our picnic and then walked through the Botanical Gardens, where Tanya told me the Russian names of the plants, including besstydnitsa (shameless), the tree that sheds its bark and stands naked. Tanya says she is lucky to have a job, but her salary is barely enough to keep body and soul together. She has decided to concentrate on her soul.

I took the trolleybus to Simferopol. My neighbour said she would agree to any government as long as people are allowed to live out their lives in peace. 'This is terrible we cannot live on our pensions.'

I am alone as the train sets off to Kiev. Sasha joins me at one of the stops. A village lad of 22 with excellent nutcracker hands (yes, I had bought a bag of walnuts from a street trader), he is going to look for work in Kiev. He has a wife and baby and would not be able to survive without help from his parents. There is no contraception available; abortion is still the commonest form of family planning. He and his wife decided to have the child. An elderly woman joined us later and railed against the present government and their 'stupid reforms'. We slept with the door open as it was so hot.

My third Tanya: Kiev, Ukraine

Taras met me and we went to his brand-new flat for breakfast. Tanya had married Maksym's father somehow by mistake. Maksym was born two days before the Chernobyl explosion. They were expelled from the Roddom (maternity hospital) to make room for expected casualties, though nothing was said at the time. The health visitor was appalled a few days later to find the baby asleep on the balcony with nappies drying in the breeze. 'Don't you know about radiation?' Tanya picked up her baby and went straight to the airport. Luckily, with the baby, she was allowed to bypass the waiting crowds and she managed to get a ticket to Novosibirsk where her mother lived. She left the child with her mother and returned to finish her studies. Now married to Taras, she watches Maksym carefully, checking for any symptoms.

Taras is a teacher. We met on a course at Woodbrooke in Birmingham, where together in the TV room we watched in horror as Russian tanks fired at the White House in Moscow in 1993. They cannot live on Taras's salary, but somehow their parents had managed to buy them this two-room flat. There are no shops, no trees and no phones here, but a metro station had recently opened to serve this new district.

We walked around Kiev. St Sophia's Cathedral is closed because the autocephalous Ukrainian Orthodox Church wanted to bury Patriarch Volodymyr there, but permission was not granted, so they buried him in the pavement outside the main gate. The grave was desecrated, so it now has a permanent guard. The other Orthodox Churches (there are apparently more than two) are afraid that if the Cathedral is opened, the body will be exhumed and re-buried inside. Demonstrations have led to violence, even death, but all is quiet today as we approach the grave mound under the watchful eye of the guard in his sentry box.

There is very little sign of celebration though tomorrow is May 9, a public holiday which is normally a noisy, flag-waving festival with victory parades. We visit Bulgakov's house, we walk along the embankment, visit the catacombs and then the Botanical Gardens, where Roger and I sat under the lilacs in 1965. The hundreds of lilacs are blooming again. A marvellous sight!

1997

JANUARY/FEBRUARY

Kiev

At short notice I flew to Kiev with Simon House on an Integrated International Health Association mission to Ukraine. Following a previous successful TACIS application for the support of cystic fibrosis families in Odessa, IIHA had decided to put in another larger application to include the whole of Ukraine in the CF programme. It was necessary to go to Kiev in order to talk to the minister of health, to make ourselves known to the two hospitals where CF patients are seen in Kiev, and to ascertain whether or not there is a parents' committee in Kiev, and if not, to encourage the formation of such a group. Our task was also to complete as far as possible the TACIS application forms, as the deadline for new grants was approaching.

Parallel with this mission was another interest of IIHA, one which is promoted with especial energy by Simon House, who feels that nothing can be more important than the health of future generations. His concerns include education and counselling for couples, good contraception advice, and perhaps most important - preconception nutrition for the man and the woman, including, where necessary, dietary supplements. We saw Raissa Bogatisova, the deputy minister of health. She already knew of the work of IIHA in Odessa. She was encouraging, supportive and grateful for our interest in health issues in Ukraine.

At the Institute of Paediatrics, Midwifery and Gynaecology, Professor Irina Vovk and Dr Larisa Novik were interested in Simon's ideas. In Ukraine in recent years, twenty clinics have opened which offer contraception and reproduction counselling and there is now a programme of sex education for teenagers, but with inadequate funding, supplies and materials, this remains somewhat sketchy. They have some videos but no video player; they have leaflets on different forms of contraception but few supplies; they can give advice on diet, but still most people are too poor to buy what is needed.

Lack of funding is one major problem for the Institute, the other is the closed public attitude towards sexual matters. All the same, figures for sexually transmitted diseases, while they remain high, fell last year, as did figures for abortion which are hard to ascertain as many are not registered. A few years ago, it was reckoned that millions of Soviet women had had five or more abortions. Figures for underweight and non-thriving newborn babies remain high. This is especially worrying in a country where hospitals are often unheated, and the few incubators which exist are switched off when the electricity supply fails. Simon is hoping to put together an application for a grant to support the work of this Institute and, by encouraging the informed choice of well nourished parents, to improve the health of the nation.

On the cystic fibrosis side, we met Dr Ludmilla Mihailets, who works in a different department of the same Institute and accepts patients from all over Ukraine. The lack of medicines and equipment means that her treatment of CF children, mainly babies, is more or less confined to diagnosis and tender loving care. A volatile woman of great energy, she is clearly frustrated by poor relationships with colleagues and by the shortage of relatively inexpensive supplies which would allow her to do DNA analysis. She also expressed the need for simple leaflets to be made available in Russian to help parents care for their CF children and to help other children, grandparents, neighbours, and schools to understand the nature of the illness. At the moment, CF children are normally barred from school because it is feared that CF is infectious.

We also met Dr Natalia Gorovenko who has a rather larger department in the hospital known as Okhmatdet and who only sees Kievan patients. Between the two of them, these doctors see about 250 patients. Statistically speaking, it is likely there are over 2000 patients in Ukraine but no figures are available. Many non-specialist doctors do not recognise CF. It is supposed many children die undiagnosed.

When we talked of the necessity, for purposes of the grant, for IIHA to be partnered with an NGO, preferably a parents' association, Dr Mihailets was astonished. She panicked a little then agreed it might be possible for us to meet a couple of parents the following afternoon. Dr Gorovenko, on the other hand, seemed to be expecting this: she had already formed a parent and patient association, of which she herself was chairman. The meeting, which subsequently took place with eleven parents and one teenaged patient, was not entirely straightforward as Dr Gorovenko, in her keenness that the application should succeed, was reluctant to take a back seat. Sometimes in order to hear a parent's voice, a question had to be put more than once. She did however agree that the Ukrainian NGO form should be signed by one of the mothers.

We were much impressed with the dedication of both these doctors and regret the stress which is caused by lack of funds, supplies and recognition. We also regretted the competitiveness and hierarchical attitudes which waste so much energy. These are partly a legacy of communist thinking but they are also no doubt caused by chronic shortages.

As there was no time to go to Odessa before the TACIS deadline (though another trip to Odessa was scheduled for later in the year), and as we wanted to include the Odessa programme in the new grant application, I rang Professor Boris Reznik in Odessa to ask whether he was planning to come to Kiev to meet us, as had been proposed, or if not, perhaps he could fax us a letter to say that he would wish his clinic to be included in the new grant. He was exceedingly angry that we had gone to Kiev 'where no proper CF work is done': his is the only clinic in Ukraine which takes CF seriously. He would ring the Ministry of Health to complain about us. He would also tell the Institute of Paediatrics that they should have nothing to do with us. He then rang off.

Our interview with the deputy director of the Institute the following morning was cancelled: it seemed he suddenly had to prepare an urgent report. The director however, Elena Lukianova, did agree to see us and even, having told us at some length of the Institute's history, awards and alumni, to listen to us. All went fairly smoothly until I said that if we got the grant, the money would be channelled through the parents' committee. 'The parents committee? What on earth do you mean? We have no parents' committee. We have no educated parents. Whatever next?'

Her subdued staff sat quiet throughout, as for the most part did Simon, who was much hampered by lack of language, even though in theory he had his own interpreter: it had been decided in advance that I would be the main spokesman, and I would be able to more efficient if I did not have to translate. The meeting lasted two hours and, towards the end, Professor Lukianova agreed to cooperate in whatever way was thought necessary. She understood that the difficulty with Professor Reznik (who had indeed rung to tell her to have nothing to do with us) was that the next grant would be for the whole of Ukraine and therefore based in the capital with funding being channelled out to Odessa, Kharkov, Lviv and any other hospital or clinic, where there was at least an attempt to treat CF patients.

We filled in the TACIS application as far as possible, walked to and on the river Dniepr, then Simon invited us all - about 11 people - to a celebratory dinner. It happened that Taras, my friend and current host in Kiev, found himself sitting between Oleg, an andrologist at the Institute, and Liudmila, a gynaecologist, and he told them of his and his wife's failure to conceive. They now have an appointment at the Institute.

Moscow

Simon flew back to England. I took the night train to Moscow and had breakfast and a long chat with Galina, FHM staff member, and then we both went to Friends House for meeting for worship at 5pm. The following day, having met with the co-clerk of the executive committee of FHM to discuss the agenda for the February meeting, I went to Yaroslavl where, after my mother's death in a hospice, I worked together with Russian doctors to establish hospice care.

Yaroslavl

Dr Sasha showed me with justifiable pride the TACIS application which the Yaroslavl Hospice team had put together during the previous three weeks. Not only had they presented an excellent argument for a 20-bed hospice in Yaroslavl, but they had also had talks with the local authority and the local health authority, who between them had identified suitable premises for this purpose within walking distance of the Day Care Centre.

We had understood the need for day care during home care visits, where dire poverty and the absence of support meant that terminally ill people were dying in appalling circumstances. 'Hopeless cases' are not treated in hospitals:

patients are sent home to cope as best they can. The local authority has helped with costs, but still the nurses and social workers are paid a pittance. Many schools, individuals and Friends Meetings have helped with fundraising, and the work of the Yaroslavl Hospice team is supported from Exeter, Yaroslavl's twin city. Fundraising will continue, as the TACIS grant is for two years only.

The team was keen to show me the progress that had been made on the Day Care Centre - the result of last year's successful TACIS application. We went there the following morning and were met by reporters and TV cameras. They wanted to film my reaction to the finished bathroom, the kitchen, the day care rooms now furnished and decorated, the welcoming entrance, then they interviewed Sasha and me partly for the news bulletin that evening, but also to show during the official opening of the Hospice Day Care Centre, now scheduled for 11 March.

The new application has to be submitted in one of the EU languages, and there were areas which needed not only translation, but also perhaps an injection of European thinking, for the applications are judged in Brussels. I was keen to get to a computer to start work on this, as time was so short, but it was important first of all to have a celebratory lunch. I do value these celebrations because it feels good to take time together to marvel at what can be achieved with divine help, on the other hand, I estimated that work on the new grant application would take about 12 hours. I managed less than three that day but sat at the hospital computer from 8am until 8pm the following day with many interruptions from well-meaning people in spite of the doctor who had appointed himself my watchdog. The last two hours were extremely useful as the team had assembled and we were able to discuss the changes I thought were necessary. I then lay on the couch being massaged by a bone doctor, while everyone else did the printing and photocopying in order to collate the required ten copies. Another celebration was in order, and yes, here are the sandwiches, cakes, brandy and tea.

Laden with paper I caught the 7am train for the nearly five-hour trip to Moscow, where I would have just enough time at Friends House for a final check through before handing the application in to the EU office in Moscow.

Chechnya

At 8.30 the following morning, Galina and I were at Vnukovo airport with Barbara Gladysch from the German Mothers for Peace. We flew to Sleptsovskaia in Ingushetia and were met by Sh.

Armed guards escorted us on the road to Grozny where we were welcomed at the Orgtekhnika, where the youth conference was in progress. An AVP workshop was timetabled for the following morning. Conversations with some of the participants helped me to see what might be useful in an AVP workshop in these circumstances, and I started to devise a programme while enjoying the local musicians and dancers and while dancing with some of the young people and with one of the armed guards, who carefully laid aside his weapon before inviting me to dance.

Galina and I put together a programme in the early hours around the theme of cooperation and awareness of the other. Of course, none of us can check the might of the Russian army, but certain skills and attitudes can reduce the tension of individual encounters. The exercise *Conflict Line* was found to be especially illuminating. In two lines facing each other, participants stand in pairs on each side of an imaginary (or in our case real) boundary on the floor. The task is to get your opponent onto your side of the line. While the eleven pairs of young people from Georgia, Abkhazia, Chechnya, Norway, Ingushetia and Russia stood frozen in their final positions, we analysed the results: several had used force or cunning, or had simply given in - the win/lose option; four pairs had compromised with one foot on each side of the line – lose/lose, as nobody had achieved the object; only one couple (and every time I do this exercise there is always at least one, thank heaven) had analysed the task, discussed it soberly and calmly swapped sides – win/win. Discussion following this was especially profound. So often do we get locked into possessiveness - my side of the line - or confrontational thinking - if he wins, I lose - instead of negotiating and trying to analyse the needs of the other. Invitations and requests for AVP books and trainings continued through lunch.

We were then treated to a dazzling display of traditional dancing by children at a dance club which had kept open through the war, even though the director and one of the children had been killed.

January 27th 1997 - Election Day in Chechnya

As an OSCE (Organisation for Security and Cooperation in Europe) observer, I was sent to a village near Naur. Instructions said we should arrive at 6.40am to inspect the polling station, the booths and the ballot boxes, to count the ballot papers, and to make sure there were no electioneering materials or weapons inside the building. At 4am, the three of us who would be in the same region were picked up in Grozny by a car sent by the central election commission. It is not desirable to drive around Chechnya at night, especially this night with the highly charged atmosphere of election fever, but the driver had no trouble at the dozen or so armed roadblocks. At Naur, the headquarters of northwest villages, I was surprised to see a telephone. During frenzied official activity, I was able to step to one side and lift the receiver: no tone - it was part of the furniture. What a nightmare trying to arrange this complicated and crucial election with the very real threats to security, haphazard transport, insufficient petrol, 40 or so official observers, and no telephone! At 6.15, with half an hour's drive ahead out to the village, I was still sitting outside the local police station in a drafty police jeep in a temperature of about -7, while indistinct orders were urgently countermanded on the car radio. The three men with me were absorbed in alternately tooting the horn and sounding the siren and then waiting. Waiting for what? None of us knew. We had simply been told to wait. After another five minutes, I said that if I arrived late, I would have to write in my report the reason why and I would probably need the number of this vehicle. With siren wailing, we set off.

B., the chairman of the polling station election commission, introduced herself and her assistant, I., and T., who is in charge of the ballot papers. In the five minutes before opening time, I had a quick look around and shook the ballot boxes by way of checking as they had already been sealed, but there was no time to count the ballot papers. Promptly at 7am, a local dignitary was invited to cast the first vote. He was escorted into the room and to the long registration table which had been divided into sections according to alphabet. He then brought his proof of registration - a small piece of paper - to the ballot paper table, and, before he was given two ballot papers - one for the presidential election one for the parliament, his right hand was checked by a special torch which had been provided by the OSCE. His hand, having been found to be clean, was then sprayed with the blue dye which could be detected at every other polling station, should he try to vote again somewhere else. He then proceeded further round the room to a cabin screened with a green curtain. Life was suspended until he re-emerged and went to the next table where his papers were stamped with due flourish, and finally to the boxes where he paused triumphant. It seemed appropriate to take a photograph, so I did, and everyone clapped. The system had worked!

Our constituency numbered 1780. It was not too alarming that only 50 had voted in the first hour, but as queues built up and still our average voting speed remained at 53 an hour, it was clear we had a problem: in 13 hours, our allotted span, less than half the electorate would have managed to pass through the system. This seemed to me to be quite a dangerous situation in this place where passions were high and every second man had a gun. True, in the first three hours almost all the voters were pensioners. In this society older people take precedence.

We analysed the situation: even if the average speed increased during the course of the day, it was clear that the problem lay in the combination of the complexity of the ballot papers, the unpreparedness of the electorate, most of whom were voting for the first time, and the fact that we only had two polling booths. I timed the people in the booths: the slowest took over five minutes, the fastest nearly two. I went out to check the queue. Because of the cold, as many people as possible were invited to wait in the building. I asked some people outside how long they had been waiting. Ten minutes. When I went out an hour later, the same people just grinned at me. When B. asked my permission to set up another booth, I reminded her that I was only observing, though I did venture to suggest that perhaps the corner would be more private than the place she had in mind. She then felt comfortable to go ahead and called for a small table and a pen to be available.

Another slow spot in the system was that T., while giving out the ballot papers, explained patiently to every voter, sometimes more than once, that the system is the following: you cross out all the candidates you don't want to vote for, leaving one on each paper. With 16 candidates on the presidential ballot, two of whom had recently withdrawn, though we were unable to find out which two, and 13 on the parliamentary paper, this was not a job to be done in a jiffy, even if you had good reading ability, good eyesight and good hand-eye coordination. How about someone, for example the policeman in charge of the queue, explaining the system to people before they come into the room? And can't the other policemen stand by the booths to help the many illiterate people, those who said they had forgotten their glasses, and those who, in their excitement at voting for the first time, had forgotten T.'s instructions? Just a suggestion, mind!

B. told me at about 7pm, when our waiting time had been significantly reduced, that she had had word that we were to close not at 8 but 10pm. No one was surprised. Everyone seemed happy, but I hoped we would see this instruction in writing. At about 8pm, I was invited to join the second sick run: every polling station had been given a vehicle and an extra couple of polling boxes, so that ballot papers could be taken to the homes of those registered as being unfit to come to the polling station. In the unremitting cold and dark, I was much impressed with the efforts to find these people in the unnamed roads and unnumbered houses. Children playing snowballs were our best informants. I was also impressed with the care taken by the policeman to explain the process and to elicit the wishes of these people, some of whom were extremely old and/or ill.

Back at the polling station, I caught the eye of a tall young man and understood that by going out I had caused him nearly an hour of anxiety. Yes, I had been aware of him during the day, but he had been so discreet and apparently busy with other things, that I had not realised I was his chief concern. He was quite embarrassed when I told him I regretted my lack of sensitivity to his needs but agreed his job as my bodyguard would now be easier.

B. closed the station promptly at 10pm, and everyone went off for their first meal of the day, leaving me on my own to sit at the table in the hall and draft my report (not observing Ramadan, I had been fed at intervals). At 10.30 I had a message from one of the volunteer helpers that a group of border guards had turned up and wanted to vote and it would be tactful to let them in. No. Well then, would I go and talk to them? No. There's no question. The polling station is closed. Did I really expect them to go away?

A young warrior came in and stood in front of me, his gun horizontal, hip-high and pointing at my chest. The door had evidently been closed but not locked. He demanded, then pleaded that they be allowed to vote. I told him I understood his frustration, but decisions are not made by the international observers. On the other hand, if they insisted on voting after the station was closed, I would have to report the matter. He left. It was good that A., my bodyguard, did not witness this conversation, though he did hear the door bang and came to check on me. I told him about the power of nonviolence. Had he met with aggression, the young man and his friends, all armed, might well have become violent.

The parliamentary count was done there and then in the polling station after the meal break. For the presidential count, we would be collected by bus and taken together with the ballot boxes to Naur. Tea and chat helped to pass the time until at about 2am, not one bus, but two drove up. Adam and I plus several other people and the all-important ballot boxes climbed into one, but there was shouting and confusion when rumour reached us that the other bus was heated. Adam and I decided to stay put, but some of the armed guards thought they could serve just as well while slightly warmer. The convoy set off - police escort plus siren in front, and another behind. When our bus broke down, the people in front of us were of course unaware, and for some reason, perhaps thinking the boxes and Patricia were in the other bus, which must at all costs be guarded, the police car behind overtook us and went off screaming into the night. The resourceful driver fiddled under the bonnet and managed to restart the bus, which proceeded for about ten minutes in second gear before stopping again. This process was repeated two or three times, until, frozen almost solid, we arrived at headquarters to the relief of the rest of our team.

Luckily there was another international observer there, so we were able to take turns at being on duty for the rest of the night. Not a single box was opened without one of us first being invited to check the seals. All spoiled papers, and there were many, passed through our hands, and our opinion was sought on borderline cases. When not on duty, I had good conversations with A. about God and death, the incompatibility of Quakers and guns, and alternatives to violence. I also marked out the local significant people – easy to spot, as everyone stands up when they come into the room - and sat with them for a while, asking their views on the election and the future of Chechnya. I had had the foresight to bring my sleeping bag, but there was no suitable place to curl up. The floor would have done, but it would not have been culturally acceptable.

Counting finished soon after 9am. It was strange to see the sun, having not had a wink of sleep. I tried to let A. go, as the buses would leave at 10 to take the people back to their villages but was told only the chief of police could release him. I told him I would be leaving as soon as I could get a lift back to Grozny, as it was necessary to get some sleep before the 5pm press conference, but he said I was to go absolutely nowhere without an armed guard. Did he not believe that Allah would look after me? Yes, but still... A lift was offered about an hour later, but I felt I must not go without A.'s permission as he was still responsible for me. Reluctantly he handed me into the care of the Chechen driver. I held his gun as he wrote down contact information in Grozny. He also wrote his own address. He was probably not thrilled with his task for election day - personal bodyguard to a weird foreign granny, but he became intrigued with Quaker thinking and the ideas of nonviolence. I do hope to see him again.

The press conference took place at the airport, which has been repaired since the bombing, but there is no heating and facilities are minimal. Anyone who wished to contribute was invited to stand on a chair and shout. Tim Gulderman, head of the OSCE mission in Chechnya, summed up thus: no one reported serious infringements, there is no indication of wanton distortions: overall he would be happy to confirm that the people in Chechnya had made their choice.

I can only say what I saw on election day: a determined effort that the elections should be internationally accepted as fair and proper. They were not helped by the complicated ballot papers, by the negative voting (crossing out all bar one), by illiteracy, and by the unpreparedness of the electorate. Some voters had not brought their passports, some had not had time to replace the passports which were lost during the war. I was impressed with the politeness, the patience with which everything was explained, and the efforts to include the refugees who were not registered in our patch, plus the lengths to which the officers went to find those too frail to reach the polling station. Almost 20% of those voting at my polling station were Russian.

Grozny

In the next couple of days, Chris, Erik and I had various meetings in Grozny – with young people, with Z., and with the Soldiers' Mothers who were living 15 kilometres outside Grozny. Flora and Maria had come again to Grozny to continue the search for lost soldiers. Maria, ebullient as ever, was not put out by the fact that the Right Livelihood Award, which had been given to the Soldiers' Mothers in recognition of their anti-war work, was now frozen in a Swedish bank account because of internal disagreements among the mothers. We wanted to hear their story but in order to reach them we had to cross a bomb crater which had turned into a frozen lake. We had no idea how deep the crater was nor how thick the ice. We drove across, praying the while. At midnight, they thawed us out and plied us with food, drink and instant sure-fire remedies, as Chris and I were coughing and sneezing and generally wilting. A warm bed was what I really needed, but it was necessary to be interviewed first by Chechen radio.

Chris took us to see the abandoned sanatorium on the edge of Grozny, which, with a lot of help from our friends, could be turned into a rehabilitation centre for children. Near a wood, it is a very pleasant site set in extensive neglected gardens full of broken play equipment. The buildings have not suffered bomb damage but they have been neglected. An estimated $10,000 would probably be sufficient for the immediate needs of 20 children in terms of safe surroundings plus heat, light and water. Médecins du Monde, who prepared this estimate, had also offered a team of local builders who said they could do the essential repairs within 21 days. Work is already being done in schools in Chechnya to identify the children most in need. About 10% of Chechen children are suffering from post-traumatic stress. There are no street children in Chechnya, unlike Moscow, because of the strong family ties: everyone belongs to someone; everyone has therefore lost someone in the war, and many will have watched their parents or siblings die. There is no shortage of children in need but there is a shortage of trained and experienced personnel.

Our last visit was to a house in Grozny belonging to M.'s brother, one of the many people who have simply disappeared. We had met M. with the Soldiers' Mothers. She was looking to rent it to someone but there are very few foreigners in Grozny now: they all moved out when the six Red Cross workers were shot in December 1996. We explained to her that we cannot afford to rent property. She said we could use the house anyway, at least while it is empty. It is luxurious beyond measure with a hot water system (in need of some repair) and indoor toilet.

Erik and I then went to Grozny airport. Will there be a plane today? 'If one comes in, it will go out: it will not want to sit here all night.' There were several other hopeful people, so we hung about for a bit, standing outside the building where it was marginally less cold, at least until the sun set. Yes, there is the rumble of an incoming flight, and in due course we boarded and flew to Moscow. We decided to stoke up a little at McDonald's on the way to Friends House, as eating had been distinctly haphazard in Chechnya, and I now knew that I would need to fight a chest infection.

Moscow

To ring home or not to ring home? To croak a message onto the answerphone is to let them know that I am ill. On the other hand, if there's no message, they will worry. I rang.

Luckily the newly appointed co-clerk of the Friends House executive committee, had already somewhat reluctantly agreed to clerk the quarterly meeting on 1st February, and we had together worked on the agenda, so it was possible on the last day in January to conserve my voice. It was not desirable for me to go out in the -15, so, for the next few days I camped at Friends House, and friends brought me tasty things to eat and remedies, including mustard plasters.

The meeting started the following morning at 11am, we had a coffee break at 1pm, and at 6.30, when we had finished, we had lunch. Topics covered included the spiritual nurturing of Moscow Meeting; the young Friends gathering in Russia; our support for the small home for street children; our involvement in conscientious objection work, including the hope that the booklet *Your Rights* will soon be republished; the support of one of our young Friends in Moscow (who had himself been imprisoned for refusing to serve in the army) to go to Novgorod to help with CO work there; the publication of Quaker literature in Russian; our support for the small school for refugee children: as the families have no status, they also have no rights and many children have not been to school for two years. We were involved in setting up this school which met for the first few months at Friends House. We also looked at the project which offers psychological support and adaptation for children who have suffered from violence: these are currently refugee families from Chechnya, but other children are not excluded. We then discussed structural and logistical problems, registration and money transfer.

Worsening health caused me after a few days to consult a doctor who prescribed strong antibiotics and rest. Luckily, at Friends House quite a lot can be done while sitting down, and as the weather was holding me prisoner, I was available for long and useful conversations (mainly listening on my part), with Russian board members, individual Friends from Moscow Meeting, a group of young Friends, peace educators, human rights activists, and of course the FHM staff, with whom I was able to do a six-month assessment, to work through the procedures handbook, and to do some preparation for the next executive meeting in April. The small group interested in AVP work came, and we had a good session on their perceptions of the work and on the concept of transforming power. They will draft some notes and publish them in Russian for use at future AVP workshops.

Margarita, who in 1995 had shown me her work in Odessa among destitute victims of Stalin's oppression, came to see me in the ardent hope that I would be able to find some money for them. I agreed to do what I could, and, when I go to Odessa, to go and see Leonid, who runs the relief programme for these people. I was still hoping to be able to accomplish the last stage of my mission: to go to the CF section in the hospital in Odessa to encourage the parents, to try to find common tongue with Professor Reznik, and to meet the project assessor, who was due to arrive from Brussels. It became clear, as my cough persisted, that this would not be advisable from any point of view. I very much regret that a replacement had to be sent out from England at some expense, especially when I later discovered that the visit had not been a great success.

If anyone has any idea how to help destitute pensioners in Odessa, please contact me.

SEPTEMBER/OCTOBER

Moscow

Galia M. rang at 7.45am. To me, having arrived in Russia the night before, this felt like 4.45. She wants to go to the International Peace Bureau (IPB) conference with me. Galia is chairman of the Organisation of Soldiers' Mothers in Yaroslavl, which is not linked, she tells me, with the Soldiers' Mothers registered in Moscow. When we met at Izmailovo a couple of hours later, she told me about her plans to go to Grozny: she feels an urgent need to continue the hunt for missing soldiers. Many hundreds of Russian soldiers are still unaccounted for after the war in Chechnya. It may be that some are still alive and could be exchanged for Chechen men who are being held in Russia.

All manner of peace issues were discussed at the conference including post war reconstruction, land mines, gender issues, peace education, mediation, a peace tax, the Hague Appeal for Peace and Nuclear 2000. It is perhaps not surprising that at the nuclear weapons subsection, only one Russian person was present. 'We feel powerless to deal with such a huge problem,' Galia said, 'we need all our strength to cope with everyday life.' Russia has the capacity to decommission only two weapons a year. The situation in Ukraine is even worse.

On Friday evening, it became known that President Yeltsin had signed the new Freedom of Conscience Law. A resolution was quickly drafted expressing our regret that Russia had passed a law which contravened human rights, and our hope that the Constitutional Court would overturn this decision. This and a resolution calling for a law to support an alternative to military service were unanimously adopted by the conference.

On my way back to Friends House, I called in at the market and stocked up with dolls, plates, wooden toys etc, which will be sold in England in aid of the hospice in Yaroslavl.

Some British palliative care doctors came to the Quaker meeting on Sunday evening. They were running a training course at the newly opened Moscow Hospice No.1. They had heard that I was in Moscow and invited me to join them for a session or two. I was very glad that two doctors from Yaroslavl were on the course.

On Monday, I went with Trina, a mediator from Norway who was in Moscow for the IPB conference, to the Soldiers' Mothers' office to hear their side of the story from the group of women who have been accused of many things, including improper use of funds. Sadly, the Right Livelihood Award is still frozen in a Swedish bank account, pending a satisfactory outcome to this dispute. Trina offered her mediation skills, but this is a complex issue: a speedy resolution is not anticipated.

Nearly three years ago, when it seemed almost ready to open, Dr Vera Millionshchikova showed me around Hospice No.1 and we became good friends. She had worked closely with Victor Zorza, who had set up the first hospices in the Soviet Union. He had started to work on this one, the first in Moscow, but withdrew when he realised simplicity would be an alien concept. There are 24 brand new beds imported from England and beside each is a hoist. No expense has been spared: the mayor of Moscow, Yuri Luzhkov, whose brainchild this is, wants it to be 'the best hospice in the world'. It must have been somewhat distracting to try to convey the philosophy of hospice care in these surroundings, and it must have been hard for the Russian doctors to see TVs, gold taps, fountains and leather sofas, knowing that in their own hospitals there is not enough money for sheets.

One of my urgent tasks this time was to try to renew my multi-entry visa. I went to the Ministry of Foreign Affairs and contacted the woman who is now dealing with British requests. Elena Dmitrievna asked all sorts of questions which I had not been asked before about the tendency of Quaker Monthly, to which I am newly accredited: the circulation, readership, political stance.

Roy Ridgway from International Integrated Health Association rang to say he would not now be able to go to Vladikavkaz, but he thought it would be useful if I could go on my own. I rang Mariam in Vladikavkaz and arranged to arrive on Monday morning. This would give me time to go down by train, thus avoiding another flight and the extremely unpleasant Vnukovo airport.

At a meeting of AVP translators, it was decided, sadly, to expunge reference to Quakers from the Russian version. This is so that facilitators cannot be accused under the new law of spreading religious ideas in schools and colleges.

The following morning, I bought a ticket for the 33-hour train journey and then took the relevant letters and visa documents to the Ministry of Foreign Affairs. Frightened lest the originals, which they now demand, might get lost in the rather insecure system, I rang to be sure that Elena would pick them up, but was told that Yuri was now in charge.

Back at Friends House, Galina and I were preparing for the board meeting, when Sergei S. dropped in. Today, 1st October, is the first day of the new draft for military service. Kolia K had organised a demonstration of public obedience, ie obedience to the Constitution, on Red Square. Conscientious objectors planned to sit on the ground forming the number 59.3, the Article in the Russian Constitution under which a citizen has the right not to bear arms. The press release had alerted journalists, who were waiting by St Basil's, while at the other end of Red Square, the demonstrators were rounded up in less than three minutes with a certain amount of force by special police, the OMON, and taken off in waiting vehicles. Sergei went to the police station where they were being held and asked in vain to speak to Kolia. 'Could you just confirm that you have him here?' No. From Friends House, Sergei rang the liberal news service - Express Khronika - and the BBC. Both publicised the event.

Four of the accused appeared in court the following day. The judge wanted the case to be heard in camera, possibly because there were a few members of the public present including Galina and myself, a foreign journalist – the very worst sort of person to have in a Russian courtroom. Kolia insisted on his right to be tried in open court, and this was eventually granted. The trial was postponed. All were given a verbal warning.

Sergei came again the next day to tell us of another conscientious objector who would need support in court. The young man should have been exempt from call-up because his father is a pensioner and is registered disabled, and his mother, though not registered, is in a wheelchair. If she were to register, she would be put into 'Group 1 Invalidity' and would be deprived of the right to work. The young man thought the call-up was a mistake and understood it would be all right not to turn up. Even though he is now married and has a child, which gives him yet more exemption points, he was arrested. On this desperately poor family, the court decided to impose a fine of 3,000,000 rubles (about £450). There will be an appeal.

I was invited to the first of a series of meetings of psychological support and adaptation for children and families - mostly refugees - who have suffered from violence. A new group of children and their mothers, refugees from Nagorno Karabakh, came for assessment. Some of the women are widows, others have a husband of the wrong ethnic group, which makes them unacceptable in both communities; others have no home to return to, either because it was bombed, or because someone else is living in it. The women nostalgically recalled Armenian traditions and recipes. They can find some of the plants they need at the Botanical Gardens.

We had a preliminary meeting to prepare for the AVP workshop which Jonathan Silvey and I planned to facilitate at Friends House, then I went to see the neighbours who had asked me to be godmother to their baby two years ago. Sasha, an engineer who works for an international company, and A. are among the most fortunate, though, as a family of four living in two small rooms, they have few luxuries. Even for them, with a good salary, things are getting more difficult now. Current fiscal reforms include a new tax on the property you live in. Many will have difficulty paying this.

Emma S, one of the peace educators with whom I have worked, invited me to lunch. Knowing that lunch here can take three hours, and mindful of my evening train, I arrived soon after midday. Her husband is a very good cook. He is also a historian and a man of firm and loud opinions. Over the excellent fish pie, he declared the Russian Orthodox Church to be a monster. 'The priests get fat trading in vodka and cigarettes, and then spend millions of other people's money on gold domes. They also trade in baptisms and so on. A friend asked a priest to pray for her deceased parents. He told her the price would be 50,000 rubles each!'

Inevitably, I arrived back at FH with only just enough time to do the emailing that had to be done before 6pm, and there waiting is Nika, one of our AVPers, a trainer in the making. She had heard I was in Moscow and had called by. It was good to see her so confident and positive. She is just back from a spell in England. I suggested we walk together to the metro so that I can catch my train.

My companion on the long train journey was Lev, an Ossetian who has lived in Georgia most of his life. He is now returning to Ossetia where he has some relatives who will help him with the all-important registration of abode. Poverty forced him to leave Georgia, where, he says, there is no work, no food, no electricity, and seek work in Moscow. As a casual labourer, he has been very successful in finding work and sending money home to his destitute mother and sister, but as a person of Caucasian nationality, he is having an increasingly hard time: physically dark and southern looking, he is easy to pick out on the metro and other places where 'undesirables' are challenged by the OMON. He could cope with being picked up once a week and paying a bribe to be released, but now that 10,000 extra OMON are on duty in Moscow he is sometimes detained three or four times a day. The bribe demanded yesterday (100,000 rubles), was the last straw. He hopes the Ossetian government will help him to register officially in Moscow. He will spend a couple of days in Vladikavkaz, then go to Georgia by bus. Since the bridges were blown up, trains to Georgia no longer run.

We took turns to fetch hot water for tea, pooled our edible resources, marvelled at nature turning from autumn back to summer as we travelled south, read a great deal and philosophised: yes, he would go back to where they were before perestroika. He blamed Gorbachev, on the other hand, he cast about for something to be grateful for: 'I would not have met you!'

Vladikavkaz

Mariam met me at 8am. A woman with a rucksack, I am not hard to identify, and we went to the department of health where the Caucasian TB conference was in progress. Delegates were there from seven Caucasian countries. The Russian minister of health had flown down from Moscow, WHO had sent representatives, and Carol Day was there from Merlin, the British medical charity which is working in the region. Doctors Without Borders are withholding their cooperation while Andre Christoph is still missing in Chechnya. This policy, while understandable from a European point of view, is much resented by the local people, many of whom feel they have absolutely nothing in common with Chechens.

Mariam, together with a small group of helpers, has set up an organisation called Rainbow to try to combat some of the worst aspects of poverty and disease. She showed me the scale of the problem: TB hospitals (there's an epidemic of TB in Russia) not only with no drugs, but also with no soap; a children's hospital so badly in need of repair that parts of it have had to be cordoned off; a sanatorium for adults with lung diseases where, of the four ventilators, only one works; a sanatorium for children which can offer nothing except fresh air; a hostel for refugees where 13 people (one of whom has recently been released from prison inevitably with TB) share a toilet, kitchen and bathroom. I greatly admired the energy and faith of the rainbow group and hope we can do something to support them. We plan to discuss this in November.

Moscow

I flew back to Moscow on my birthday and was quite relieved that no one had come to meet me, as the plane was two hours late. I made my way back by bus and metro and there, at Friends House, was a delegation of well-wishers with flowers, champagne and cake!

Jonathan, Raffi and I met early the next day to plan the AVP workshop. The meeting with interruptions lasted nearly four hours. One of the more annoying interruptions was that I had to keep going to the phone to try to find Elena Dmitrievna at the Ministry of Foreign Affairs. She answered her phone at 1.30 and said the authority would be ready at 4pm. I duly collected the piece of paper from the Ministry at 4 and dashed across town to register the visa. The registrar was not a bit pleased to see me at 4.45, but she cheered up when she found a mistake on the Ministry's form. The thing will have to be redone. I rang Elena. 'Well, it will have to wait till Monday.'

Local AVPers had asked for another training for trainers. They want particularly to explore teambuilding, leadership, transforming power and role play. Highly valued were the games plus the open clinics, in which co-facilitators analyse what worked well, and how things might have been done differently. The role plays were again not an outstanding success. Why is this? How would it be if the mother were to react differently? 'She cannot react differently because that is how mothers react.' Oh dear, back to the drawing board.

My trip to Yaroslavl had to be postponed because Monday must now be devoted to visa battling with a good deal of frustration involving office and bank. Yes, the visas will be ready tomorrow morning. I will collect mine when I get back from Yaroslavl.

Yaroslavl

Nina, the hospice director, and Sasha, the oncological consultant, met me at Yaroslavl station. We had a preliminary meeting straightaway, parted at midnight, then spent the whole of the next day shuffling papers. We need to meet the needs of the local banking, tax and employment laws, while at the same the European grant monitors demand original documents. The herculean task now facing us is to produce a final report on our TACIS grant.

At last, I have time to spend with patients and staff at the Day Care Centre, but first we must help one of our home care patients to get to hospital for an urgent procedure. Neither the driver nor I had met the woman - 46-year-old Alla - who is too ill to come in for day care, but we knew her home care nurse would be with her. To add to the misery of lung cancer, she now has pleurisy. Speechless and grey, she winced at every bump in the road.

I was pleased to see they had moved the furniture at the Day Care Centre. A small thing perhaps, but since their visit to hospices in the Exeter region in the summer, the director and senior nurse had understood the importance of the intimate circle for fellowship and group support. The other nurses were mystified: they could see nothing wrong with the patients on arrival wandering off into corners with knitting or a newspaper. They had listened politely as I and others talked of community building - using the power of the group to create a supportive atmosphere. Today they joined the circle. There is a skill in encouraging a group conversation, but today one of the patients, describing the range of feelings connected with her illness, said that the diagnosis had caused immediate, and she thought terminal, depression - she wanted to die straight away. Now among people who care about her, she has changed her mind. She called for the guitar. There are two small quiet rooms for anyone who needs a bit of space, but it is now expected that people will join the circle for the first half hour or so of the day.

The health department phoned to say that we would have to pay a fine because someone had sent us several thousand syringes which were not certified; not only a fine but we must also pay storage, as they had been in customs care for two months. It seemed a good enough reason for me to go the following day to see the local health minister whom I know quite well. Galina Morgunova agreed it was most unlikely that someone had sent a consignment without letting us know; she also agreed that we should pay nothing until the matter had been investigated. Yes, she remembered that her department had offered to cover the hospice staff salaries at the end of our grant: 'But we have no money. What can we do?' We spoke of the funding model in England, where hospices engage in serious fundraising, and the government pays about a third of the costs.

She acknowledged that the hospice work was a real service to the community and confirmed that she would try to help us with some tax concessions. At the moment we pay 40% tax on all salaries, and, under Russian tax law, for every monetary donation, both donor and recipient must pay tax. This is why companies have given a carpet, cooker or TV, but there is a limit to the number of carpets we need. We are trying to devise a scheme whereby a nurse could be sponsored, but this is apparently not possible under employment law. We have put in for another TACIS grant, but at the moment hospice work in Yaroslavl is almost wholly financed by donations to the Yaroslavl Hospice Trust based in Exeter.

Moscow

At 7am I caught the train back to Moscow and without too much difficulty picked up my visa on the way to Friends House. Most people had by now arrived for the annual meeting of the international FHM board. We agreed an agenda and timetable and found times for the committees to meet – programme, personnel, and finance; the executive would meet at the end of the board meeting. During the three days we revisited our employment practices, looked at programme weightings, discussed interim plans to agree a budget, and tried to envisage where we should be in three years' time. Of course, all this may depend on future attitudes to religion in Russia and on the interpretation of the new law.

In short, the Freedom of Conscience Law seeks to establish 21 religious organisations which will have various rights. Only four will be recognised automatically – Orthodoxy (only the Moscow Patriarchate) and one branch of the following: Islam, Judaism and Buddhism. Other religious associations can apply for recognition, but only if they were registered in Russia 15 years ago. One of the Baptist churches will probably have no difficulty, as will one or two Catholic churches; religious groups can apply for registration, but they will have no rights to own or rent property, they will have no right to indulge in charity work, and their worship and teaching must be confined to their own followers.

The law is supposed to come into effect on publication. It has not been published yet, but it has already been invoked in various parts of Russia. Lawyers have told us it is written in such vague terms as to be open to all manner of interpretation. Zealous officials and police chiefs in the provinces, where there is a tendency in the public mood to return to despotism and good order, have taken matters into their own hands: there was trouble at a Ukrainian Orthodox service in Riazan; a church has been confiscated from the Orthodox Abroad; Pentecostalists have been expelled from a school; even in St Petersburg, the Salvation Army is suddenly no longer allowed to use two meeting halls.

We cannot predict what will happen to Friends House. We will have faith in the future and continue to support our staff at this challenging time.

Galina, Natasha and I went to the Helsinki Watch office to witness the birth of an organisation which seeks to defend the rights of citizens in Russia and to fight the Freedom of Conscience Law in the Constitutional Court. Speeches from the floor expressed the horror of human rights activists that such a law could be passed with almost no opposition. 'This is not just a law about religion. We must defend our society before we return to the Middle Ages. Our people do not know how to stand up for their rights; they do not even know they have rights.'

Galina, Bonnie and I met all morning to discuss their concerns as FHM staff and to prepare for the evaluation which is due to take place in February. Emma S, the peace educator, came with a cake. She very much wants me to understand the Russian situation before I represent Russia at the peace education congress planning meeting in Graz next week. As she talked, the situation became even less clear, but perhaps this in itself is useful to know.

I spent my final evening with the S. family. They are not sure they can send their six-year-old to the special English school attended by his elder brother. In theory the education is free, but charges are imposed all the time, and the donation now required to register a child is several hundred dollars - such is the premium associated with English.

I left the following day. My next trip will be January/February 1998. These are some of the people whose paths I crossed during the four weeks and some of the issues which were raised. I have tried to sketch out their energy, anxieties and aspirations. Thank you for your interest in this work. I have more Russian toys, bowls etc to sell in aid of the hospice.

1998

JANUARY/ FEBRUARY

Oslo

This trip started in Norway. I was a facilitator at a congress of women peace workers looking at reconciliation, post war reconstruction and possible ways forward. From three conflict areas in the former Soviet Union: Nagorno Karabakh, Georgia/Abkhazia and Chechnya/Russia women came to meet each other and to meet Norwegian peace organisations. We looked at the causes of war, propaganda, prejudice, the interests of a third party, and the huge unwieldy Russian army, and we wondered how to counter these forces by improving communication, empowering peace groups, building up cross-border organisations, and encouraging young men to resist army service. Against a background of poor or broken telephone lines, brutality at border crossings, a shortage of basic services, and extreme poverty, we knew that some of our ideas were destined not to flourish in the immediate future, but still it was encouraging to be with such determined and energetic women.

Moscow

Because it was cheaper to do so, I flew from Oslo to Moscow via Heathrow and arrived at Friends House just before midnight. Waiting to let me in was one of my former students, Jane Whitechurch, who now works for Oxfam, and the director of the Oxfam East European desk, Tony Vokes. Jane had rung me some weeks earlier saying that Oxfam wanted to research the possibility of working in Russia, and they needed to start by meeting some people already working there. Could I arrange some introductions in Moscow and could they come to Yaroslavl with me? I had fixed up some meetings for them in Moscow and I bought the tickets for Yaroslavl the following morning, then went to the British Embassy for a meeting about kidnappings in Chechnya.

Yaroslavl

In Yaroslavl, Jane, Tony and I had a series of meetings. The staff and patients at the Day Care Centre were as keen as ever to organise a celebration, but this time the joy of meeting was tempered with disappointment: we had heard on December 31, 1997, that the grant application we had worked so hard to prepare had not been accepted by the European Union. It seems the ratio of salaries to equipment does not fit their norms.

I rang the office in Brussels and told the young man that palliative care, especially in Russia, where computer-controlled mattresses and bath hoists are not available, depends largely on nursing and personal care. He was not to be persuaded. We can resubmit in April, cutting out a couple of nurses and adding some expensive foreign equipment which, when it goes wrong, will probably not be repairable. There seemed to be no room for negotiation. We are unwilling to cut out a couple of nurses but is there something we can buy, preferably something Russian?

The new two-year grant would have enabled us to work together with the local authority to open a 20-bed unit in Yaroslavl. We have had talks with the local health authority and have been offered a rundown wing of a hospital. Yaroslavl would then have been able to offer a complete hospice care service with trained personnel, some of whom are ready to train others in palliative care, but now the chairman of the health authority, having been warned that she may be forced into retirement on reaching a certain birthday in January, took matters into her own hands. When she heard we had been refused the grant, she simply stuck a notice by the door of a hospital ward declaring this ward to be *Hospice No.1*. She then recounted a list of her successes, including the single-handed opening of a hospice, while the local Duma debated her position. She has kept her job for another year. We hoped it would still be possible to work together on this development, perhaps by offering training to the staff, but we were refused permission to see this ward.

Equally frustrating, as Oxfam is particularly interested in women's issues, was our attempt to find out what provision is made for women in Yaroslavl. Is there a refuge centre? A crisis telephone line? Adequate childcare? 'Yes, we have everything in Yaroslavl,' Jane and Tony were told by the chief administrator of the gynaecological hospital. Why was the meeting arranged here? Well, we were told, this is where women are dealt with. Could we see the crisis line? Where are the counsellors trained? What problems concern women in Yaroslavl? Unencumbered by language, of which there was a great deal, Tony was the first to understand that we had entered the realm of the imagination: none of my women friends had heard of the crisis line. It seems it is due to start next week.

Rather more satisfactory was our visit to a support centre for people with disabilities. The director, himself an amputee, was very much aware of the reality of the problems: social attitudes, unemployment, poverty, a shortage of aids and prostheses; he did not mention access until we did, struck by the ramp, one of the few in Russia, outside his office. He then threw his arms out to gesture the scale and hopelessness of this problem.

Moscow

Back in Moscow, I had confirmation that the English doctor, with whom I was to go to Vladikavkaz, had not received his visa. Our trip was postponed, so I was free to go to Minsk: Educators for Peace had invited me to join their 10th anniversary celebrations.

Minsk

I was particularly cheered to hear many of the teachers using the vocabulary of nonviolence and being enthusiastic about introducing these ideas into their schools. There are serious problems now that Belarus has taken a hard line on reforms. I was glad to meet the director of the Human Rights Centre and to be able to suggest one or two ideas for funding.

Moscow

Together with the Russian co-clerk of the executive committee of FHM, who had agreed to clerk this quarterly meeting, we sifted through the reports, documents and projects and planned the agenda for the following day's all-day meeting. In the evening, an American historian came to tell us about new findings in Buzuluk and Samara, where Quakers engaged in relief work during the refugee crises and the famines in the 1920s. David had also discovered that the Quaker office in Moscow, which had been closed by Stalin in 1931, was in Borisoglebsky Street, just a short walk from our present office.

It was now necessary to plan with Victor and with Erik, who had just arrived from Norway, for a major assessment of FHM which opened on January 1 1996. We received paper reviews from members of the international governing board, talked with partners and project managers and discussed with staff their self-assessments; we looked at the efficiency of office management, communications, money-handling, filing etc.

Somewhat worn out, Erik and I gladly accepted the invitation of Emma and Yuri to spend the evening with them and their son, who has emigrated to Mexico and married a local girl. He is now having trouble with registration and cannot invite his parents for a holiday. They have been talking of visiting him for some years, but now it seems they can no longer afford to go. Yuri retired some years ago for health reasons and is on a very meagre pension; Emma, in her mid-sixties, is now doing two jobs, partly to earn more money, but also because she is afraid if she refuses to do her colleague's work as well as her own, she will lose her job.

While Friends House filled up with refugee children, mainly Chechen but also some Armenian and Azeri children who are still living in unsuitable hostel accommodation in Moscow, Erik and I continued to write a report of our findings. We decided to go to Izmailovski Park for an hour or so in the bitterly cold bright sunshine, so that I could stock up on dolls, toys and brooches to sell in aid of the hospice. Thanks to friends taking boxes of goods to sell before Christmas in places like Dundee, Croydon, Shetland and Newbury, and also thanks to the sales in and around Exeter, plus the donations from a carol concert, the hospice service in Yaroslavl gained £1200 - enough to keep going for a few weeks.

Erik, Victor and I finished the first draft of our report. We discussed it in outline with the staff and Russian FHM board members, after which I had a meeting with Natasha, who told me of some of the problems among the refugee families: one family, where there is a sick child, is threatened with eviction - it seems the neighbours had discovered they were from Chechnya; another mother, whose child is now ready to leave hospital after several months of treatment for a blood disorder, has been refused permission to take him home, because she cannot afford the medicines he needs. What will happen to him? He will probably be sent to Khabarovsk, eight days away by train. Children's homes in Moscow are overcrowded, and yet the small family home - seven children - which is supported by FHM not only gets no help from the local authority: it is threatened with closure.

Galina and I were invited to celebrate the first anniversary of a self-help group for children with special needs, which is supported by FHM. It was a freezing night of thick snow, but the drama, feasting and dancing cheered us, as did the smiling faces.

I went to see the Red Cross in Moscow to talk about training in first aid. Doctors in Yaroslavl had told me of the damage done to accident victims by untrained ambulance staff. Yes, they said, they had looked into this, but the cost is prohibitive, and it is really hard to keep the poorly paid staff.

The British Embassy rings frequently because of the unrest in the Caucasus. On 29 January, they rang to say that the head of the UNHCR mission in Vladikavkaz has been kidnapped. Together with Dr John Stephen, who had at last arrived in Moscow, I was invited to a meeting at the British Embassy where we were strongly advised not to travel. Accepting the advice with regret and feeling we had let down the people there who are struggling with appalling problems, we repaired to Friends House to work out a useful programme of activities in Moscow and to make arrangements.

We went to the Republican Children's Hospital to see the cystic fibrosis doctors, whom I know quite well. To me, having worked for some years on encouraging the parents to form an association, it was thrilling to meet Irina, the secretary of the Moscow CF parents group, and to hear her talking of networking and of supporting parents in other cities, even fundraising. The doctors, who had been reluctant to work with the parents, now seemed more confident and the unit more secure.

The department had had to move out of the Institute of Paediatrics, because the children adversely affected the mortality statistics. Now, after links with Southampton Hospital, the children are much healthier. On the ward was a baby whose mother was refusing to go home to the Russian garrison in Sevastopol where the personnel (who are viewed with suspicion by the local Crimean population) have not been paid for several months. Could she move to Moscow, where she can get treatment to the child? No.

John and I also went to see the sanatorium for children who have had treatment for cancer at the invitation of Dr Grigori, whom I have known for some years. This is housed in Stalin's dacha, a palatial place of balconies, chandeliers, and buckets to catch the drips. We also met Marina who runs the Magic Key, an NGO which supports the families of these children in various ways, for example organising meetings with teachers, psychologists, lawyers; together with two volunteers she also runs a rudimentary palliative care service for children. As she was talking, it occurred to us to put Irina (secretary of the CF group) in touch with Marina, as both sets of parents have problems in common: the stress, problems with the availability of treatment and medication, poverty and human rights: despite protestations, in September last year, a CF boy was drafted into the army, where within six weeks, he died. We are now looking into the possibility of a European Union grant for an association of parents of seriously and or chronically sick children. John is hopeful the IIHA, with whom he is linked, will help to take this forward.

As usual I went to see my former neighbours to catch up with my godson, P., now nearly three, and his older sister, who used to come to my kitchen for recorder lessons. Their mother has at last got a part-time job though this was not easy. She told me it is perfectly legal for employers to dismiss women who become pregnant, or to refuse employment to mothers of young children, especially if you have two children which is unusual. It is also perfectly normal to stipulate what sort of hair and legs applicants should have when advertising for clerical staff.

There are many other gatherings and meetings with old friends and new. I went to see Shapi, whom I had met in the Caucasus. He is editor of a major Caucasian journal and I wondered if he had any news of the kidnappings. Alexei rang FHM for help with a democracy grant application; Sergei came by several times, and together we wrote a grant application for a conscientious objection seminar in Novgorod, where it seems only two young men have ever refused army service. When we had done enough work, we would sit quietly in the kitchen with the Friends House magic teapot while Sergei talked of the difficulties at home where his wife's mother is dying. Oh no, they cannot talk of death, not with her nor among themselves. The children have been told she will get better. There was also the usual horror of standing in queues trying to get painkillers. She died the day I left, so I was not able to be with the family for the funeral.

Maria, one of our ecumenical links, told me of the fate of Fr Georgy, a liberal Orthodox priest: his church has been closed and some of his parishioners arrested, but he is allowed to use a room in the lending library.

M. came from Chechnya on her way to a landmine conference in Germany; L., from Ingushetia, where there are still many thousands of refugees, has been invited to Poland; L. and L. are looking for a European partner with whom to apply for a grant in the realm of women's and ecological issues; Grisha came to read out a newly published poem he had written about me. With the poem ringing in my ears, I left for the airport.

APRIL/MAY

Yaroslavl

Every moment since I got back from this trip last week has been spent on finishing the new EU TACIS grant application for the Yaroslavl Hospice. The Russian team and I had spent four days together in Yaroslavl mapping out our objectives and desired outcomes, justifying our requirements, trying to be true to the needs, as we saw them, of terminally ill people and their families in Yaroslavl, but at the same time mindful of the norms in Brussels. Our previous grant had been rejected because the ratio of salaries to equipment was too high. 'How much is too high?' I asked them in Brussels. 'There's no specific guideline but it's felt that in your case, you need to cut staff and buy some equipment.'

In Yaroslavl I had worked on the detailed timetable while the Russian team, looking for ideas as to how to spend the equipment money, pored over a catalogue of articulated beds, hydraulic hoists and spa baths - all available in Sweden. There was of course a distinct danger of being carried away. We shared a moment of doubt - perhaps we should not be reapplying for this grant if it makes us lose sight of our own reality; on the other hand without a major grant we cannot think of establishing a residential unit, and the day care patients will continue to dread the day when they are too ill to come to the Centre and have to stay at home, some of them alone, waiting for a visit from the home care team.

The Day Care Centre has no computer (yes, two computers are already included under 'equipment' in the grant). They had a typewriter until that was stolen in the break-in last July, so now they write out everything by hand. I had brought a disc with me to try to save time, and a friendly hospital allowed me access to their computer. Dr Sergei came to encourage us to stop for lunch. Thinking to improve one of the settings, he pressed a few keys, and the morning's work disappeared. We knew of only two people in Yaroslavl who have email addresses - a doctor who is currently in Japan, and L., the hospital bookkeeper. It was Saturday afternoon. I left a message on the answerphone at Friends House asking anyone who might hear it to forward the forms to L. I had emailed them to FHM from Exeter before leaving home. Meanwhile we continued in pencil.

It was a beautiful day with snow under the birch trees and thin cracking ice on the rivers. I have got used to the lack of springtime here, but it still seems unnatural to go from winter one day to summer the next: it was too hot to sit in the sun, and the bare trees gave no shade. Nevertheless, from time to time, we allowed ourselves to escape from the great heat of the office, where the central heating cannot be controlled, to sit on a bench outside with a chilled drink.

Good work had been done in the intervening weeks to improve relations with the local health authority, and agreement has at last been reached on future collaboration. We were invited to see the municipal 'Hospice No.1', a basic, overcrowded, rather run-down place with a strict regime, no hot water and inadequate supplies. Both toilets are inaccessible by wheelchair, of which there were two for 26 patients. The patients were all in neat lines of beds under grey blankets. The very pleasant doctor was interested to know that there is a philosophy associated with hospice care: it is not about lying still waiting for death; it is rather, as Victor Zorza said, living to the end. Let us hope that we get this grant this time! There are budget lines for training and publications, and there is such fertile soil here: between us all, we could offer comprehensive end of life care in Yaroslavl.

Moscow

I returned to Moscow with sheaves of paper, notes in pencil, and a barely comprehensible budget: we had added, subtracted and moved figures from one column to another, as we changed our minds about purchases and other expenditure. The clever Friends House computer wizard, had converted a Word 7 disc to Word 6, which saved me a lot of time, but still for several days I worked on this grant for two or three hours early in the morning before the staff arrived.

Before going to Yaroslavl, I had managed to finish the notes and minutes of the FHM executive committee meeting. Friends from Russia, England and USA had met for a few days at the end of April to look at staffing needs and at programme and accommodation. Our landlady wishes to sell the spacious flat which we have used for over two years. Do we need living accommodation? Do we need large rooms for workshops and meetings, or just an office? How to continue to support the refugee and other groups which currently use our space?

Galina, Bonnie and I went to see Irina O, chairman of the Independent Peace Service, who has recently been elected to the Moscow Duma. She told us to get in touch with an organisation in her constituency which works with young people: there may be scope for collaboration, especially in the work with young drug addicts, and it may be possible to rent a large room for AVP and other FHM projects; we could then look for a smaller flat not too far away for the office.

We found the place and spoke to the director, or rather Galina did with admirable patience. I had understood from introductory remarks that it would be better to keep quiet. Sadly, we deduced from the director's assertion that all Russia's ills come from abroad, that this would not be a cosy place, not only for our western visitors, but also for our many refugee families from Chechnya, Azerbaijan and Armenia.

We hope these families, who currently come to FHM on Sundays, will be able to continue to meet. Without friendly premises, the chances are slim as rents are extremely high in Moscow. The psychological support group for children who have suffered trauma, who also meet at FHM, has been awarded a grant, and again the money had to be spent on things rather than people: they now have a video camera and a huge homeless photocopier which at present sits at Friends House.

On my last visit I had helped Sergei and G. prepare a grant application for a conscientious objection conference to be held in Novgorod in September. During my time in England, I met the potential grantors in London (including another former student) and was told it was a good application, but helping a few young men avoid army service is not democracy. Really? When people are deprived of their constitutional rights, arrested and sometimes imprisoned for breaking no law? A grant would be considered if 1) the denial of constitutional rights applied more widely, for example if we could include refugees being denied housing, Chechens being denied passports, and sick people being denied medical treatment, and 2) if the conference took place not in one place but in five.

Sergei and I doubted we had the strength and the time to expand the application in this way. I had heard from another former student that it might be worth trying the British Embassy first. I faxed them the project proposal, and we were invited to come and discuss it with the political secretary, whom I already knew, by chance. They asked us to make some changes, but we were quite hopeful. We heard the following day that the grant had been approved.

Sergei invited me that evening to a meeting of human rights groups at the Sakharov Centre. A recent government decree invited runaway soldiers to give themselves up: their citizen's rights would be restored, and they would be treated leniently. The hundred or so who had trusted this announcement found themselves rounded up and shipped off to a military posting in Vladikavkaz or to a prison in St Petersburg. What is now the proper response of the human rights activists? The soldiers' mothers proposed a mass gathering of deserters, conscientious objectors and human rights activists, but this was thought to be too risky. The OMON, the special forces, who wear black helmets and black jackets, have become much more numerous in Moscow.

Luzhkov, the mayor of Moscow, pledged to clean up the capital and purge it of 'undesirables'. There are now fewer beggars, fewer people lying homeless or drunk on benches or in the street, and the packs of stray dogs have disappeared which is a mercy, but so have the women at the metro stations who provided a valuable service by selling homegrown produce including wonderful radishes and cherries, while the tarted-up kiosks, which sell mainly imported goods including violent videos and neon kiwi liqueur, flourish.

One of the soup kitchens was raided recently by the OMON who confiscated the equipment which had been bought with an EU grant, and there were scuffles when people were arrested at the Ukrainian Orthodox Church; street children too have been rounded up, and the authorities are even insisting that those who have been adopted should be given up to the state orphanages - the same places from which many of them escaped. Katerina, an aircraft engineer, who left her job six years ago in order to take in some of the homeless children who huddled beside the warm air vents in the metro, has had many brushes with the authorities. She is now threatened with eviction from her two-room flat, one room for the girls, one for the boys; she herself sleeps in the kitchen. For a while, two of the boys had taken turns to go to school in the winter as they only had one pair of boots. FHM has been supporting her and the children in a small way for some years.

By chance, my companion on the 16-hour train journey to Kiev was the Russian editor of a monthly journal devoted to questions of religion and society. As we talked, he invited me to contribute an article for the journal. Is that wise in the present climate? Well, perhaps not. A year ago, I cheerfully spoke about Quaker concerns to chance fellow travellers; I even had a few leaflets in my rucksack in case people wanted to know more, but now that it has again become legal to persecute people on grounds of religion, I am more circumspect. Is he optimistic about the future of Russia? 'No, the best we can hope for is a measure of stability, while a different world outlook permeates the minds of the people, but this seems unlikely. Patience is already running out. People are hungry, actually hungry.'

Kiev

Taras met me and took me home for breakfast. I was terribly keen to find out if the fertility treatment had worked, but it seemed impolite to ask. Taras said nothing though he grinned when I asked how Tanya was, and I was thrilled to see their four-month-old daughter.

Simon House and I had returned to Kiev to continue working on his project - the health of future generations which seeks to counter the poor record of abortions, teenage pregnancies, and underweight babies by promoting knowledge of sexual matters, planned parenthood and the health of potential parents, including the importance of diet. We were told by the director of the Institute that only 7% of babies born in the Ukraine are healthy. The current child allowance is 12 griven/month, about £3.75.

Our other important mission in Kiev was to re-establish contact with the parents of cystic fibrosis children. This is another second application to TACIS in Brussels. Practically speaking, we needed to get some signatures on the new forms, but we were hoping to be able to introduce group skills, management, networking and co-counselling, so that the parents' association could work to maximum efficiency, but first we wanted to listen to the parents to hear how things have changed since our last visit and what their current needs are.

How shocked we were to learn of the deterioration in circumstances since we were here two years ago! Things were not wonderful then, but now several of the tearful parents told us that they cannot get enzymes for love nor money: a three-day supply is handed out twice a month. They are not interested in newsletters or psychological support: they want inhalers and antibiotics. What is the good of a parents' association when they are watching their children starve?

We promised to try to include these essentials in the grant application, but too much of this and the grant will be turned down. It is designed to strengthen East European non-governmental organisations and to build civil society, not to supply drugs. We can put in for computers and modems etc. for efficient networking, but not enzymes to keep children alive. The oldest patient in Kiev is 25-year-old Mario who is now seriously ill, and the parents begged us to take him to England to save his life. The nurse accompanying us doubted that any treatment would help now, and the stress of the journey could kill him. There is no counselling of any kind and no preparation for the final stage. One of the parents is a doctor. The other parents agreed it would be sensible to bring him to England for training, so that they could all benefit by being better informed. This could certainly be included in a TACIS or other Know-How grant.

The parents' association in Moscow, with whom we have worked for about five years, is organising physiotherapy and the publication of information leaflets. I contacted them before coming to Kiev to see if there is anything they could share with the parents in Kiev. Tatiana brought me some documents. It seems that Irina, the energetic secretary of the Moscow CF parents' group, is in hospital herself undergoing tests. I managed to speak to her in hospital before leaving Moscow. Her future is still uncertain.

Before leaving Kiev, I called at the Ministry of Education to ask for a visa support letter to the Congress of Educators for Peace to which I had been invited, and which takes place at the end of June in Sevastopol. I got the letter and waited an hour for the all-important round stamp, but have I got the energy to go back at the end of June and then again at the end of July for a Quaker gathering near Moscow; possibly also at the end of August for Exeter Day in Yaroslavl, and at the end of September for the FHM Board meeting? The revised IIHA cystic fibrosis grant application has been sent off, so has the application from the Yaroslavl Hospice: five copies of 35 pages plus various annexes, including a map. There must be a more equitable and efficient way to redistribute wealth to benefit disadvantaged people!

JULY/AUGUST

Gratz

Vienna, if one takes a broad view, is on the way to Moscow. In theory I could save time and money by going straight from the European Congress of Peace Educators in Gratz to FHM. Not so. Pricing policies have little to do with distance it seems, and timetables are not always kind. I did half the journey by train.

At the congress *Building a Culture of Peace in Europe*, Bernhard spoke about using drama with troubled teenagers in Germany, and Toivu, an Estonian social scientist, painted a gloomy picture of his society, where real changes in attitude and perception are very slow indeed, and where, if there is a problem, people will look for an enemy, rather than try to solve the problem. More positive was the presentation from Macedonia, where Nikolina is working on a UN scheme of prejudice reduction, which includes bilingual kindergartens in Macedonian and Albanian, and structured youth camps. Many who came to my workshop were struck by the style of experiential learning: could they have more? Would I come to Ukraine?

Moscow

But first to Moscow. Friends House has moved from our very pleasant location on the Arbat. We are now between the main ring road and Kurski Station. The flat looks spacious partly because there is almost no furniture. I wondered how we would manage when I discovered that the landlord and his wife were still living there while working on repairs. There is only one small bed. Well, they are both slim, and there is a spare mattress which I unrolled in the minstrels' gallery while coping with the great heat, the noise and the mosquitoes.

Yuri and Polina gave up trying to eke a living as artists in Moscow. They turned their backs on the stresses and false values of the capital and moved to Pskov, Yuri's hometown, where they tried to become self-sufficient with sheep and vegetables. A serious fire ended that phase of their lives - there is no insurance - but now, with the rent from FHM, they will again try to live off the land.

Yuri is standing in the hall gazing at the toilet walls. Today he is going to paint them, a job which would take me 20 minutes, but for him this is no slap it on/get it done job, but a deep experience: it will take him three days. Polina understands my need to talk priorities, for example we have no washbasin, no cooker, no light in the office, but well, today is Yuri's birthday, so we celebrate with a watermelon and with shortbread and real coffee brought from England.

Because of a new law, Yuri, who is not registered in Moscow, can no longer go out on his own. He is frequently stopped by the OMON possibly because of his artistic hair, and, without the protection of his legally registered wife, he would be detained, possibly beaten as an undesirable, and after the third offence he could be deported. He looks forward to getting back to Pskov, though even in those remote regions, things are not what they were: the border between Russia and Estonia is now wired and guarded with soldiers and dogs so that grannies can no longer collect mushrooms or visit their sisters. Permission to cross can only be granted in Moscow or Tallinn with passports and signed documents. Yes, he understands about the taps, cooker etc: they have been waiting all week for a plumber; yes, I understand about the toilet walls – it is his way of clinging to sanity and self-respect. Yes, it is a bit awkward, but it could be worse.

Bonnie and Galina have arrived. As there is no table, Bonnie is scrabbling frog-like on the floor coaxing the photocopier, and Galina explains to a woman on the phone how to find us: Larisa from Kazakhstan needs help with her application for refugee status. She tells us when she arrives that a human rights journalist, a young woman, was recently murdered, and she and her husband have good reason to fear that they are next on the list. Unfortunately, in her state of heightened anxiety she asked the guards at the entrance to our block where to find Friends House. They immediately became suspicious and asked for more details. She gave them our phone number. Luckily, it was Galina again who picked up the receiver when they rang, and with her calm Russian voice she managed to placate them when they threatened to call the police.

Final preparations were underway for the first inter-regional gathering of seekers, those people who have come across Quakers one way or another and have made contact with us, often via London. Thirty five people from Lithuania, Georgia, Belarus, Ukraine, Chechnya, Tatarstan, from Volgodonsk, Novgorod, Electrostal, Gatchina and Moscow, and also from Japan, USA and UK met in Zvenigorod for three days. For some, this is their first meeting with Quakers, others have been Friends for decades. In workshops, talks and meditations, we examined Quaker thinking and values, looking at examples of service, including the history of Quaker work in Russia; we read *Advices and Queries* and explored the sources of our testimony to peace, equality, simplicity. We also swam in the River Moskva, circle danced, walked in the woods, and worshipped in the open air in the manner of Friends. How to accommodate the dozen or so people who need to spend at least one night in Moscow before going back to their corners? Well, somehow, we managed.

Galina was worried about her husband's impending operation. This had been scheduled and postponed several times. She had already paid $1000 but she herself had to find and buy suitable blood in case he needed a transfusion. She located the rare blood by telephone, travelled to the centre, booked it, and asked them to store it. But it now seems they have sold it to someone else who needed it urgently. They will ring the donor. He will probably agree to give more, especially if he is short of money.

She has also bought antibiotics, painkillers and other drugs, tubes and catheters – the hospital gave her a long list. The operation was postponed again. Should they have paid someone a bribe? How much? Under the old system it was clear - no treatment without a bribe - but now nothing is clear. Who pockets the $1000? Are the nurses paid at all? For some time, hospitals have offered no food or laundry service: you come with your own sheets and take them home and wash them. Now there are no needles or bandages. No wonder desperate people beg on the metro for money for an operation.

Hospitals and illness were to become a major theme of this visit: it seems that one of the major difficulties with cystic fibrosis children is the lack of communication between hospitals and polyclinics. Is there any mileage in our trying to improve the situation? Might the health authorities be interested in new ideas of collaboration or are hierarchical attitudes so entrenched that such a project would make no difference. IIHA has been encouraged to look into the idea.

Also on the agenda was an urgent meeting with Marina and Grigori to finalise, so I thought, a grant proposal to encourage the establishment of an association of parents of children with cancer. Marina has already started to work along these lines, but with no funding and a general disbelief in the power and competence of parents, she has met with scepticism and has all but given up. No draft proposal was ready at the first meeting, and Marina was dispirited and hostile - a different person from the one I met in January. It seems she has lost not only hope but also her job at the Oncological Institute. Did she wish to continue, or should we postpone or cancel the application? It was certainly not the intention of IIHA to ride roughshod over the group in Moscow, in fact nothing can be done until they have an outline of what they want to achieve. Our second meeting was far more productive: they had some good ideas about support and networking, and we incorporated a bit of western thinking into monitoring and outcomes.

Another project which needed some attention was the support group for children with heart and vascular problems. I rang Vera to make an appointment and she immediately asked for my passport number, so that she could add me to the eight busloads of children with heart disease that she was planning to take to an outdoor concert at the Kremlin, where Monsarrat Caballé would be singing with the Kremlin bells. The vast concert was spectacular, even though the children and I nearly suffocated, as we were not allowed to get off the sweltering buses while we waited about half an hour for the police escort and then another 45 minutes for Naina Yeltsina and her entourage to be welcomed and seated. Such a different approach to sick children and family support!

When I did manage later to speak to Vera privately, I found I could make very little headway in putting the IIHA vision of family support: to promote self-help, to empower the most interested group, the parents, and to encourage them to ask questions, to make demands and play an active part in the child's wellbeing, and to acquire skills in networking, co-counselling, and publishing useful materials for schools. In her own way, Vera does a lot for these children, sometimes persuading the hospitals to operate free, getting free supplies of fruit juice, needles, yoghurt, sometimes free holidays and outings such as this concert; she also tries to respond to requests from hospitals to get hold of certain drugs. Can our visions match? Does she need us? It was a useful meeting, and we decided to continue with our collaboration at least for six months.

Alexander Viktorovich had heard about the hospice work. He got the number of Friends House through the British Embassy and came to see me. He was an army doctor until invalided out after an accident. The army fixed him up with a job, something of a sinecure, in Hospital No.5, which is run by the Orthodox Church. He had heard about palliative end of life care and wanted to introduce some of the ideas into his wards. The Church sent him to America for training, but when it was discovered that he had specialised in the care of AIDS patients (thinking that this would be useful in Russia), he lost his job. AIDS is seen as God's punishment. If Alexander wants to work with these people, it must mean he is one himself, in which case he is not fit to work in the hospital.

He really needs a job but the health authority does not allow us to accept AIDS patients for hospice care in Yaroslavl, besides, we employ only local people and cannot afford to take on more. He had not tried the Moscow Hospice, but they do not (or cannot) take AIDS patients either. He worked for a while in Poland and then with a US-financed project in Gomel and Svetlogorsk - two of the regions worst affected by Chernobyl fallout. How frustrating to be highly specialised in something for which there is no employment in your home country!

I was pleased to hear that a grant proposal which I had helped with in January had been accepted in principle, though funding would be delayed. Valeri from the Rainbow Camp told me this group has already started work on promoting knowledge of human rights, especially in the field of religious tolerance, even though this year's camp had been broken up by OMON troops with dogs and weapons. I spent a night under canvas at the camp two years ago with Bonnie and Natasha and was struck by the generosity and trust among the campers for whom a warm fire was a shareable resource and extra water was boiled in case a stranger needed a cup of tea.

Vida told me about the deterioration of life in Lithuania; Sergei will be defending another young man in the Criminal Court for refusing army service; Galina's husband recovered well from his operation. Yaroslavl beckoned.

Yaroslavl

Nina, the hospice director, is ill. In line with our policy of networking and building up a literature in Russian on hospice philosophy, she had gone together with Olga, our senior nurse, to visit the hospice in Ulianovsk. Nina lay on the top bunk on the return journey complaining of headache and then back pain. As things worsened, it occurred to Olga to get her off the train and to seek help at one of the stations. Sensibly, she did not do this, but went herself to telephone Yaroslavl to arrange for an ambulance to meet them off the train. Our close links with the doctors and hospitals probably saved Nina's life: although they arrived at night, a swathe was cut through the normal reception process. Doctors were waiting, and drugs, needles and drips were found. She had an acute infection of the spinal cord and lost all sensation from the waist down. She is still in hospital. Some control has returned to her right leg, so she can now stand and hobble with a stick. One of her worst plagues is the catheter which gave her a bladder infection, which spread to the kidneys.

As we talked, her neighbour, Valentina, tried to get up, gingerly testing her feet on the ground. The door flew open, and a nurse shouted: 'You're late for your injection!' Valentina had had a kidney removed 30 hours earlier.

This was not the first time I had donned a white coat in order to be smuggled into a hospital. We keep a couple in the hospice van, just in case. Without it, you are challenged at every corner; properly clad you can get on with your task. Was this something of a metaphor for life here?

Moscow

Back in Moscow, Bonnie, Raffi and I facilitated a three-day AVP advanced workshop with some interesting participants at the Sakharov Centre. The following day, I flew to Vienna, then took the train home.

SEPTEMBER/OCTOBER

Moscow

It is wonderful to have the hostages safely back but shocking that three more Britons and a New Zealander have now been seized in Chechnya. I was in Yaroslavl at the time and heard on radio Russia that the British ambassador has forbidden British people to visit Chechnya until 2002.

Ten people were due to arrive for the annual three-day meeting of the board of FHM. Preparations for this gave way to other meetings, sometimes four a day, for example grant-writing with Marina on the project to support children with cancer, and meetings with project managers, including the plan to publish a book on human rights; there was also a preparation meeting for the conscientious objection seminar in Novgorod, plus other essential activities such as renewing my annual multi-entry visa, a frustrating but eventually successful job involving many phone calls, faxes, photos and visits to registration offices. And there was time for talking with staff and our new intern, David, and for drinking tea with them and with our many visitors.

Questions discussed at the board meeting included how to support local Friends in the worsening crisis, and how visible should we be in light of the new law on religions? Projects approved included work to promote healthy attitudes towards drugs and drink, a theatre workshop for children with learning difficulties, psychological support for children and families who have suffered violence, and the promotion of AVP workshops.

Yaroslavl

October 1st is Old People's Day. The hospice patients invited me to lunch at the Day Care Centre in Yaroslavl. For most, this is now their only meal. As we celebrated and reminisced, they brought out their plastic bags and gathered the uneaten food. Here comes the samovar, and today's cake, a rare luxury, was a present from the bakery, which is itself on the brink of bankruptcy. Pensions, which would now be worth about £15/month, have not been paid since June. Medicines, which in theory are given free to war veterans, pensioners and the chronically sick, are no longer available, or if they are, they have to be bought. How to survive?

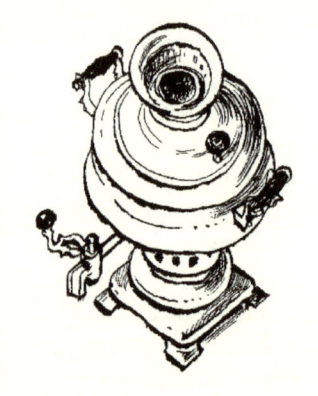

The hospice team has become expert in public relations and in lobbying. There were TV cameras and radio interviews, official doors were opened and cups of tea drunk while we had talks with the local authority and sought permission to open a charity shop for second-hand goods. We have been thinking of this for years but have allowed ourselves to be defeated by bureaucracy and tax laws. Surely its time has come. There are many unanswered questions, including how to avoid the attentions of the mafia, and how to reach agreement with the tax inspectors. Might we lose our charitable status in Russia? Nobody knows. Shall we start in a small experimental way?

It was good to see Nina on her feet again and working, at least part time. She is chronically tired after her recent serious illness and walks with difficulty. She has been longing to return to work, and this was her first day back at the hospice. She says she now feels a complete person again. We sit together looking at the hospice grant application to Soros. Is there a slim chance they will help us keep going until we hear from TACIS?

Our meeting with the deputy mayor was postponed because of a local demonstration of despair which closed several roads. Some of the hospitals are heated but most homes are not, at least not yet, even though it is -3. People have no control over heating which comes from a central source, as does the hot water.

Quote from my notes: 1 October

I'm wearing a thermal vest and a long-sleeved vest, my three sweaters, both pairs of tights, a long skirt and a hot water bottle. Last night I was snug enough with the Exeter Meeting quilt thrown over the bed, but, after handing it over to the hospice today in the presence of TV cameras and the local press, I could not very well ask for it back. The only other garment I have is a warm jacket borrowed from FHM's emergency clothes store, having given away the coat I was wearing. 2 October – no electricity today but the hospital administrator's office is warm. He is duty-bound to keep open and provide some sort of service for the 163 patients under his care. He has no money and can pay no salaries, though oddly enough, as long as the cooks will work for nothing, he can provide lunch as the funding for that is from a different source, and they have gas cookers.

Some of his patients had health insurance but there is no hope now of reclaiming that. His funding from central government comes through the Sberbank system, but the behaviour of the banks is totally unpredictable: sometimes they are shut for days, sometimes they agree to give out a ration of rubles. Today they have given him 3000 rubles about £160. He has some expensive diagnostic equipment bought with German money, but this will be useless when the three-week supply of reagent runs out. He cannot buy painkillers or bandages, and there will be no question of repairing or replacing anything. He glanced at the silent phone/fax, the blank computer. It must be tempting to accept the bribes of the people who beg to be taken into hospital for the sake of the food and warmth.

We decided to write out a letter by hand to take with us to our meeting with the deputy mayor. Yes, we were received and politely heard, but no, we could not be given answers. 'You have permission to open a shop? Open it, and then we'll see about the charitable status.' We do not want to risk this. We see the venture as a public service and as a way to help finance the hospice, not a commercial venture.

October 3rd is Teachers' Day. I am invited to celebrate with the teachers at School No.4 who came to Exeter on exchange in the early 90s. There are flowers, speeches, songs, poems, comic turns, and the inevitable table with sausage, cakes, and bottles and yes, tea. Teachers have not received their miserable salary for two months, and many have started giving private tuition. Education is becoming a privilege. The Medical Academy now accepts few non-fee-paying students.

The phone is ringing as I get home. Drs Sasha, oncological consultant for the hospice, and Natasha will pick me up in ten minutes to take me to their dacha for an evening of shashlik with their children. Shashlik cooking is strictly a male preserve, so Natasha and I gather in the last harvest. This is how many people survive: this not very large garden has yielded countless bottles of jams and fruit preserves, mounds of potatoes, cabbages, onions and beetroot, plus green peppers and tomatoes from the homemade greenhouse. Frozen fingers are revived by the fire, and when the meal is ready, we repair to the cosy, candle-lit, wooden building, where the inevitable cure-all in the -7, a bottle of vodka, is waiting.

Telephone conversations, meetings and another meal with friends leave me little time to shop for dolls, bowls etc, which can be sold in Britain to boost hospice funds. Feeling somewhat under the weather the following day, I was not too sad when another radio interview was postponed. Dr Anatoly, who happened to be on duty at the hospice, prescribed rest, so I was tucked up on a sofa and looked after by the patients.

There seemed to be a subdued mood in the Day Care Centre that day which I felt sure could not be explained by my own unusually prone posture. When the patients had gone home in the hospice minibus, the nurses told me in low voices that Maria, one of the patients, had recently died, and news of this had filtered through and was being discussed in whispers. Can it be that in all the trainings and seminars we have not covered death itself? How to bring light and air into the situation? What do they normally do when somebody dies? 'Nothing. We leave it to the priest. We are not qualified to talk about life after death.' Oh dear, the 'expert' syndrome again. We had a conversation about death and dying. Might it be helpful to encourage the group to share their memories of Maria?

Many of our nurses are also the family breadwinners: Irina lives in one room with her husband and 20-year-old daughter. For six years they have applied in vain to be rehoused; Julia is trying to save for her daughter's education; Olga supports three generations on her meagre salary.

One of the collective farms (yes, they still exist here) was moved by seeing us on TV to donate a ton of vegetables - huge sacks of cabbages and carrots lie in wait for us in the corridor. They will be distributed but meanwhile the nurses help themselves and prepare cabbage soup for lunch. Most of our patients lack the strength to cut up a cabbage, still, it was a kind gesture and the warmth of it cheers us up.

Moscow

Back in Moscow safely before the general strike scheduled for 7 October, I attended a planning meeting for the upcoming AVP advanced workshop to be held in the Sakharov museum. This was a three-day workshop which went very well on the whole, though we ran into difficulties with the role plays when participants got carried away, some playing parts dangerously close to their own suppressed painful memories. Two women were unable to surface from the tensions, so the three of us had lunch together away from the group, and they talked for the first time about how it had felt to be the child of divorcing parents. They had never met before but were able to draw strength from this new shared openness. We celebrated my birthday at this workshop then celebrated again at FHM, being serenaded by young Friends who had met to discuss business of their own, with a song, cake and candle.

I had been warned that trains could be cancelled because of the strike and was half expecting some violence and lawlessness, but although there were huge numbers of police and OMON, I had no difficulty reaching Red Square, where several thousand people had gathered for a pro-communist, anti-Yeltsin rally. I was circumspect with my camera, having once been threatened at a similar rally, but this crowd, perhaps cheered by the red flags and the old national anthem, was in good humour though some of their solutions to the present problems seemed to miss the mark: 'All our problems are caused by the dollar! Ban the dollar!' 'Order of the noose for Yeltsin!'

Irina, chairman of the CF Family Association, shared with me some of her desperation: they have enough enzymes to last until the 22 October. There will be no point in any more projects because the children will be dead. Devastating to hear this! Together with IIHA, I have engaged with these families for nearly five years, encouraging them to form an association to work on co-counselling, group skills, grant applications, lobbying. They had achieved the almost unthinkable – they had persuaded the Russian government to accept responsibility for these children, but now their official documents allowing them to collect enzymes and antibiotics from certain chemists are no longer being honoured. If they had money they could buy whatever is left in Moscow and last another month or so. I alerted the expat community to this sudden emergency and over £800 was found almost straightaway. We will try to take enzymes out in November.

Chris and I were invited to the embassy to meet the new political secretary. Charles seemed pleasant enough but somehow too green to cope with the present crisis plus the new kidnapping. We decided not to worry him with our plan for me to do a workshop in the Caucasus. If it is not possible for us to go to Grozny, then we will bring young Chechens out. Some of the young men had already done a basic AVP but since most had not, it was decided to do another basic before launching into an advanced workshop.

Nalchik

I flew down to Nalchik, capital of Kabardino-Balkaria, with Bonnie, FHM staff. It was wonderful to be with these warm and hospitable people again, not to mention the +25 balmy evenings. It was good to make new friends and to see again some of the people who had given shelter to us during the war and shared with us whatever there was to eat. The workshop was very energetic and much appreciated, and as usual the free time was perhaps equally valuable.

What are their hopes, fears, plans? A group of young people had already completed a tree planting project. Now they want to restore Grozny Park which still resembles a bomb site. Nothing was left whole - no play equipment, no benches. We danced late into the night - circle dances, traditional Caucasian dances and yes, amazingly, I danced rock and roll with Ibragim. No, these people must not be abandoned.

NOVEMBER

Am just back from an extra trip to Russia. I was asked to accompany a British doctor on a mission supported by the British government to look at the changes in the provision of healthcare in Russia. Of course, I took the opportunity to stay an extra few days to attend the conscientious objection conference in Novgorod, for which I had helped to find funding; I also took some cash to the Yaroslavl Hospice: dollars in a belt round your waist is currently the only way to transfer money.

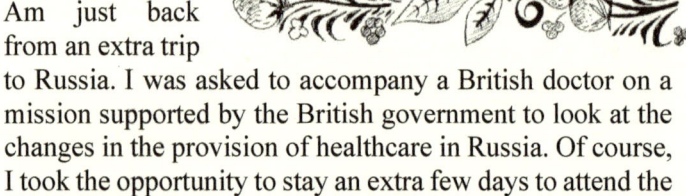

Moscow

In the provision of healthcare, we were looking particularly at the link between hospitals and polyclinics, at the continuity of care as a patient moves from one institution to another, and at family support. We went to the Russian Medical Academy where, senior personnel having been trained in England, there is now a department of general practice and family medicine. After a two-year postgraduate training, the first Russian family doctors graduated last year. Could we meet some of them? Apparently not. Where are they now? Working in remote regions and villages. It seems not to be possible at this point to alter the polyclinic system to make it more efficient. In the polyclinics we visited, we found no change from last year or the year before: patients wait in shabby corridors (there is still no booking system) while 'the experts' sit in their immaculate rooms. They were happy to take the plastic covers off the expensive X-ray and ECG equipment to show us, but these cannot be used for lack of film and paper.

We spent a good deal of time at the Republican Children's Hospital which I know well and where the IIHA has a new project in family support medicine for CF patients. A Russian nurse was trained in England to teach parents to cope with intravenous treatment at home. The families are very pleased about the possibility of treating their children at home, but in Russia this is against the law. Similarly, it is only possible in Russia to train a doctor in physiotherapy, not a nurse. The one Russian doctor who was trained in England to teach the parents this skill is overworked, short of time and frequently ill. Information leaflets and booklets have been published in Russian but, classed as drugs, they are stuck in customs. The families are desperately anxious about enzymes and antibiotics. (Does anybody have access to Creon? I could take some on my next visit.)

Yaroslavl

The Yaroslavl Hospice team, also somewhat desperate, had made some progress on the second-hand shop idea. They were thrilled with the children's clothes and shoes I took them. They now have no simple painkillers and there are none available in pharmacies. I could take out a few packets of paracetamol in January. The patients joined the staff in sending warm greetings to all our supporters.

Please let me know if you are willing to take a box of Russian toys, bowls, Christmas cards to sell in aid of the hospice.

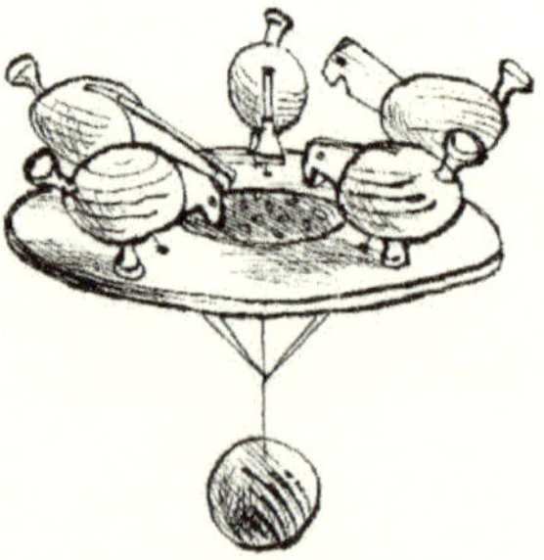

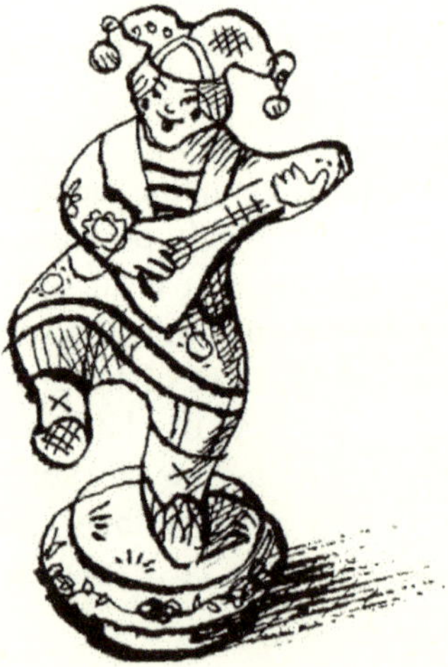

1999

FEBRUARY

Again I arrived at Sheremetevo with no luggage. The young official was not very helpful, but I was unable to leave without the all-important lost property form and customs stamp. Only two stamp officers were on duty at the time. A crowd had gathered around one, and when I approached the other, she shouted: 'Can't you see I'm busy?' Without luggage, I can easily get about by bus and metro, but a friend had come to meet me. We paid his parking fine and set off for a proper Russian welcome at FHM. Last time this happened the luggage turned up about five hours later.

Together with the staff, we planned the agenda for the next day's meeting of the executive committee. It was not ideal that I had arrived only the day before the meeting. I had agreed to postpone my trip to Moscow in order to help with a visit to London of a high-level delegation from the Russian Ministry of Health. It seems that Luzhkov, the mayor of Moscow, wants to open another ten hospices in Moscow. They cancelled two days before they were due to come - too late for me to change my ticket.

The new lock on the front door no longer works. The only way to gain entry is to ring ahead of time or to shout, or bang on the metal door with a stone so that someone comes down and lets you in. Sergei volunteered to go down and hang about inside the front door in the cold waiting for luggage which might or might not come on the last flight from Frankfurt. He returned triumphant just after midnight with two rucksacks destined for Yaroslavl. Small victories are much appreciated.

At the executive meeting we checked up on existing projects, discussed proposals and wondered whether it would be a good idea to write to Cadbury's to remind them of their Quaker heritage, now that they have opened a factory in Russia. One of our partners asked us to find volunteers to work with children with special needs. Under present economic conditions, it is not reasonable to expect people to volunteer for nothing, and yet to pay a volunteer could cause problems when professional staff are receiving so little. We decided to set aside an allowance which we hope is neither exploitative nor overgenerous. Three people from the Quaker meeting offered their services.

For many reasons, not least because our neighbours had complained about our numerous visitors, including 'undesirable' people, and had threatened to take us to court muttering about a foreign sect, it had been decided to find another location for the weekly meeting for worship. Friends now meet in a pleasant hall belonging to the Society for the Blind. We are still much exercised by the problem of registration. To what extent should we be visible?

The director of the Moscow Hospice rang and apologised for the cancellation of their visit, although of course she was in no way to blame. I took her some post from the British Russian Hospice Society, and she agreed to sell a hoist for a very reasonable price to the Yaroslavl Hospice: Moscow has more than it needs, and Yaroslavl has none. Equally importantly perhaps she introduced me to Irene, the British palliative care nurse who is on an East European placement, and offered to lend Irene to Yaroslavl for a short training course.

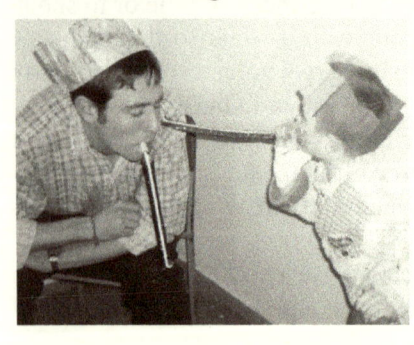

I went with David, the new intern at FHM, to the Republican Children's Hospital to talk about the grant which is intended to train the parents of cystic fibrosis children in physiotherapy skills and to encourage parents to treat their children at home with intravenous drugs. A nurse has been trained to work with the parents, and the families are glad to be able to avoid hospitalisation, but there is a lot of fear and resistance. Moscow Quakers have been asked to organise another party for the children.

Trudging through the snow on the way home, I was startled to hear 'Patreeesha'. It was M, a young Ingush man from North Ossetia - one of the participants at the AVP workshop in Nalchik in September. He had come to Moscow to talk about setting up an email network among young people in the North Caucasus. Natasha came to discuss plans for work with refugees: what would be needed to get started on a self-help project so that women could learn a craft and sell their wares? We looked at start-up costs, marketing and how to write a grant proposal.

David and I met the following day with Chris, G., Misha and Sergei to discuss the learning opportunities from the Novgorod seminar on conscientious objection which had taken place in November. We also discussed what to do with surplus funds - between receiving the money in dollars and spending it largely in rubles, the ruble had collapsed. We composed a letter to the funders putting forward our suggestions for the best use of this money – a conscientious objection video, another seminar and an email network for information and support. Young men have the constitutional right not to serve in the army for reasons of conscience, but with no law to back up this right, COs face harassment, criminal charges, and imprisonment. Misha suggested starting with placements in hospitals or care homes, then perhaps the law would follow, but even this is not easy in the absence of a culture of volunteering.

Misha S, whom I had met at the seminar in Novgorod, came to FHM to collect the book I had brought for him from War Resisters International. He wanted to pay for the book but could not buy it from me. If I would agree to sell it to a second-hand bookshop, he could then buy it from them. 'Can't I just give it to you?' He rang the bookshop to check which documents are necessary and to ask if the buyer and seller can be the same person. Yes. He gave me some money and took the book and his passport to the bookshop.

Marina came to FHM to meet Galina with a view to resubmitting a grant proposal for the Magic Key which supports children with cancer. The previous application was turned down because it was felt to be too doctor and research oriented: our grants are more family-based. It may be helpful for Galina to meet the families and to encourage them to have more input into the next application.

David and I went to see Vera and Julia who work with children with heart disease. This is an ongoing project with the International Integrated Health Association, and the funders wanted answers to some questions. What had impressed Vera and Julia most on their visit to England was the attitude of the health professionals to the parents: parents were invited to be present as the children were examined, they were informed, consulted, consoled. Vera and Julia doubt they can make much of an impact in the short term in Moscow on the 'doctor is king' philosophy, but who knows? They are planning to start with translating and publishing materials so that parents can be better informed.

Galina, Raffi and I did another advanced level AVP workshop in the Sakharov Museum. I had knocked on the director's door while visiting the museum shortly after it opened and asked if we could rent this space for occasional workshops. He wanted to know more. He looked at an AVP manual and agreed that our work promoting civil society was in line with the spirit of Sakharov and therefore no rent would be charged. It is an excellent place in central Moscow, but we sometimes feel a bit frivolous as we are watched by the sculptured heads of Russia's recent liberal thinkers, most of whom suffered imprisonment or worse.

For many of the participants, this was their third workshop, and most want to do the training for facilitators which will be offered in April. There was a high level of active participation and, as everyone wanted to act, we did three role plays which participants found illuminating, even though two of these ended in no solution to the problem. One of the role plays gave rise to some interesting discussion about changing the culture of violence among teachers in schools.

G. rang: the CO office in Novgorod has been burgled. His computer with a lot of the CO work on it has been stolen. The neighbours have complained that the flat had turned into a den of vice – more hints of undesirable people linked to a foreign sect. The police have imposed a closure order. Sergei S. will go to Novgorod to support G. He came to FHM to borrow the fare.

Yaroslavl

David and I set off for Yaroslavl. It was more difficult than usual to buy tickets this time. The woman on the second floor, where there were no customers at all, told me there was no such train, and even if there were, she would not sell me a ticket as her services were for long distance travel only - nearly five hours is not long distance. I went back to the ground floor where only one window out of 17 was open and went the manager's office to ask how I might get served. 'Go to window 6.' 'But window 6 is closed.' 'Well then, you'll have to go to the one which is open.' I queued and was then told that I could not travel to Yaroslavl without an invitation from the receiving organisation. David could, as a tourist, but I could not, as I had a different visa. OK, but what has happened to the train I always catch, the 16.25? It no longer runs on Mondays, Wednesdays or Fridays, but there is a train to Yaroslavl at 18.25. I went back upstairs to the same woman in the empty hall, and without much argument, bought two tickets on the 18.25 to Yaroslavl.

We were met by Nina, the hospice director, and Dr Sergei, and the following morning we set off with a sizeable delegation in the hospice minivan for Rostov, another ancient city on the Golden Ring. The health department in Rostov, having read about the Yaroslavl Hospice in the regional newspaper, wanted to start a similar service for their own citizens. They had made contact and had identified two nurses who had volunteered for training in hospice care. This visit was to meet the mayor's health adviser in the town hall and to discuss possible collaboration. It was cheering in the freezing weather to meet such enthusiastic people and to know that the hospice philosophy had spread itself in the most natural way at grassroots level.

At the Hospice Day Care Centre in Yaroslavl, we coincided by chance with the new priest who comes visiting, our very pleasant, round and cheerful Fr Aleksei having been moved to a different parish. It seems the new priest insists that all should attend his sessions which can last up to three hours. The staff have won a concession for patients who object to this for one reason or another - they can go in another room. There is a quiet room set aside for prayer or serious conversations, but when the new priest, who feels an urgent mission to save souls, including apparently David's and mine, insisted on an icon and an oil lamp in every room not only in the quiet room, the staff meekly agreed. How to cope with this new unforeseen hazard? Russian Orthodox believers used to be persecuted but here we seem to have another manifestation of the new 'freedom of conscience' law under which anti-semitism flourishes, Lutherans have lost their licence, Catholics have lost seminaries, the Salvation Army has lost premises, Pentecostalists are again meeting in the woods, and Jehovah's Witnesses are on trial.

I stayed for a bit while the silent audience was told to repent while there was still time or face fire and brimstone, then realised that Anna was missing. She smiled as I joined her in the quiet room. I told her it was nice to see her smiling. 'Oh,' she said, 'I've only recently learnt to smile. It was impossible before.' 'Why?' 'I was a teacher.' 'Aren't teachers allowed to smile?' 'No,' she said fiercely, then smiled.

Home care for terminally ill patients has become increasingly burdensome to the Yaroslavl Hospice as costs mount and public transport deteriorates. The local authority was asked to provide some support for this service, including a car, but instead of this they decided to start a service of their own taking their cue from Luzhkov in Moscow: local authorities are now keen to say that they are offering hospice services.

With some speed they have set about renovating a pleasant single storey building. We were shown around with pride by Irina, who is to run this new venture, and a senior official of the health department. One spacious room was already furnished with imported black desks, swivel chairs, computers and telephones; the large room next door, which was not quite ready, would be for Irina herself, and the third large room would be for the bookkeeper. 'Do you need so many large rooms for administration?' 'Oh yes, you see there will be three bookkeepers.' 'What about the patients?' 'Those that come in for the day can sit in the entrance hall, and those who come for treatment will be seen in the procedure room at the back of the building. We will offer specialist treatment.' 'What treatment? How many doctors/nurses?' 'We don't know yet if we have been allocated any money in the budget.' 'But you have nearly finished this expensive renovation...' 'That was a different budget.' 'Will there be a budget for training?' No.

As we talked over tea, it became clear that neither Irina nor her superior from the local authority had seen a hospice, nor had they read anything about hospice philosophy. Nina, Olga and I were told not to confuse the needs of ordinary patients with those of cancer patients. What did she mean? Cancer patients do not like watching TV. Nina and Olga, who have had years of training and practical experience in this field, kept quiet. Were they frightened of losing her support, or did they see no point, or did they lack the confidence? After some photos and another cup of tea, in proposing a toast to the future of hospice care in Yaroslavl, I suggested that we work together on training. It seems clear that this building will not be used for sick people, but still, some training might be helpful if the local authority is now talking about hospice care. Now more than ever we need the grant from Brussels.

There is still no news of this. With this grant and with the collaboration of the local authority we could at last offer a proper service to many of the people on the waiting list; without it we do what we can. This is not a good moment to open a second-hand shop, even though it would be a useful public service. To lose our charitable status now would be a severe blow, not only in terms of money. The children's clothes which I had brought will be auctioned to raise some money. They will also bring a lot of cheer.

Dr Valeri made contact. He was the first doctor I worked with on establishing a hospice here. He now has a much easier job with the oil refinery sanatorium, but he offered to abandon his work for half a day in order to take us to Kurba, a village near Yaroslavl.

By some miracle, the abandoned isolation hospital which we opened as a hospice in 1993 keeps going. Three more beds have been added to try to cope with demand, half are for end of life care, and half for respite or post-operative recovery. Valeri and I could not avoid a moment of nostalgia: standing in this warm, clean building among smiling nurses and patients, we remembered the rot, the cobwebs and the padlocked door.

In between visits and serious pancake eating, David and I saw a splendid production of Hamlet at the Volkov Theatre, the first theatre in Russia. We also indulged in a sauna with its attendant eating, drinking and singing in the company of various doctors and nurses, and I found time to stock up on traditional bowls, dolls and brooches which will be sold at Christmas in order to support the hospice.

I went to see Tatiana with whom Exeter University signed the student exchange agreement from which followed the city twinning link, which celebrates its 10th anniversary this year. Could I please come in June, and could I persuade Roger, my husband, who had started the process with a letter to the Pedagogical Institute, to come too? I will try.

My last visit in Yaroslavl was to the Red Cross in the company of Galina E, one of my oldest friends in Russia. No longer supported by the city, the Red Cross is still expected to care for people on the lowest rung of the ladder. They desperately need bandages, syringes, clothes, soap, almost everything. Do contact me if you have anything useful that I can pack into a rucksack for my next visit. Meanwhile destitute people queue up to donate blood for 90p and a cup of Red Cross tea.

APRIL/MAY

Nationalism is rife in Moscow. Volunteers have offered themselves to rescue 'our Slav brothers', there is a call to unite Serbia, Belarus and Russia, and we were advised not to speak English in public. The American embassy, which is roped off, is daubed with multicoloured paint hurled by passers-by. Nationalists and communists have found common voice and the heightened tension is marked by an increase of armed and flak-jacketed militia on the streets and in the metro. The borders between Russia and the Caucasian republics were first reinforced and then closed.

R., a young man from Chechnya was taken off the bus on his way to Piatigorsk to make accommodation arrangements for our workshop. This was to be an advanced workshop for those who had attended the basic AVP last

September in Nalchik. He managed to ring us to say that his experience showed that the young people from Chechnya would not be able to reach Piatigorsk. He suggested Nalchik, but the British Embassy strongly advises against Nalchik now that there have been so many kidnaps, so we arranged to try to meet in Rostov-on-Don. Would we be able to find somewhere to live in Rostov? Who do we know there? Would they be able to reach Rostov from Grozny? Shall we fax them an invitation? Can the satellite phone except faxes? We puzzled long over the fax trying to avoid provocative words like 'violence' even 'nonviolence', which could look threatening to a border guard on a train, as could 'conflict resolution' or even 'peace'. We settled for 'communication skills' and sent the official-looking document from FHM, duly signed and stamped with an antique rubber stamp which I had found in a junk shop in Exeter some years ago.

ROSTOV ON DON

When we showed this document to the two Rostov militiamen on the platform, they seemed satisfied and allowed the group to emerge from the train. As we were trying to leave the station, Boris, a local man whom I had not met, a friend of friends from Winscombe, came towards us. In a loud voice he said to the armed special police who were blocking the exit: 'They have come to a seminar. I'm in charge.' The seminar went well, and we look forward to working with these spirited people again.

MOSCOW

The next stage in the AVP programme is a training for facilitators, and we were able to offer one of these workshops in Moscow. Ute came from Germany to work with me, and of the 12 newly trained Russian facilitators to emerge from this workshop, three have now facilitated a basic workshop.

I was staying this time with Alina, who is totally deaf, and her hearing assistant cat, Tishka. After working for 35 years, Alina receives a pension of about £20.00 a month. The professor of defectology ('yes, we are looking for another word') who came to lunch, told me that she cannot afford to give up work, as she will have a similar pension. The chairman of the Russian Association for the Deaf is Ossetian and because he is darker than most Moscovites, he is picked up by the police every day, sometimes five times a day, and because his speech is poor, they often assume he is drunk. The previous chairman was murdered in May 1996.

Alina's daughter is involved in imaginative projects for deaf children and adults: some videos have been made so that small deaf children can be introduced to Russian culture, and a Russian sign language dictionary is ready for publication, but the funding was lost when the ruble collapsed in August 1998. She is constantly short of funding. If anyone has any ideas or links with deaf studies, do let me know.

Yaroslavl

The amazing news on funding is that the Yaroslavl Hospice seems to have been pre-selected for a grant from the European Union, as has the cystic fibrosis project in Ukraine. We are not quite sure what this means, though it is perhaps encouraging that we are being tormented with questions and requests. The questions refer to things we wrote in January 1998, and the requests are for another copy of the Russian statutes with translation, plus a letter of support from the mayor.

After many times of asking, we were finally granted an audience with the mayor of Yaroslavl. If we do get this grant, we would like to house day care and residential care under one roof; in fact, home care could also be administered from there. Is this possible? Again we raised the question of the charity shop – can we open a shop to raise money for the hospice? This would not be approved, at least not yet.

The donated children's clothes I took to Yaroslavl have been sold. They have given much joy to the people who acquired them, mainly for grandchildren, and with the money raised the hospice team bought some things they needed including an up-to-date piece of equipment to measure blood pressure. They have asked for more nearly new clothes for children, including shoes. Do let me know if you have any, as I could possibly collect them on my travels.

Moscow

At FHM, Galina has a problem with her eyes. It looks like conjunctivitis. She went to the polyclinic where the queue was so long, there was clearly no chance she would be seen that day. Is there a system of making an appointment for the following day? No. Zalima rang: her niece Khava was injured with shrapnel behind her eye in 1995 during the war in Chechnya. Khava has had a series of operations, but they are now frightened for the sight of the other eye. Such a pity! Surely it's time to abolish war!

This week's visitors included A., who came to see us from Grozny, or rather since there are no flights from Chechnya, he had come from Dagestan and was then held for questioning for three hours at the airport: is it possible that we can help with registration? No, but we know people who may be able to help; Z.'s flat was raided by armed police at 5.45 this morning; Ira came from Tosno. She works in a women's prison and there is a chance that she could get permission for us to do a workshop there. We have not been successful in getting the AVP programme into prisons in Moscow; Timur came with his crisis of nerves: he needs help in getting 90 Russians to The Hague.

The executive committee of FHM discussed various projects including how to help the Dukhobors. Quakers worked with Lev Tolstoy a hundred years ago to rescue this nonviolent sect from persecution after they had made a bonfire of their weapons. Most went to Canada, but some stayed in Georgia, whence they have now had to move to Briansk. Still refusing to bear arms, they are still experiencing discrimination. We also discussed the setting up of a woodworking workshop in Ingushetia to provide useful employment for some of the thousands of refugees who are still living in railway carriages after the 1992 Ingush-North Ossetian war. L., who would be in charge of this project, came to talk to us. There are severe tensions in the area.

The Hague Appeal for Peace - Peace is a Human Right. Time to Abolish War, 11 – 15 May

Nine thousand people attended this centenary of The Hague Appeal for Peace. The huge programme was divided into four main sections: the prevention, resolution and transformation of violent conflict; disarmament and human society; international humanitarian and human rights laws and institutions; and the root causes of war and the culture of peace. We were reminded that more people have been killed in war in this century than in all previous centuries put together. Issues of landmines were addressed, as were child soldiers, third world debt, colonialism, feminism and post war reconstruction. The Russians are here, as are people from the former Soviet republics, and also from Europe, the Americas, Africa, the Middle East and the Far East including survivors of Hiroshima and survivors of rape, land mines and other horrors of war.

Snippets from my notes for those of you who would like to have been there: people are fed up with fighting; we must not bring the baggage of violence and injustice into the new century; it is time to abolish war; national security threatens human security; every 22 minutes someone is killed or maimed by a land mine; 53% of the world's children are undernourished; we must seek new diplomacy, new thinking; we must teach peace in our schools; deep ethnic problems cannot be solved by violence; we need a new message, a quantum leap based on reverence and respect for every human life, for the environment and for creation.

Is this the most dangerous moment since the Cuban crisis? Russia's conventional forces are in tatters but her nuclear weapons are intact. We are asleep at the wheel. Let us build nonkilling societies! Let us share and listen and rediscover solidarity! We must work on social and emotional learning and learn how to manage anger. We can learn to go beyond what looks irreconcilable and listen to what people agree on, to transcend not just words but attitudes, behaviour and contradictions. The truth and reconciliation process in South Africa helped people to heal just by telling their stories and feeling heard.

Archbishop Tutu: 'If people tell you human beings are weak, they're lying. People destroyed apartheid. We have the capacity to end war if we are determined.'

The women's movements of many countries were well represented. Many stood with us - Women in Black - as we remembered war victims. I particularly remembered the women with whom I had stood in the Women in Black demos in Belgrade during the war in 1992 and in Moscow in 1995.

There was much emphasis on the situation in Yugoslavia. Large passionate meetings every day included analysis and academic presentations about the history of the crisis; there were also vigils, marches and calls to stop the bombing, while the Kosovar Albanians made sure we did not forget about the ethnic cleansing - most had experienced the horrors of forced migration.

There were calls for the UN to take a firmer hand in conflict prevention and in peacebuilding. Kofi Annan: 'Perfect justice may not always be possible. We must do our utmost to spare the living and those yet unborn from armed conflict and its consequences.'

Vandana Shiva: 'The politics of food is creating war with our bodies, with our fellow creatures and with the earth. Present policies are to feed the well fed and to make profits for multinationals. We do not want to grow the perfect plant; we want diversity, nonviolent technology and nonviolent economics.'

We were invited to join the following campaigns: 1) the international action network on small arms - the need for a global campaign to halt the devastating impact of the spread of small arms, 2) the global campaign for peace education - a culture of peace will be achieved when citizens of the world understand global problems and have the skills to resolve conflicts, 3) the global ratification of an International Criminal Court, the establishment of which would constitute one of the greatest advances in the rule of law and protection of human rights, 4) the international campaign to ban landmines - work continues to enforce the implementation of the treaty which bans the use, production, stockpiling and transfer of anti-personal mines, 5) the campaign to abolish nuclear weapons, 6) global action to prevent war - moving towards a world in which armed conflict is rare and peacekeeping is promoted together with disarmament, human rights, nonviolent solutions and the rule of law, 7) the coalition to stop the use of child soldiers, particularly in countries where child recruitment and participation in armed conflict continues.

The vision statement, which calls for us to find the moral spiritual and political will to do what must be done, includes the following points:

* Abolish nuclear weapons, landmines, and all weapons incompatible with humanitarian law.
* Abolish the arms trade or at least reduce it to levels compatible with the prohibition of aggression enshrined in the charter of the United Nations.
* Strengthen humanitarian law and institutions for the transition to a world without war.
* Examine the causes of conflict and develop creative ways of preventing and resolving conflict.
* Overcome colonialism in all its forms and use the resources liberated by the end or reduction of the arms race to eradicate poverty, neo-colonialism, the new

slavery and the new apartheid, and to benefit peace and justice for all, plus the preservation of the environment.

There were workshops on human rights, on conflict resolution, on post trauma rehabilitation and on how to make paper cranes. Stairs were decorated with thousands of drawings of the feet which have taken a bold step for peace and of hands held out in friendship. There were demonstrations of arts, crafts, singing and dancing; there were organised entertainment events and spontaneous groups of drummers or singers, and at the last evening party, we felt we were dancing with the whole world.

I have taken the liberty of assuming that most people who read my reports will also be interested in The Hague event, since my work in Moscow is mainly about peace, right relationships and building a civil society. It was written in some haste as I have only had two days at home, that is to say, four days in all, but have been involved in a two-day prison workshop at HMP Channings Wood. I was a prison minister in a former life. I return to Russia tonight.

JULY/AUGUST

Yaroslavl

This time I went straight to Yaroslavl where the Norwegian lorry was eagerly awaited. A chance conversation with my friend Erik when we were in Moscow had led to this. I had told him about our successful application to the European Union for a grant to establish a 20-bed unit for the hospice, and only a few days later, when he returned to Norway, he was asked if he could find a use for 20 beds plus all sorts of other things – wheelchairs, walking frames, commodes, grab sticks etc - as a care home was closing, and these perfectly good items of equipment were going for scrap. To cut a long story short, after much telephoning, faxing, grant writing for the transportation costs, the loaded lorry was at last ready to leave Oslo. A final phone call from the customs in Oslo - have we got a licence to import disinfectant soap and the skin creams into Russia? No? Well, they will have to stay in Norway. Heavens, soap! We thought we had been careful in avoiding contentious items! Let's not hold up the 82 cubic metres for the sake of a box of soap! Another phone call two days later from the Russian border - more questions: can we send a fax?

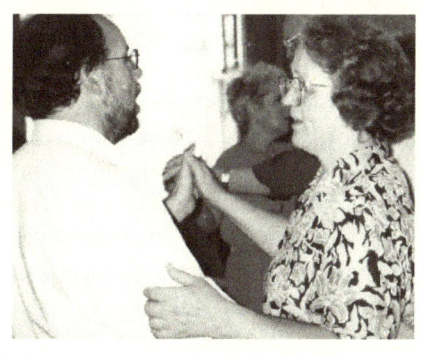

Meanwhile another conversation had led to a musical treat. Over a coffee after a concert in Exeter, I idly wondered if a small group of Cathedral singers might like to perform in our twin city in Russia. Why not? They found the money for their fares, coped with visas and flights, and here they are - six men singing to packed audiences in Yaroslavl, including a joint concert with a Russian choir and a much-appreciated performance at the Hospice Day Care Centre, followed by a dancing session with Tatiana Kasatkina (the woman who had facilitated our link with Yaroslavl) dancing with Stephen from Exeter Cathedral. Not to be outdone, the patients and nurses gave an impromptu rendition of popular Russian songs under the energetic leadership of Tamara, who has made such a good recovery from her breast cancer that she is now more volunteer than patient, though she can no longer reach the extremities of the piano.

A telephone message reached us on the evening of the farewell concert with speeches, flowers and fond farewells, the lorry had arrived. Another phone call summoned me back to Moscow but not before we had had a chance to talk to a young, slightly disabled, brilliant, to my mind, local artist. I had met her some months previously at an official function and wondered if there could be scope for collaboration. I bought some of her painted wooden items for fundraising resale in England, but more importantly perhaps, she expressed a real interest in visiting the hospice with a view to designing a logo. It surprised me that the hospice team was thinking of a logo, when there are so many serious problems to contend with, but I understood that it was an expression of confidence: they are now ready to be recognised as a force for social change in the region. Two nurses from Rostov have been trained in Yaroslavl in the care of the terminally ill at home. This service has become very popular in Rostov, and the health authorities now want to open a centre for day care. Another health authority at nearby Pereslavl has also heard of the Yaroslavl Hospice. Could they be linked into a training programme? We are still waiting for the funding from Brussels.

The contents of the lorry were locked under seal while the paperwork was sorted out. As I write five weeks later, the load has still not been released. Nina, the director of the Yaroslavl Hospice, has relayed to me some of her almost daily conversations with customs officials:

<u>Customs</u>: Why do you need all this stuff?

<u>Nina</u>: Because it will make a real difference to the service we can offer our patients.

<u>Customs</u>: These things are available in Russia, or if they are not, it means Russians don't need them.

<u>Nina</u>: Many of the things are not available here, and even when they are, we cannot afford to buy them. We cannot even afford to buy incontinence pads.

Moscow

In Moscow there were problems with one of our FHM projects. This was the result of another chance conversation. Sharing a bench at lunchtime some months ago with a participant during an AVP workshop at the Sakharov Centre, I asked about his life. He told me he tries to keep young people out of prison. 'How? What are your challenges?' 'We are getting ideas from books. We need proper training in mediation and restorative justice.' I rang Mediation UK: would someone come to Moscow? Yes. FHM raised funds for Marion's fare and other costs, the dates were fixed, a venue found, and here they are.

Despite detailed communication between the English facilitator and the Russian organisers, still the first two days had demonstrated that there were mismatched expectations. There were also problems with the interpreter who missed nuances and continued to use the word 'criminal' rather than 'offender', despite repeated requests. A small group of us met over a pizza and a cup of tea to talk about where to go from here with restorative justice, mediation and conferencing. It was of course unreal to expect one interpreter to work at this level all day. I shared the last two days with her and learnt a lot about restorative justice. The participants' final evaluations were very encouraging. Some of the social workers and psychologists present were hoping to take the ideas further. What a challenge for them in a society where offenders are imprisoned for years, sometimes three to a bed, so that they have to take turns to lie down!

At the FHM executive committee, we discussed among other things the local Quaker meeting and the FHM sponsored retreat for Russian Friends which is due to be held in September. We also heard about arrangements for the Baltic peace gathering, looked at new project proposals and received reports of ongoing projects, including the CO work, the psychological support for children, and the support of refugees: one family is Russian and it would not be safe for them to return now; others have nowhere, nothing and nobody to return to. Many are desperately poor and are living in overcrowded flats, usually with a relative who is registered in Moscow. FHM has supported a programme to teach computer skills to those who want to learn; we are also encouraging them to register as an organisation so that they can officially apply for funding. We will of course help with grant writing and other support as needed.

Galina, Sonia and I facilitated an advanced level AVP workshop in an orphanage in Moscow. Our youngest ever participant was a twelve-year-old boy. What a joy he was with his unspoiled vision! He threw himself into the various discussions, eg how to raise self-esteem without falling into what some call the 'sin of pride'. Also present were two of the people whose project proposals we had discussed at the FHM executive committee. The successful one was to support conscientious objection information work in Dzerzhinsk, which is only 7 hours by train from Moscow, and Andrei was very pleased to receive the money straightaway so that he can prepare for the autumn draft; the other was to support an emergency telephone line for women. FHM had had no previous links with this group and were not convinced that the work must be done by trained and experienced psychologists who need to be paid. I took the opportunity to get to know Albina during breaks and accepted her invitation to visit the room where the psychologists wait for the phone to ring.

They did not have to wait long. Albina showed me the results of a questionnaire that had recently been filled in by

1000 women in Moscow. Number one on their list of problems is money, 2) a worsening of human relations, 3) the threat of unemployment, 4) the deepening divisions between rich and poor, 5) a weak and inefficient government, 6) the drugs problem, 7) crime, and 8) many are afraid for their lives. People are shutting themselves off from their neighbours and concentrating on survival as tensions worsen.

Chance conversations (and cups of tea) can solve some problems, but there is more work to be done as the level of violence, including domestic violence, increases.

SEPTEMBER/OCTOBER

Buzuluk

Isn't it wonderful to sit quietly and to know that what you see from the window will still be there in five minutes? I am back home after a journey through five time zones involving four countries, planes, trains, buses, cars, a minibus and the metro. With two friends from Moscow, I went last week to Buzuluk (27 hours by train) to facilitate an advanced AVP workshop in a teacher training college.

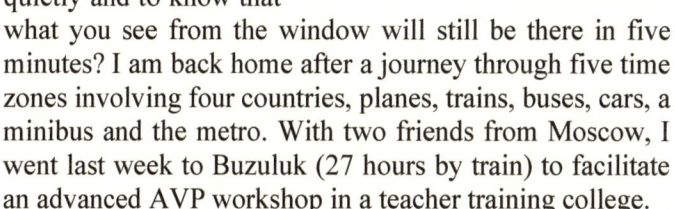

Reading about Quaker work in Russia, many of us had come across this unlikely sounding place where Friends had worked among refugees after the First World War and during the typhus epidemic, and where some had stayed on through the post-revolution civil war, though there was a gap of about 18 months when it was thought to be too dangerous. Sergei, FHM staff and amateur historian, had taken it upon himself to travel there to visit the archives and the museum and to see if the Quakers were remembered. Yes, a few people remembered being fed by Quakers during the famine, and although there is no mention of this work in the local museum, the buildings still stand - the office, orphanage, hospital and storerooms. On this occasion

Sergei had brought with him copies of photographs taken in Buzuluk in the 1920s which are stored in Quaker archives, and the museum curator agreed to display them. Sergei also had with him $300 - a gift from Friends - with which to buy equipment for the children's rehabilitation centre. What an entertainment the children put on for us!

The workshop went well, and it was good to be in this place so far from the centre of things, and as we froze on the train, we remembered early Friends - Nancy Babb, Theodor Rigg, Ernest Rowntree, Ruth Fry, Ruth Pennington and others - who travelled this route 70 years ago in far worse circumstances.

Odessa

This visit to East Europe had begun five weeks earlier in a heatwave in Odessa with a project organised by the International Integrated Health Association. I had gone with a team of four from the Royal Brompton Hospital to work with doctors, nurses, social workers and parents of cystic fibrosis children. Trying to counter the prevailing opinion that the expert has all the answers and concentrating on the importance of the contribution of the parents to the care of these children, we were especially dismayed with the official translation of the last slide: *'above all, a multidisciplinary approach is needed'* as *'strong discipline is essential'*. But the discussion which this caused was in fact very helpful. It was one of those mistakes which led to deeper understanding.

We had expected parents and some children to be present at some of the sessions, but were told this was not possible because of procedures, lunch etc. Two of us went to the ward to encourage the parents. Yes, they knew the English were here. Some parents had come from miles away - Minsk, Kharkov and Lugansk - in the hope that we had brought medicines and could cure their children. Yes, some drugs were available, enzymes for example, which took four days to be released from customs, and painkillers for

Kay, a 12-year-old boy, whose sharp decline had been brought about largely by a lack of physiotherapy, but there is no cure, only training in care and physiotherapy.

After some negotiations, five of the parents agreed to come and meet the physiotherapist from London, who again emphasised the vital role of the immediate family and the importance of simple techniques – breathing exercises, clapping and huffing. For most of us this was not our first visit to the University Hospital in Odessa, and for some of us it was depressing to find that attitudes had shifted so little: still the hierarchy is firmly in place, still the nurses have no status and still the parents do not believe that their contribution matters. Should we be doing things differently? Is there another approach?

Kiev

The team flew back to London, and I caught the overnight train to Kiev in order to meet the CF parents' group there. I went to the newly opened Tsentr dlia Invalidov (Centre for Disabled People). A great deal of money had been spent on this building which now gleams with plastic windows and modern furniture (I was told this was a vote catching measure). There is even a ramp up to the front door - a rare sight - but how useful is this, since there is no lift, and the meeting room is on the third floor?

About ten parents had gathered and more arrived during the next hour. Clearly, Vera, who took over when the previous secretary's business partner was shot dead in Kiev last year, is overburdened with the single-handed running of the CF parents' group. She is also anxious about her child's condition. In the general confusion and noise, her only option seemed to be to shout. I suggested looking at choices – what is the first thing you need? 'We need a place to meet.' 'What is wrong with this place?' 'We don't know if it's available.' 'Have you asked?' No.

It is not surprising there is so much negativity in the circumstances, and yet it is disappointing that after years of work with these and similar groups in Russia and the Republics, still so many meetings are a matter of shouting and anecdote. How can self-help groups be encouraged to help themselves when the odds are so heavily against them? How can ordinary people begin to solve their problems when it seems to be nobody's job to book the room? How has it happened again that for 70 minutes of this meeting nobody is taking notes except me? 'When did you last meet as a group?' 'When you were last here.' 'So this is your AGM. Will you not need a note of your decisions and a record of who has offered to do what?' Burdened as they are with sickness in the family, poverty and isolation (their neighbours fear the coughing is catching) they still don't believe that they have any power.

Four CF children had died during the summer. The parents said this was because the hospital doctor they normally see was away on holiday at the time, and there was no one else to give advice. I went to see this doctor at the Mother and Child Hospital. A specialist in genetic diseases, she told me she is not paid to consult CF parents, in fact she had not been paid for a lot of her work over the last ten years, and since she has now lost her assistant, her time has become more precious. She complained that the parents, instead of following her advice about exercise and diet and generally maintaining a good level of health, use weird magical cures including urine drinking, and then demand that she save their children's lives when they are in crisis. To whom should these parents now turn?

I went to the Institute of Paediatrics and was introduced to the head doctor at the children's polyclinic next door. She is also a geneticist, and by chance she was planning to leave work early to go to a meeting at the Institute of Genetics: would I like to go with her? The director of the Institute was sceptical, but he told me to come back when the grant money finally comes from Brussels. 'Yes,' he said, 'we could do a serious job in the education of the parents, of the doctors and of the community if we had some funding for publications and training.' Meanwhile where should these parents go? To the children's polyclinic at the Institute of Paediatrics. This run-around was exhausting and it must be so much worse for the parents (usually mothers), worn down by anxiety and the very real fear of losing their child. But what choice do the doctors have?

Yaroslavl

In Yaroslavl is another group of people waiting to hear from Brussels. We had applied for a grant for a 20-bed hospice unit in January 1998, and we heard in December that we had been preselected. Nearly a year later, all we have is a file of correspondence. We have had to justify a), b) and c) and explain why we have not asked for d) for example interpreters' expenses, which we don't need. We were also warned to increase the per diems for the European 'expert', ie me, otherwise the grant will not be taken seriously. But I have no need of taxis or of accommodation expenses, as I have plenty of friends, and we eat simple home cooked meals, with ingredients from the market or from somebody's garden.

Marc Delmartino from the EU in Brussels asked me to meet him in Moscow and he showed me what other Europeans claim in per diems – 300 euros a day each for hotel expenses plus three meals/day. I had claimed 15. I added a zero on the end and, in due course, gave the extra cash to the project, though we did have one multi-course hotel meal to celebrate.

A document from Brussels in July said that we would have to start the project within two months, and this caused a flurry of meetings at high level in Yaroslavl, but there is still no agreement and no sign of funding. We have had to describe exactly what we will do in month one, month two, three and so on, but of course it is not possible to remain in a state of readiness with no end in sight. After several false alarms, we have lost credibility in Yaroslavl.

Rostov Veliki (Yaroslavski)

Meanwhile the hospice team, while continuing to do what they can for terminally ill people and their families in Yaroslavl, have won a Soros grant to help with the establishment of palliative care in Rostov. The changes that have been brought about by the injection of not very much money are quite remarkable. At first sight it might seem that redecorating two rooms at the polyclinic is not the best use of grant money, but this, and the acquisition of a washbasin, a bit of furniture and a telephone, has done wonders to raise the self-esteem of the local staff. Galina B, the energetic polyclinic oncologist, runs the service in addition to her normal work.

There are now three trained nurses and three volunteers. Two of these came forward as a result of a newspaper article, the third is Vera who, to our way of thinking, has volunteered her services too soon after her loss: her husband died in April just short of his 47th birthday. Her ultimate aim is to move to Kazan, where her parents live and her daughter is in college. The paperwork will take many months and meanwhile her only interest in life is the hospice, to whom she reckons she owes a huge debt. In fact, she wants to give her flat, the only thing she owns, to the hospice, so that they can open a centre for day care. It seemed churlish to refuse the offer, but at the same time dishonest to accept this gift from someone who is not quite stable. We agreed that nothing would be done for six months and meanwhile she could find out the cost of a suitable flat in Kazan.

We had brought to Rostov boxes of warm clothing, bandages and soap, all gifts from Norway. The lorry load was eventually released after much argument and negotiation, though three boxes and 20 sacks of clothing and sheets were missing; the disinfectant soap, which we had been told had been removed in Oslo as it could not be imported without a licence, was found tucked in one of the boxes of incontinence pads. Of course, the second-hand computer caused a lot of bother with the customs officials, as did the syringes, but surprisingly enough most troublesome were the bandages. In the interval of time between the lorry leaving Oslo and the load being released in Yaroslavl, a new law had been passed: brand new cellophane wrapped bandages from Norway cannot be imported into Russia without medical tests and a licence from the Ministry of Health in Moscow. Each small box of bandages needs its own certificate and each certificate costs $7.00! What to do? It seemed that the only option was to burn the lot because customs wanted to charge for storage, and the cost of sending them back was huge. As so often in Russia, the problem was solved by a personal appeal to a highly placed friend.

Moscow

Friends from America, Japan, Norway and England had gathered in Moscow for the FHM annual board meeting. This year, apart from the usual agenda items connected with priorities, policy and budget, we gave a lot of thought to the current level of violence in the country. An advertisement in The Friend had raised enough funding for one of our projects in the Caucasus, a woodworking shop for refugees in Ingushetia to provide skills training, work and eventually furniture and shelter; another project in Ingushetia for work with traumatised children was also approved, as were two projects for supporting refugees in Moscow: one for training in computer skills, the other to encourage women refugees in Moscow to form their own association, so that they can organise activities to meet their needs and apply for funding; also approved were two projects a) to encourage volunteering and b) to promote the idea of an alternative to military service.

With daily reports of the appalling war in Chechnya and after the bomb attacks on housing, Moscow is a very tense place. Thousands of special force police have been drafted in to help check every flat in Moscow - who is living where?

Are they registered? The whole of Moscow is undergoing a process of reregistration: notices on doorways encourage citizens to ring and report any suspicious-looking people in their area; vigilante groups are meeting; new locks are appearing on entrance doors; some blocks of flats now have guards on the door asking questions of all visitors. The spot check on our block took place early in the morning on the day after I arrived. Alina was asked to show her passport as she left the building, and luckily I was too sleepy to respond to the doorbell, which is more light than sound, as Alina is deaf. She told me in the evening that she had worried about this all day and begged me to say if asked that I was a distant relative, otherwise there might be all sorts of questions.

Adding to the atmosphere of fear and suspicion, posters of men wanted in connexion with the bombings have appeared in prominent places in Moscow and other cities. The men are all demonised and dark, and the wording invites citizens to help catch these criminals. Because of the bombs and the campaign to incite xenophobia, there is now a great deal of public support for the Russian attitude towards Chechnya. Many of our Chechen friends in Moscow live in a state of fear. Z. told us she and her brother had been threatened by the police.

Lillehammer

In the middle of this trip, Chris and I flew with Z., who was anxious for her brother and phoned home every day, to Norway for a weekend congress of peace builders and change agents. Together with people who work in the Balkans, in South America, and in the African Great Lakes region, we looked at obstacles to peaceful change: how to overcome passive dependence on authority, and how to encourage people to believe that they can play a part in creating a different future, especially if they can find a way of working together. Yes, but sometimes, just sometimes, one can get discouraged.

2000

JANUARY/FEBRUARY

Let me start at the end. There had been no heating or hot water for three days, and on my last evening in Moscow there was no electricity or gas or water of any sort. I arrived home on the bus from Heathrow at 2am a couple of days ago with a four-year-old Chechen girl and her father. Her mother welcomed us. The child had hysterics when I met her in Ingushetia, and the father was not at all well. We doubted this trip would be possible, but here we are.

Nazran, Ingushetia

Galina and I were in Ingushetia to conduct an AVP workshop with human rights workers and refugees in Nazran. We had planned to do an advanced workshop, having previously done two basics, but there were problems in gathering the group: one had recently lost her mother, two more potential participants were unable to get out of Chechnya, and one had not been in touch. It was agreed to gather a new group and do another basic; we hope to form an advanced group from the two basics in due course.

Piatigorsk Region, North Ossetia

We stayed in a house in the Piatigorsk region of North Ossetia, where many displaced people from Chechnya also seek refuge. As we drove through the checkpoints, I was advised to take off my woolly hat and my glasses, as they marked me out as being non-local. I already knew from years of similar journeys not to look at the guards, as this seems to provoke them into activity.

Accompanied always by Chechen armed guards, we helped to pack boxes of essential foodstuffs for 1200 needy families. Many refugees are not registered - some have simply moved in with their relatives, and others somehow survive in outhouses. We visited one of the camps where hundreds of refugees live in railway carriages and tents in the mud. Here is the pity of war.

The stationary train consists of 105 carriages. The carriage we entered houses 17 families, 64 people in all. In each tent there are 20 double bunk beds with a narrow gangway. Gas has recently been provided by the Russian Ministry of Emergencies to heat the one stove at the entrance to the tent. The stove itself is a danger to children, though it does give some welcome heat. Many people were lying on their beds - the old, the sick, those with nothing to do. There are few medicines available to these people and very little medical attention.

Because the authorities wanted these people to go home to their ruined houses, they had not provided food, apart from bread, for five days. Some told us they had tried to return but were forced to come back to the camp because of military activity.

Most of the people participating in the seminar were living in these conditions. It was not surprising that during the construction exercise in which, in small groups, they can build whatever they like, using only newspaper and masking tape, and communicating only nonverbally, these young men and women built houses. One group built a whole complex, including a tree and a bus which could bring guests, and R. sang a song about home to his battered guitar, one of his few remaining possessions.

We wondered how we dared to offer this workshop, including light and livelies and the brainstorm - *what is violence*? It was difficult to imagine what these people who had experienced real terrifying violence could gain from this. We were tempted to abandon the address list required by funders, but our anxieties turned out to be groundless: participants were eager to write down their addresses even though their houses for the most part no longer exist, and for us it was one of the best workshops we have done. We very quickly found common tongue, the participants were full of infectious enthusiasm and energy, and the evaluations were extremely positive. They were keen for us to come again, and we all look forward to an advanced workshop, though we cannot predict where or when.

Meanwhile the outlook for tolerance and democratic rule in Russia is not good: there is no plausible alternative presidential candidate, key government ministries have been given to the communists and ultranationalists, and the more liberal factions, ie nearly half the deputies, having been given no positions of authority in the Duma, have staged a boycott. During a TV interview, the leader of the nationalist party advised these people to join a majority if they want positions of power. There is no democratic opposition.

Only one TV channel dares to criticise the war in Chechnya: it suggests that we multiply the official figures for dead, wounded and missing by three. Interviews and news broadcasts on the other channels promote the ideas of defeating the enemy, of victory and heroism. The newscaster congratulated one of the generals on his birthday: 'With generals like you, Russia need fear nobody.' The word 'Chechen' is inseparable from the word 'bandit', and anyone a bit dark is liable to be challenged. As we entered a metro station in Moscow, the swing doors separated me from my young Chechen companion. I turned to finish my sentence, but he had gone. The OMON held him for several minutes in the street before releasing him. It seems this happens several times a day.

Other victims of this hardening attitude are conscientious objectors. More are now being arrested and brought to court, and more cases are ending in defeat. The harshest is that of Alexei whose mother has long been a conscientious objection activist. He was sent to prison for two years in October 99 and spent the first two months on severe regime, ie he was on his own in an unheated room in freezing temperatures.

Yaroslavl

Yaroslavl was several degrees colder than Moscow and the deep crunchy snow was splendid. The hospice is still functioning well but not without problems. The local minister of health suddenly declared that the rental agreement for the Day Care Centre would not be renewed. Why not? 'Because you are over the norm: you have 10 square metres beyond the statutory limit.' What norm? What limit? There isn't another hospice day care centre in Russia. We tried to approach the situation nonviolently, but she would neither see us nor speak to us on the phone. Appeal to higher authority brought immediate reassurance and a renewed agreement, but we recognise that the problem is probably not solved. We are still waiting of course for the grant money from Brussels, and our dream is to incorporate a centre for day care into the 20-bed unit.

Rostov Veliki

Meanwhile Rostov continues to be a success story. We borrowed a hospital van, one of the few with a heater, and set off at 6.30 in order to see the local health minister who had a gap in his diary at 8am. He was most appreciative and welcoming and told us there would be no problem in finding premises in Rostov. Nina and Olga brought some bandages, incontinence pads, stoma bags, creams and medicines to the tiny hospice department in Rostov; they also brought one of the anti-bedsore mattresses - a gift from the hospice where my mother had died in Tiverton. This was urgently needed. Patients who spend their last days on such a mattress say it is like lying on a cloud!

In spite of the heater in the van, we had to stop several times so that the driver could scrape a chink of visibility in the ice on the inside of his window.

Pskov

Pskov was not much warmer. Galina and I went there on the overnight train. Yuri, our FHM landlord, had invited us to see his work and to look at one or two possibilities. He and his wife, having lost their smallholding after a serious fire, live simply on the rent from FHM while they work on issues of nonviolence and ecological awareness. Polina, who has a theatrical background, has managed to open an after-school theatre where a lot of creative work is done on tolerance and self-development.

Yuri and his friend Igor told us of their plans to renovate abandoned greenhouses; they also want to repair a natural spring which could provide ecologically pure water. What about an international work camp? Why not put in a project proposal to FHM?

Yuri also wanted us to see a home for children with severe learning difficulties and disabilities, which is a good two hours from Pskov and beyond the reach of any public transport. On the way there we called in on his friend Tatiana, a school psychologist. She it was who had alerted Yuri to the appalling plight of these children.

Because no trained teacher would choose to work in this remote place with such poor conditions and miserable pay, the 120 children, all of whom have been abandoned by their parents, though some may be genuine orphans, are taught by untrained women from the local village. It was sad to see the blank faces of these children, all sitting in neat rows at empty desks, all hopelessly looking at the alphabet. There was no music or movement, no exercise equipment; there was not even enough food. Of course, there is no hot water, but the bathhouse is heated once a week, so that the children can be bathed and given clean clothes.

Back in Pskov, we went to a small school for children with special needs which has been set up by a German organisation. The staff here, having received a great deal from Germany, are glad to have an opportunity to share their training. We encouraged Yuri and Tatiana to put in a project proposal to FHM for the Pskov personnel to train the village teachers. We cannot fundamentally alter the structure but perhaps this will help the children to reach their potential. At least it will be more fun.

Moscow

At the executive committee meeting of FHM we received reports from ongoing projects including conscientious objection work, AVP and a new NGO run by and for refugee women in Moscow.

New projects agreed:
- to support the dissemination of restorative justice in Russia
- to pay the expenses of a local Friend while he works with a human rights group
- to equip a resource centre to help handicapped school-leavers in their search for education or work and
- to promote conflict resolution in schools.

APRIL/MAY

Ingushetia

Well, who'd have thought it? Here I am in the baggage check shed at the airport in Ingushetia being challenged to play my recorder! London's Burning does not seem quite right, nor does Jingle Bells. I strike up a hearty rendition of the Bells of Norwich. We danced to this tune with the children and with the AVP participants. In two ticks we'll have the border guards dancing right here round the conveyor belt and the buzzing arch. Normal life - tickets and visas and 'empty your pockets' - is suspended for a moment. Galina was asked my name, so I am now on first name terms with the officials in this busy little transit zone, including the woman who had discovered the rogue instrument (could it be a weapon?) in my shoulder bag. She takes me by the arm and introduces me to the ticket lady. 'This is Patreesha. Can you stamp her ticket, please?' Meanwhile the luggage lady has become anxious: 'Patreesha, don't forget your rucksack!'

After the stresses and sadness of the last few days, it feels good to have shared a moment of common humanity with these people in the shed. Now on our way back, Galina and I had set off from Moscow in faith not knowing what would happen when we arrived in Ingushetia. Would it be possible to do the advanced AVP workshop, as we had promised? Would we be able to link up with the local FHM project managers? Would we be met? We had sent a message with someone on the previous day's flight from Moscow but had it reached anyone? We had one-way tickets and open minds.

So many people met us that it was hard to decide what to do first. After some loud discussion in the hot sun, L. and her bodyguard took us to Nazran. FHM currently has two projects here: the Sparrows work with refugee children. A car collects the four women who run this project and takes them to the week's location. They set up a temporary base and let it be known that children between the ages of 6 and 14 are welcome. To the more remote areas which have been largely ignored by other charities and agencies they bring their programme of music and song, dancing and storytelling, and materials for modelling and painting, plus puzzles and games in an effort to create a framework in which children can be children. Many have lost members of their families in Chechnya; some have seen things which no child ought to see. They all live in appalling circumstances: we were shown a room 3 metres by 4 which is home for 10 people. They have now acquired bedding from Denmark but through much of the freezing winter they were sleeping on the concrete floor.

The other FHM-funded project which was set up by L. is a woodworking workshop, which is intended to provide employment to skilled refugees, to train young men, and to produce windows and doors. Y., who took us to see the foundations and the mounds of bricks and sand, explained the many difficulties he is having: the costs, the frosts, the unreliability of the young workmen, some of whom had gone back to Chechnya. In short, the money had run out. It had not occurred to him to apply for further funding, nor, though he had the figures somewhere, could he let us have a report including a financial statement. It is a revelation to him that if he could produce a simple report with some figures, we might prefer to find more money to complete the project, rather than blame him.

It was a great joy to see the AVP participants again, though we also shared sadness: Zh had spent a month in hospital and was now skin and bone; F. was in severe pain from kidney stones and could not afford the treatment she needs; R. is worried about his children who are still in Grozny, where there are now rumours of typhus; A., who was the life and soul of the previous workshop, is having difficulty being present in mind, and 29-year-old S., who, when we were last met, told me of her longing to have a child, was widowed in February. She counts herself lucky that she knows how her husband died and knows where he is buried.

What shall we do? Is it appropriate to try to do an advanced AVP workshop in these circumstances? We consulted with the group. It was decided to go ahead as planned.

The theme for an advanced workshop is chosen by the participants. Galina and I had worked out a starting agenda which was designed to empower them to make a group decision by consensus; our task was then to think up a coherent programme so that their chosen theme could be explored. How we tormented ourselves that evening! How to work positively on the abuse of power, bearing in mind the appalling stories that we had heard? We offered an agenda, the workshop was much appreciated and all the participants want to enrol for the next stage - the training for trainers - but when and where? Where will these people be in June or July? They long to go home but it is still too dangerous, and many have nowhere to return to: villages have been reduced to rubble, there is no water, gas or electricity; the rivers are polluted, and fields mined.

It was good that we had taken the advice of our friends who warned that it would not be wise for us to stay in North Ossetia at this time and to risk crossing the border each day: all the houses were checked and eight young Englishmen arrested in the night. It is time for us to leave Ingushetia where the population of 300,000 has been augmented by 200,000 refugees, and where the electricity comes and goes, and water is stored in the bath. But first we are invited to lunch with B.'s family. So pleasant to sit next to the summer (open air) kitchen in the comfortable seating area shaded by a prolific vine, but it was shocking to hear that the local maternity hospital has no running water!

The plane is packed. No doubt within a few hours of landing in Moscow, some of these young men will be stopped by the police because they are dark-skinned. Which one will be arrested I wonder - the one who gave up his seat, or the one who helped with the luggage or…?

Moscow

Galina and I catch a minibus to the crowded metro. 'Where are you from, Patreesha?' Heavens, it seems the woman I find myself sitting next to on the metro was also in the baggage shed! She writes her name and address on my metro ticket so that I can visit her when next in Nazran.

Yaroslavl

Yaroslavl seems a distant memory and yet it was only two weeks ago that we sat for hours with the samovar, checking every detail of the agreement for the TACIS grant. We were slightly alarmed to see that according to Brussels, in spite of the mountains of paperwork and correspondence, the 20-bed unit is meant to be in YARISKAVU - three mistakes in one word! Worse, under a new rule any journey further than 200 kilometres is now deemed to be an international journey. Well, this might make sense for people traversing the countries of Western Europe, but in Russia, where we can travel for eight days before meeting a frontier, few journeys worth the effort are less than 200 km. Yaroslavl, only 230 km from Moscow, is considered to be next door! Does it matter? Yes. When we filled in the forms two years ago, the only choice under *travel* was *local* or *international*. Under *local travel* we calculated the travel costs of hospice networking within Russia - attending seminars in Petersburg or Perm, inviting hospice workers from Astrakhan or Kazan. According to the new rules, we will not be able to use the money in this budget line, as there are no hospices within 200 km. Should someone tell them in Brussels that Russia is big?

The truly major problem is the strange behaviour of the local minister of health. For years she supported the hospice movement in Yaroslavl: it was largely thanks to her that we were given the premises for the Day Care Centre, and we always tried to keep her informed of developments. Having signed over a building for the 20-bed unit for which the funding is now within sight, she has suddenly withdrawn her agreement. The building is still there and it is still in need of repair, rather more so now, and there is funding for this in the grant budget, but without her support, it is beyond our reach. What caused this change of heart? Could it be connected with the fact that her husband died of cancer in December?

Can we help her recover some balance so that we can move forward with our joint project to provide comprehensive hospice care the citizens of Yaroslavl? She refuses to see us or even speak to us. Does she blame us for the delays? About a year ago she seemed to give up on us when the money was not forthcoming. There will now be further delays as we hunt for alternative premises. Not easy: once the contract is signed, we are committed to certain activities in the first month, second month and so on; how to do this when the building we had surveyed is no longer available? We met with Victoria, the hospice psychologist, to think what to do.

In search of some relief from our problems, we gather at the Day Care Centre where Tamara is playing the piano. The patients entertain us with wonderful Russian songs, and I play a couple of duets with Tamara, but I cannot help noticing that Rimma, who was part of this group and who always sang so lustily, knowing every word of every song, is missing; Raissa died recently too - such a busy little woman always wanting to do the washing up or mop the bathroom floor: 'I never knew what it was to sit still till my legs swelled up'. And Svetlana, who still treasures the memory of dancing with the Exeter Cathedral singers after their concert here last July, is now too ill to come in for day care. She will be visited but we cannot offer adequate care. She faces her last weeks largely alone. It is for her and the many like her that we need residential care.

A woman rang the hospice: her father is dying at home and his passport runs out next week. The woman is desperate. Her father must apply in person for an extension, but he is too frail now even to be transported to the office. If he dies within five days all will be well, but if his passport runs out before he dies, it will be impossible to bury him, and there will be endless arguments over tenure of their flat. A notary has agreed to come to the dying man for a fee so long as he is transported there and back by a person connected with the case. The man is not our patient and we have only one vehicle, but how can we refuse? The essence of life in Russia is still to be found in the classics: Tolstoy, Dostoevsky and above all Gogol. Here Gogol and Dostoevsky meet Thomas Hardy.

Rostov Veliki

A major celebration has been organised in Rostov to mark the successful completion of the Victor Zorza Trust grant which was awarded to the Yaroslavl hospice team to promote the theory and practice of hospice care in Rostov. This was a small grant to train social workers to join the Rostov nurses who were trained in Yaroslavl last year. With a grant from Soros an office within the polyclinic has been refurbished and some equipment bought. The celebration is out of all proportion!

Amazing to think that when I first talked of establishing a hospice with Charity Know How money in 1992, nobody in Yaroslavl knew what I meant! Even when the small hospice opened the following year in Kurba, a village outside Yaroslavl, it was not possible to name it because the local people did not want it known that there was a hospice in the village: hospices are not nice - people die in hospices. Now the room in Rostov is packed with medical personnel, social workers, relatives of patients, city administrators and radio and TV journalists. The Soros representative is here, as is the chief oncologist of the region, and the proceedings are chaired by the pro-rector of Yaroslavl Medical Academy. Yes, the Yaroslavl hospice team is expert now at PR, but is this a shade over the top?

Moscow

At FHM we received reports from our three projects in support of conscientious objectors: seminars and consultations have been held for young men and their families in Dzerzhinsk, Gatchina and Perm, and alternative service work has been found for volunteers in a care home and in a park. We feel these projects are particularly important now as young conscripts are being pursued with greater energy. Under the Russian constitution, young men have the right to opt for alternative rather than military service, but there is no law to back this up nor is there a structure for civilian service. FHM is attempting to establish a model of alternative service simply by doing it. It could also be helpful to the young men when their cases come to court to have a record of voluntary service. We were glad to hear that Alexei, whose mother is known to us as a human rights activist, was recently released from prison: in October 1999 he was given two years (the maximum) for opting for alternative service. He has spent much of his time with 20 other men in an 8-bed cell.

Reports were received from:
- Sparrows - FHM agreed to increase the funding to include training, and to allow for two extra staff to be employed, so that in two teams of three, they would be able to reach more refugee children in Ingushetia

- AVP - four more workshops have been held in communication skills, personal empowerment, problem solving and conflict management. There are now 20 trained Russian facilitators, and the advanced manual has been published in Russian. Funding for this work was also increased.

New projects adopted included:
- A summer camp for our partners over many years who work with children with special needs and their families
- An international ecological work camp in Gatchina
- A long-term project in Pskov of collaboration between the children's theatre group which concentrates on self-development, peace building and ecological awareness, and the orphanage for children with disabilities
- The development of a conflict management programme, co-funded by the Swiss Embassy in areas where there is a high concentration of refugees
- Support for local Friends in their quilt-making initiative
- The young Friends summer gathering and
- Spare time activities for teenagers, including art classes, cooperative games and camping, organised by young Friends in Novgorod.

Thank you for your interest. Good quality children's clothes are much appreciated. We also need musical instruments for a school in Chechnya. They have asked for a violin and a guitar.

JULY/AUGUST

Nazran

Clowns? What do you want clowns for? Don't you have clowns in England? Médecins du Monde had told us that the clowns - an Englishman, an Irishman and a Frenchman - would be performing to refugee children at a market in Nazran, capital of Ingushetia, at 7pm. We scoured the markets – the old one which is called *Newmarket* and the central market, which is on the edge of town, and eventually found, in a small camp, the shining faces of children enthralled by the motley trio, one of whom is the son of friends in Exeter.

Malgobek

Galina and I had gone to Ingushetia to do the AVP training for facilitators with the group of Chechen refugees who had done the basic workshop in January and the advanced in April. They had arranged for this third and vitally important workshop to take place in Malgobek, a place visited by very few foreigners, so few in fact that the police came to investigate. Where was our permission to travel? Who finances us? Where was the rubber stamp? Why was there a Ukrainian visa in my passport? The policeman and the FSB agent were given copies of the manual in Russian, and these inspired more questions as they read about prisons, violence and volunteering. Why would anybody want to do something for nothing? How can communication skills reduce violence?

We had been called in from the field next to the hotel. We had been admiring the full moon while singing and dancing and playing the guitar and reminiscing about home, which for most is only a memory, and now at midnight, after a ladder was found and lads had forced an entry through our window (Galina and I having left the only key in our room and shut the door), we are sitting on the floor in the hotel discussing the philosophy of AVP with the officers of the law. Arresting a foreigner could be more trouble than it is worth. They decided to arrest two of the participants instead but agreed in the end they were no more guilty than the rest of us. The options were to arrest all eleven of us, something of a logistical and bureaucratic nightmare, or to wish us good night. An hour later they chose the latter.

The interlude, though not pleasant at the time as we had no way of knowing how it would end, was a useful demonstration of the philosophy of AVP which is based on transforming power to which we can all be open if we choose: in short, faced with a potential conflict, respect yourself, respect the other, keep calm and look for a nonviolent solution. The guitar and the cup of tea may have helped.

It was an excellent workshop with some memorable moments as the participants prepared and presented their agenda. The evaluations were full of the thrill of new discoveries: 'I had only ever seen myself as a victim', said one woman; others used the words *fascinating, challenging*. For us, the thrill was to see our friends grow in stature before our very eyes. The nine newly trained AVP trainers were presented with manuals which they took back to their tents and their cow sheds. Of course, we will try to keep in touch, but they agreed to support each other as they gain confidence.

The Moscow Friends meeting quilt was presented to A., whose birthday it was; and S., whose musical instruments had all been lost in a fire in a school in Chechnya, went home with the guitar and a violin - gifts from friends in

England who had read of the need. She invited us to the next school concert.

Moscow – St Petersburg

After a somewhat frantic day in Moscow, I left in a monumental downpour for the midnight train to St Petersburg. Among the four of us in the compartment, it was agreed that I, in spite of umbrella and raincoat, was the wettest. They left me alone to strip naked and to don some only slightly damp garments from my rucksack, I then went to wring out my dress in the corridor, the loos being locked, while the next person took her turn to change. We dangled our clothes from all available hooks and slept in a sort of sauna in the great heat. What a beautiful day dawned in St Petersburg! In the almost empty local train to Gatchina, I spread my wet things in the sun to dry. Oh dear, these eccentric people, first they skip through torrents, dodging thunderbolts, and then they display their laundry in the train! I got some funny looks but became hugely popular when it turned out that I had the only timetable, soaking wet it's true, but still legible.

Gatchina

FHM has three projects in Gatchina. I went to look at the pottery studio where K. and M. work with children who would otherwise be at home on their own or on the street. They had used an FHM grant to make their roof space habitable so that they could invite more children as there are so few out of school activities, especially in the winter. The pottery classes have become very popular.

I also talked with A. who runs the advice centre for conscientious objectors. He is having problems with the local militia because of his activities - his support for the young men, his newspaper and other publicity. It may be that he should look for an office: in the current climate, could it be dangerous for him to continue to use his home address? He will look into the possibility of renting a room with a phone.

The third project is an international work camp in Gatchina Park. After breakfast in Karl Marx Street, I joined the FHM group of ten volunteers in their primitive but charming abode in the stable block of the park. Imagine Kensington Gardens and Hyde Park with only three gardeners plus two part-timers to pick up the rubbish, all litter bins having been stolen because they make good barbecues!

What on earth do we hope to achieve in two weeks? My back not being what it was, I knew that pond-clearing was not for me (for pond, think Serpentine times three), so I joined the acacia pruning gang. We looked for tools in the pitch dark, there being no electricity or windows, in a storeroom big enough to house a plane, then Masha, Sveta and I, after very little instruction from the site manager, got going on the acacia walk. In a charming garden designed for the royal family to enjoy the delicately scented arched walkways - twelve of them, each 25 metres long (nothing by halves in Russia) - with marble statuary and gryphons and a graveyard for pets, the acacia trees had had their way unattended for several years. It was our job to wrestle with the unruly and thorny branches and to saw off the ones which refused to yield. Of course, while you are at full stretch up a ladder - string in teeth, secateurs biting into stubborn wood – the mosquitoes attack behind the knee. How thrilled we were at the end of the second day to have finished one elegantly shaded walkway, and how we enjoyed the shashlik party by the river with songs and football, and then the walk home in the daylight late at night! This is the first time we have done this project but there is surely scope here for practical work in international relations and, though this is a long shot, in alternatives to military service.

Yaroslavl

Yaroslavl beckons. How to cope with the new decree that for every hospital patient there must be 300 square metres of space? What problem is this designed to solve? Is it going to help the patients who have to provide their own sheets, soap, needles, drugs, bandages, oxygen and blood? Or will it help the technicians who are unable to use expensive equipment for lack of paper? Or the patients who would starve if their families did not feed them? Or the doctors whose salaries, miserable at best, are not paid on time? Besides what does the 300 metres include? Are hospice patients included in this decree?

After three months of serious premises-hunting, the only building which has been made available to us for the 20-bed hospice unit project is a rundown, almost to the point of no return, sotsward, where 25 socially deprived people are given a bed and not much more. They share a total space of about 200 square metres. How does this fit with the new law? 'But you'd only be renovating, so that doesn't count.' 'No, we would want to make radical changes.' 'Well then,' I was told, 'you can include territory in your calculations. There's a wood at the back.'

We asked the chief architect of the city – is there really no alternative? What about the empty kindergartens? 'You can't put a hospice in a kindergarten.' Why not? 'Because although it's true people are not having babies now, in ten years' time they might, and if we give away all our kindergartens, there won't be anywhere for the children.' 'If there are no suitable premises, there will be no grant.' He promised to give it a thought and let us know on Friday.

He did come up with two suggestions: one is already a bank; the other has been sold commercially. What to do? Can we turn a crumbling sotsward with 25 beds, a huge corridor in typically Russian fashion, one minute bathroom with no room for a wheelchair let alone a hoist, and one WC into a hospice? There are some pros of course, not the least being that there is no choice. We have commissioned reports on the state of the building and feasibility and will then decide to go ahead or return the money, the first tranche of which is imminently expected.

Moscow

I went to the 25th anniversary of the Helsinki group in Russia - not a happy atmosphere as those who had served hard labour for setting up the group could see parallels in today's trends. From the point of view of civil society the news in Russia is not good. Putin is often to be seen in the company of uniformed personnel saluting, giving out medals, even firing a gun. The arrest of the head of independent television coincided with the refusal by its hard-hitting satirical programme *Puppets* to remove the Putin character. In a recent programme the doll explained what is meant by the dictatorship of the law: 'Easy. I change the law and then dictate.'

At the FHM executive meeting we received reports from six ongoing or recently completed projects:

- The summer camp for children with disabilities and their families at which the parents of a 12-year-old boy, whom they had rejected at birth, expressed their wish to take him home and to look after him
- The small school for Chechen refugee children in Moscow
- The mediation group in Odessa who have prepared materials for mediation and anti-bullying work in schools
- The seminars of support for elderly refugees
- The restorative justice project
- The resource centre for orphan teenagers with learning difficulties.

We approved projects to translate restorative justice material into Russian; to provide sewing machines and other materials for a group of forced migrants in Krasnodar;

to continue to support the small school for refugees in Moscow, and to make a contribution to the *Culture of Peace* children's camp.

OCTOBER

Penza

Have you ever heard of the Leonidovki? Neither had I until I met Oksana and Lydia who had come with their children to the Sunday classes for refugee children in Penza. Ethnic Russians are having to flee from some of the former republics of the Soviet Union to which their great grandparents had been sent as part of Soviet policy. Many, having lived in Kazakhstan, Kyrgyzstan or Latvia for three or four generations, are no longer welcome, but they have nowhere to return to. There are 80,000, mostly Russian, refugees in and around Penza. A few local residents led by Misha, himself a refugee from Grozny, set up a self-help group - the Little Fire - which bravely does what it can with a Soros grant.

They bought a computer so that they can register the refugee families and their needs and, thus organised, they can link the families with medical and legal support. More importantly perhaps, the internet gives them access to other potential funders. The UNHCR provides a minibus, and, with another grant, they set up the Sunday classes for the children, all of whom have had disrupted schooling. The minibus still exists and the space is available for classes and meetings, but the grants have ended and the teachers have not been paid since July. For the children from Leonidovka this is their only schooling. The immediate worry is that there is no money for petrol to bring them the 15 km into Penza. Galina and I, who had gone to Penza to do an AVP workshop at the invitation of the Little Fire, gave them the money which we had on us in various currencies. This will be enough to run the minibus for about four months. There is no other transport to Leonidovka.

Why did these 350 people all from Kazakhstan decide to settle in this place where there is no paid employment, no medical service of any sort, no schooling and no transport? Their families had come originally from Penza and they had heard that property in Leonidovka was cheap and the soil fertile. They thought that together they could survive these hard times by growing their own food. At the beginning the school was functioning and there was a bus to Penza. Only later, having spent their meagre savings on buying properties, did they understand why the local people were keen to move out: this is a major storage zone for weapons of all kinds – chemical, biological and nuclear. Thirteen of their children have died in the last 18 months.

Little Fire took the local authority to court a few months ago when Lydia was threatened with the loss of her status. It was claimed that she had deliberately made herself homeless in order to get treatment for her husband, whose cancer had reached the third stage. They won the case and the advocate, who charged no fee, is confident that they will win the appeal.

Yaroslavl

For some years I have had a multi-entry, automatically renewable 'charity' (because of the hospice work) visa, but the local authority has been questioning the hospice team, and the mayor's office rang me at the hospice office in Yaroslavl to ask all sorts of questions. Why, for instance, had I landed on a certain date (they knew the date) at Domodedovo airport and not at Sheremetevo? 'Because that's where the plane landed.' Not wanting to involve the hospice team in trouble, I took it as a warning and did not apply for an extension.

With my newly acquired tourist visa, it was thought to be too dangerous for me to accompany Galina this time on a trip to Ingushetia and Chechnya to support the recently trained AVP facilitators in their first workshop. A., a young Chechen woman living in Moscow, accompanied Galina. This turned out to be a wise decision. Galina was thoroughly searched at the airport, and it was probably the presence of A. as a witness which prevented her from being relieved of some of the money she was carrying (this is now a known hazard). The workshop went well, and, on this occasion, there was no police check, though the timetable had to be adjusted to fit in with the recently imposed curfew hours.

Galina and A. managed to reach a couple of villages in Chechnya where they were able to give a small amount of FHM emergency relief money to the destitute families who are still living in ruined houses with no services. These and the other survivors of war are facing another winter with no heating or running water.

Moscow

At the FHM annual board meeting we received reports from:
- An initiative of young people in Novgorod to run an environmental activities club for teenagers
- A group which works with people with disabilities and their families
- The restorative justice project, a small group of dedicated people who organise trainings in mediation and restorative justice
- The newly formed organisation for forced migrants in Krasnodar
- The Sparrows, a programme for refugee children in Ingushetia
- The Russian young Friends summer gathering
- Open House, which supports refugees in Moscow
- AVP
- Projects in support of conscientious objectors

- Odessa mediators, who have run courses in nonviolence and bullying awareness in schools and in the community.

FHM agreed further support for most of these organisations.

Many of the grantees have come to talk to us and to explain their needs. Especially impressive was Marina who is running the project in Krasnodar. FHM had given money for the purchase of sewing machines and other materials so that a group of refugees could make goods for themselves and for sale, and could offer skills training. Marina came with tablecloths and shawls. She predicts that the group will be self-sufficient within six months. She asked for another rather expensive sewing machine which can handle embroidery.

She also came with a proposition from another small group of refugees in Krasnodar: if we could lend them $4,000, they could start up a honey producing cooperative and could return the money, some of it perhaps in the form of honey, within four years or so. We feel this is a good opportunity for community building which could lead to self-sufficiency among deprived people. We have asked Sergei, FHM staff, to visit these groups in Krasnodar, and we could look for funding for this project.

Yaroslavl

What about Yaroslavl? After the epic six-month struggle to find premises in Yaroslavl for the 20-bed hospice unit which is at last to be financed by the European Union TACIS grant, Larisa, a good friend to the hospice team, published an article in the local paper: 'Can no home be found for a hospice in Yaroslavl?' She made it clear that if no premises are offered, then the money will have to be returned to Brussels. Having read the article, Dr K., whose hospital in the village of Dievo Gorodishche was under threat of closure, contacted the Yaroslavl Hospice team.

Larisa was so thrilled at the success of her article that she immediately published another: 'At last the hospice has found a home!'

This of course had dire consequences for Dr K. who was simply making preliminary inquiries and had not sought the permission of his superiors nor of the Ministry of Health. A major scandal was averted when the hospice team, who have had training and experience in nonviolent communication and in public relations, invited all concerned to the Hospice Day Care Centre for a meeting for clearness and lunch.

Yes, we have permission to proceed with the plan to convert a spacious village hospital in a poor state of repair into a 20-bed hospice unit. Dr K. has agreed to be the site manager for the renovation works, and we drove the 17 km to Dievo Gorodishche to reassure the remaining staff that they would be offered jobs at the new hospice after training, if this is what they want. Yes, there are challenges ahead but this is something of a triumph.

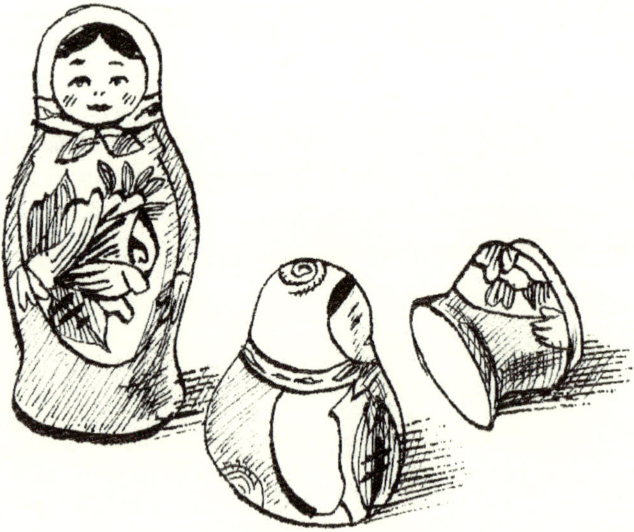

2001

JANUARY

Moscow

What? sounds like tennis racket? By some miracle, a Chechen family had managed to ring me in Moscow. The line from Chechnya was so bad that shout as we might we could still only glean information from random syllables. It is -12 there, and there is no heating and little running water, though most people have electricity for part of the day. The children go to school but only for about 3 hours a day, partly because of the cold and partly because of the shortage of teachers, books, and other materials. It seems that schools were bombed deliberately and this is a major worry: Chechens are proud of their educated children - their engineer sons and doctor daughters. What is to happen now that thousands of these children have had little or no education for five years? What hope that they will be accepted for higher education?

They speak of frequent murders, bombs, arbitrary arrests, and disappearances; you still have to bribe your way through checkpoints, submit to searches and respect the curfew. A tennis racket is no less logical than the violin I took them last year. In the circumstances it is probably exactly what a 9-year-old boy needs. Has anyone got such a thing, perhaps recently outgrown?

The small Chechen school we support in Moscow has recently had a major setback: they have had to suspend most of their activities because of a fire which did serious damage to the building where they meet. Nobody was hurt but they suspect the firemen of making off with their safe which contained the recent grant from Friends House Moscow of $1500. What to do about this? There are no reliable insurance companies in Russia - loss is loss.

FHM supported a grant to the new project which runs a drama and play studio in Moscow: thirteen war refugee children are to be offered trauma counselling and play therapy; the parents will also be offered a course in stress management.

FHM agreed to pay for a website to be set up so that hospitals throughout Russia can be informed about services which are available for children with heart diseases.

FHM also offered continuing support for the alternatives to violence project - eight more Russian facilitators have been trained. There are now trainers in St Petersburg, Penza, Novgorod, and Ingushetia as well as Moscow.

Among the other project proposals approved by FHM in January are support for
- An ecological work camp in the summer in Gatchina
- The crisis centre for women in Gatchina
- Work with COs so that young conscripts, having opted for voluntary work instead of military service, can be supported through the courts.

Funds were requested to continue the work with the children with special needs at the orphanage near Pskov. FHM had been alerted to the plight of these children by Yuri, our landlord, who now lives in Pskov, and we were invited last year to go and see for ourselves. The children sitting at their desks in serried ranks hopelessly trying to learn the alphabet were indeed in a pitiful state, and the teachers - untrained women from the nearby village - were working for a pittance.

What to do? FHM is not big enough to cope with such a challenge. I rang a young woman I had met at the Anglican Church in Moscow (I sometimes sang in their choir), had tea with her and showed her the photos. It was decided they would hold their July youth camp in the area and the inspiration came from some of the young campers: why not raise money for some fun equipment and for training the local teachers in simple life skills and craft work which they can perhaps pass on to the children? FHM agreed to contribute $1500 to this project, which has expanded to include a psychologist, a legal advisor and a specialist doctor. We are hoping that some of these children can be rescued from the fate which awaits them in adult institutions.

Another new departure for FHM is a loan scheme: two groups of forced migrants in Krasnodar need some capital in order to become self-sufficient. The women's group has asked for a new and even more expensive sewing machine, and the men's group would like to expand the bee-keeping co-operative.

Krasnodar

Galina and I went to Krasnodar - 28 hours by train - to meet Marina, formerly an oil engineer in Grozny, and Victor, also an engineer, who had to flee from Kazakhstan last year because of ethnic tensions. Krasnodar is in an area of 5m people of whom 600,000 are refugees or forced migrants. Was the machine really necessary? These are more or less destitute women, most of them widows who fled from war in Abkhazia and Chechnya. They are so glad to have the work and the company. They are afraid to meet all together: they meet in small groups where they will not be challenged by the neighbours or the authorities.

The potential beekeepers are equally circumspect. Hives are placed in the villages and only one person knows where they all are. These people who have suffered discrimination, persecution and exile prefer to take no risks. We understood from the enthusiasm of those we met that bee keeping is not just an income, it is rather a respect for the wholeness of life. We were enthusiastic about this venture and will continue to fundraise so that more families can be accepted onto the programme. We have agreed that some of the repayment can be made in kind.

Yaroslavl

The Yaroslavl Hospice meanwhile has challenges of a different sort. The money has now arrived from Brussels, the first tranche of the EU grant, but as more bits of the building are uncovered, so more rot is exposed. Why does the new roof leak? Why did the ceiling fall, crashing through the floor? Why have small doors been fitted onto the new loos, when larger doors were specified for wheelchair access?

Brussels sent the money in November 2000 and they expect us to have completed the repair of the building within the first month. This is probably not realistic anywhere, certainly not in Russia in the winter. Conditions were not pleasant on the building site in -20: the building inspectors have their own ideas about timing, the architects have attitude, and the builders have a thirst. It was hoped that we could deal with some of the issues over a civilised cup of tea, but this was not to be.

Lacking the rich vocabulary they were using, I was able to sit serenely as they pointed fingers at each other while shouting something about a dog. I took a photo of the row, and the flash shocked them into silence and then to an awareness of the futility of the noise. How to move forward? We did manage to establish a working relationship and parted if not friends at least collaborators on a project. No, the hospice will not open in February or March. April perhaps, God willing. Let us hope that Valentina, who wanted to be our first patient, lives that long. At least the kitchen has been made ready, and a hot lunch is now provided on site.

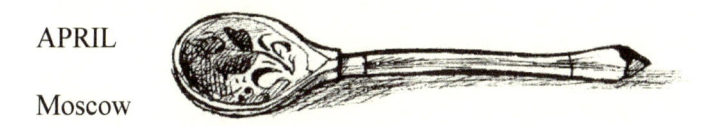

APRIL

Moscow

On my last morning in Russia in April, I settled with my breakfast and switched on the TV as usual partly for language practice but also to keep up with the news, and on this occasion I was seeking reassurance as I had heard that NTV, the independent channel, was off air. I was surprised to see grainy pictures of the police raid on the studio running on a loop before the screen went blank. The other channels, including the Russian news service, offered no explanation; BBC radio - nothing.

Grigori, who runs a centre for children with cancer, came early to collect some gifts from well-wishers. 'Have you heard about NTV? Armed police raided at 3am. That's it. That's the end of independent telly in Russia.'

Galina came to collect the keys. 'That's it. There's nothing more to be hoped.' Yeltsin had had his disagreements with this hard-hitting liberal TV station, but its doom was writ when they refused to remove the Putin puppet from the spitting image show. There were accusations, counter accusations, meetings, demos, protests. NTV addicts watched the unequal endgame, some even took part. A trailer was shown for a Saturday evening feature on journalists in the Chechen war which threatened to challenge the official line. Was this brave or foolish? The raid took place early on Saturday, only hours after I had returned from facilitating an advanced workshop in Sergiev Possad for human rights activists.

Yaroslavl

I was in Russia for the quarterly meeting of the FHM executive committee and for our monitoring visit to the Yaroslavl Hospice project. Our expert, a Russian speaking Greek of Bulgarian extraction, knew nothing about terminal illness or hospice care, which embraces the whole family and seeks not to deny the process of dying or to add days to life, but rather adds, were possible, life to days.

Plamen was moved by the atmosphere at our Day Care Centre, where he helped to celebrate the birthday of a patient. He subsequently wrote glowingly about this, about the project as a whole and about the dedication of the staff, but his expertise was in accounts.

He spent a lot of time checking the 147 pages of the project report, which I had sent to Brussels in February together with the four document binders, each an inch thick, and he tried to help us fit the prescribed parameters for petrol and other receipts. We have to justify local travel by giving the purpose of each journey made by each individual, and each person's allowances must be on a separate piece of paper. You feel sorry for the trees.

Moscow

At FHM we received reports from several of our projects including:

- A club for refugee children to enjoy drama, painting and storytelling - all of which help with their social adaptation.
- Oleg wrote to express gratitude for the wooden apparatus and toys: the play shop gives the children confidence in handling money.
- Forum, which is developing a programme for preventing and resolving conflict in migrant NGOs.

- Roof, which has been working with children with special needs in an orphanage in Pskov, wrote about the handicraft and skills training.
- The beekeeping project has taken on another eight people, of whom four are disabled and one is a single mother.
- The school for refugee children, which is run by university students in Moscow, applied for funding to replace the textbooks which had been lost in a fire.
- The restorative justice group we support had held a seminar in Kiev, where the ideas are new.
- The club for teenagers in Novgorod and the crisis centre for women in Gatchina also wrote about their activities.

Successful funding applicants included AVP which has recently run three basic workshops in the Moscow region; the bee programme for forced migrants; the Odessa mediation group which plans to run a training programme *Through Integration to Civil Consciousness*; Sparrows who work with war refugee children in Ingushetia; the orphan outreach project and the orphanage youth club, both in Moscow, and the crisis centre for women in Gatchina. We also agreed to fund a seminar for volunteers and a volunteer information brochure.

MAY

Moscow

Having been invited to the Moscow Hospice Conference, I returned to Russia in May, not just for the two days, but for two weeks as FHM was short-staffed. At the restorative justice seminar, which was organised by one of our grantees, we discussed the enormous challenge of translating these concepts into

Russian, for example 'shame' which as well as being verb or noun is, in this context, a process of recognition of responsibility on the part of the offender, linked with the need for forgiveness.

Always interested in breaking the cycles of violence, Galina and I joined the Warm House *Tolerance in Schools* project. Children at a school in Moscow were shown a video of Chechen children talking about bombs, ruins, dead bodies, hatred and revenge; some spoke of escaping at night running through fields and begging not to be left behind as they fell over. It was clear to us all that life should not be like this. In small groups we processed their reactions, and many of the children drew pictures of their vision of peace or wrote friendly letters. These will be taken to the refugee camps in Ingushetia.

L., our link in Ingushetia joined me for a couple of days. Russian authorities are encouraging the thousands of war refugees still living in tents and railway carriages to return to their homes, but how can they when their homes are in ruins and there are no public services? World Vision has joined the emergency feeding programme.

Galina and I celebrated Sakharov's birthday together with liberal politicians, human rights activists and others. It was a sombre affair with speakers bemoaning the fact that the process which had started was now grinding to a halt. A decade of democracy is not enough to establish a tradition which would encourage people to believe that their views matter. 'How can we build civil society without a free press?'

How indeed when even the Yaroslavl Hospice team comes to an important congress of Russian hospice workers with no proposals for the development of hospice care in Russia, no brochures or visiting cards, even though we had discussed the opportunity for networking, community building and lobbying. Nobody knows how many hospices there are now in Russia or where they are, and as no list of participants was available at this conference, we still do not know which ones were represented. No, ten years of democracy is not enough: there is still no tradition of identifying a problem, looking for allies, defining a strategy and getting things done.

Yaroslavl

Still, the Yaroslavl Hospice 20-bed unit was declared open even though it is not quite ready. It was a jolly occasion with speeches, TV cameras, champagne and a concert. It is also a triumph of human endeavour. The Brussels grant is for two years only. The fundraising and community building efforts continue.

SEPTEMBER/
OCTOBER

Moscow

Participants at last week's seven-day residential workshop on human rights, democratic processes and peacebuilding were invited to present a vision of Russian society as it could be in 2020 in terms of government, education, health, the media, relationships and attitudes, and then to consider how they might get there from here. What skills, knowledge, support do they need? We looked at human rights, having downloaded the declaration in Russian from the internet, and how these rights link with responsibilities and our needs. For that matter - what are our basic needs?

Constantly drawing attention to the techniques and tools we were using, we worked on nonviolent communication, ie how to move from defending an adopted position to one of hearing the needs of the other; we practised negotiation and mediation and looked at how to facilitate a meeting. This being an experiential workshop, we prepared to re-enact a court hearing of a case brought by the family of a young demonstrator who was shot dead by a soldier. In four groups of three - the family, the soldier, the army, the government - we discussed our rights, responsibilities and needs.

The last day was devoted to workshop design. What sort of workshops do your constituents need in your areas? How can you empower them and encourage the growth of civil society? The placards from all our brainstorms, lists, agreements and diagrams were valued as resources and the four facilitators were on hand to challenge, provoke and encourage. For this workshop, Erik and I had successfully applied for funding from the peace education budget of the Norwegian government.

The participants in this training for trainers were all from organisations in southern Russia who worked with migrants and other disadvantaged groups in their areas. Many of them are themselves war refugees; one had to leave early when he was recalled to Rostov-on-Don to deal with a new influx of refugees from Abkhazia where the fighting has intensified again.

Yes, there is hope for civil society in the development of hospice care in Russia. During conversations over coffee at the hospice conference in Moscow in May, it had been suggested that while it is thrilling that the Russian ministry of health has at last recognised that courses in palliative medicine are a legitimate part of medical training, and that two such courses have already been set up in Russia, the most efficient way to spread the ideas of hospice care to the widest number of medical personnel would be for the professor of palliative medicine in Moscow to come with a team to the regions. Since it was our idea, why not hold the first such perambulatory seminar in Yaroslavl, where we now have a comprehensive hospice service?

Yaroslavl

Hospice is still something of a mystery for many of the regional doctors. A seminar for the medical personnel of Yaroslavl Region (population 1.5m) addressed questions such as - what is a hospice? What can it offer? How can you make use of its services? This was followed by a week's intensive training for the personnel already involved in hospice care. To get maximum benefit from this opportunity we decided to invite someone from the Exeter Hospice to share their experiences.

Thus it was that Bridget Boxall, who has been managing volunteer services at the Exeter Hospice for more than ten years, presented a paper. There was a great deal of interest in her talk which for many was somewhat revolutionary: the horizontal model of patient care, the multi-disciplinary approach, collective decision making including the patient, and the daily team meetings where different opinions are heard were all new to the local medical practitioners. The serious attitude towards volunteers who are encouraged, trained and supported was particularly surprising for many of the Russian hospital doctors who do not encourage visitors of any sort; they were also shocked to hear about the group of young people from the schools where I used to teach in Exeter, who came to Yaroslavl to work as volunteers in the gardens of the hospice in the summer. Of course, they had fun singing and dancing and swimming in the Volga with local young people, but they also worked every day. The fact that they walked in and out of the hospice to use the facilities helped to reinforce the message that dying is part of life.

Bridget stayed to do some training with local volunteers and staff, while I struggled with the paperwork for the next report on our EU TACIS grant. This year's monitoring visit had gone well, and our previous report, which had needed some late night and early morning work, was accepted with one or two amendments.

Moscow

While in Moscow I visited a couple of FHM projects: 1) the school for children with cancer where Suzanne, our third staff member, has been teaching English. She has managed to replace herself by contacting the English students in

Moscow, two of whom have volunteered to visit the hospital once a week and 2) the school for refugees, which started at FHM in 1996 with student teachers from Moscow University and a handful of children who, as war refugees, had no educational rights in Moscow. The children now do attend school, but most are a long way behind, as they have missed four or five years of education. Suzanne is seconded to this evening school for half a day a week to help with the teacher training and lesson planning.

At the annual meeting of the FHM board, reports were received from the group of young and dedicated people with whom we are working on a programme of restorative justice; from the crisis centre for women in Gatchina; from the school for refugees in Moscow; from the conscientious objectors group and from the women's club in Krasnodar who borrowed money from us to buy sewing machines and who are now beginning to make a little money; from the AVP facilitators who are now making some progress in their attempt to introduce the programme into prisons, and from the service for reconciliation in Petrozavodsk.

Applications were accepted to continue the work of AVP in and around Moscow, and to continue the work of the play therapists in the refugee camps in Ingushetia; we also agreed to support the Russian Quaker website and to continue supporting the crisis centre for women, with the emphasis on encouraging them to find funding from elsewhere. We also agreed to step up our support for conscientious objection; to help establish a peace school in Volgodonsk; to work with conflict resolution among migrants in Astrakhan and Kaliningrad, and to support the teaching of tolerance in Petrozavodsk and in Moscow. Regrettably, we felt unable to support the projects seeking to equip a school and a dental surgery in Chechnya. If anyone has ideas about these, I would be glad to hear from you.

Postscript: first published in the Hospice Bulletin

Is Volunteering Catching?
Students, a Saw, a Scythe and a Hospice

The students had just finished their A-levels at Exeter School, the saw was borrowed, the scythe found in a shed and the recently opened hospice by the Volga was being shunned by local people because hospices are not nice places: people die in hospices and the diseases are believed to be catching.

The ten students plus two teachers were housed in nearby drafty barracks with one cold and dripping tap and a dodgy loo, and nobody complained, not once. Of course they soon began to use the superior facilities in the hospice itself. Local people were astounded to see the casual comings and goings as Pete, Kate or Alistair, dressed in a towel and carrying a toothbrush, would toss a passing 'zdravstvuite' - or the more user-friendly 'privet' - to staff or patient, as they headed for the EU-funded bathroom.

With much support from Exeter, Yaroslavl's twin city, the Victor Zorza Hospice Trust, and from the local health authority plus a €240,000 TACIS European grant, including budget lines for training, publications and a conference, we set up a 20-bed inpatient hospice unit in Dievo Gorodishche, Yaroslavl region. This was the second EU grant for the Yaroslavl Hospice, the previous one had enabled us to open a Hospice Day Care Centre. The home care service had been established with Charity Know How and local grants.

The school looks for challenging opportunities for their students, especially those which will broaden social awareness, and the new hospice needed help, especially with its rather neglected garden. We had spent vast amounts on the roof, the drains, wiring, windows, doors, floors, bathrooms etc, but we had no budget line for the grounds: what about a work camp?

It was on the third day that the young Russians joined in. We first met them down by the river where we cooled off after a morning's work by diving in off the jetty. We invited them to an evening barbecue/picnic; they invited us to a party in the village hall. They offered to help with the carpentry, the enormous hedge and the paths. Excellent progress was made with minimal shared language, but with lots of laughter and energy.

The hospice has lost its pariah status, and to this day local young volunteers maintain the hospice garden. Not only that but they and their parents and friends help in other ways too: with shopping, cake making and companionship. The local people were afraid of catching cancer; it seems they caught volunteering instead.

2002

JANUARY

Like the other grannies here, I have learned to avoid the lethal bare patches, to take small steps and to fix my head at 45 degrees to the vertical, the better to navigate a safe course through these treacherous surfaces. You would walk right past your best friend if you didn't recognise her boots. Conditions are especially bad in Moscow this year as temperatures fluctuate between +4 (hazards concealed by slushy puddles) to -26 (ice rinks after a thaw). The hospitals are full of seasonal victims. On the other hand, what can be more beautiful than a crisp sunny day in St Petersburg with the architecture outlined in glistening snow? I had gone to collect the invitation for my multi-entry visa from the friends of St Petersburg Hospice. Let's hope it works!

It was equally cold (about -20) and equally beautiful in Yaroslavl, though we spent much of the time indoors knee-deep in paper, for this was the annual hospice audit. We also took the opportunity to discuss the virement of funds from one budget line to another in the usual way, that is with constant interruptions, full volume and no set procedure. Somehow agreement was reached after two days, and a letter was written to Brussels asking permission to increase the publications line and to allow for two more training seminars. We had planned to go to the theatre (Russia's first theatre, the Volkov, was built in Yaroslavl), but had to work late into the night, and so we consoled ourselves with some fiery liquid and zakuski - tasty bits to eat including home preserved vegetables. A young local reporter, who seems to have taken the hospice project to heart, asked if she could come with me to visit the in-patient unit, and could she bring a photographer this time?

Viacheslav took some inspired photographs, one of which appeared the following day on the front page of the Severny Krai, a newspaper with a distribution of about 3m. He later said the hospice visit was a life changing experience for him. We arrived within an hour of Anna's death. This is not a tragedy of course, but still the moment must be marked with respect. We sat quietly with the nurses on duty before going to talk with the other patients. We avoided ward 2, one of the single-bed wards, where a couple had just arrived to take their leave of a dying relative who had, according to Dr Sergei, just a few hours left.

As usual my rucksack was full of gifts mainly from the Exeter Hospice - incontinence pads, stoma bags, pain relief, skin creams – all essentials, and I wish I could bring more. The pretty nighties in which women can be buried are especially well received. One was selected straightaway by Anna's daughter. How to dress the deceased matters a great deal in Russia where coffins are kept open until just before burial. I took a risk this time with painkillers and was not too sorry when my luggage, which had gone to Frankfurt, had to make its own way through customs a day after my arrival.

My neighbour on the flight was embarking on a gap-year in Russia, and no, he would not be averse to volunteering his services for some Quaker projects in Moscow, for example at the children's cancer hospital or the school for refugee children, mostly Chechen, which started at Friends House with an FHM grant in 1996 and now has its own premises. He took several of my cards to share with the other school leavers on the flight, and yes, eight of them have already started working with Quaker projects in Moscow, and one will make contact with our orphanage project in Novgorod.

At this quarter's FHM executive committee meeting, reports were received from the psychological rehabilitation project for war refugee children; from the refugee school in Moscow; from the school in Chechnya for which we are trying to find funding for basic furniture; from the conscientious objection programme; from the peace school in Volgodonsk and from the children's reconciliation project: data gathered during the course of these two projects will be used as the basis for an application to the EU for serious work to be done on violence in schools.

Workshops on conflict management will continue to be funded during the next quarter, as will some conscientious objection work; refugees in Penza will be able to buy three sewing machines. Support for young people includes volunteer training in Dzerzhinsk, activities for young people with special needs in Moscow, befriending young people in a children's home in Novgorod, and a life skills programme in Lipetsk, including some emphasis on sex education and drugs avoidance: there is a major AIDS problem now in Russia.

Two days after our meeting, we heard that the Duma has approved the second reading of the draft law on conscientious objection. the law which might come into effect in February will allow a young man to opt for four years as a hospital porter, or three years in the dangerous and much loathed stroibat (a building battalion under the command of the army) instead of the normal two years in the army. We were hoping for a more liberal law which would give a young Russian man the choice as to where and how to do his civil service, in the same way that M., a young German conscientious objector, has chosen to come to work on some of our projects in Russia for his alternative service. Teaching refugee children and networking with non-governmental organisations, he is developing useful skills while promoting civil society, not sweeping the floor in a TB hospital for four years.

A historian friend of mine is worried by the growth in national pride. He has been told by the Ministry of Education that Russian schools need only one history book and this must be officially recognised. Y. pointed out 38 places in this new compulsory textbook where peace could be mentioned, where in fact this would be the honest thing to do, but pride in victory and heroism is apparently more important. Another friend told me of her research: 15-year-olds from five nations were invited to place words such as power, money and freedom in order of priority and to list associations with each word. For the young people in Russia, power, which was associated with strength and not responsibility, came high on the list, as did money, which alone in Russia was not associated with banks or giving; patriotism was high, and the individual was in 31st place.

How to encourage a culture of peace? Perhaps we should redouble our efforts towards a civil society while there is still time? The Salvation Army has been expelled from Russia, and the Quaker meeting was interrupted by the police in January. They wanted to see the registration documents and the rental agreement with the Blind Centre. We hope there will be no consequences.

APRIL

Yaroslavl

'What wonderful tomato plants you have!' Well, sometimes you can't help sounding like a character from a Gogol story. Despite all the changes, Gogol is still the key to Russia as he was 150 years ago. Valentina beams, broom in hand. Our yard is spotless until it rains when the whole area turns to mud. She explains her tomato strategy – you sow them in batches of ten, so that when something terrible happens, you only lose a few. She uses my windowsills to spite the cat. There must be a hundred plants! They will provide her with a neat income in due course. She also uses my fridge, and she likes to catch me in, so that she can impart the usual doom-laden gossip, and tell me how to behave so that the milk won't turn.

A chance would be a fine thing! The Yaroslavl Hospice team and I again worked all hours to prepare the report for Brussels. We started at 9am, stopped for a cheese and gherkin lunch at 4, and went home exhausted and starving at 9pm. The next day was worse: we left the office after midnight, though some of us did manage to have soup and pancakes at about 3pm at the hospice. We had gone to get the signatures of those who had received salaries, also of course to talk to the patients and staff and to give them the nighties, creams, medicines and incontinence pads from Exeter. One of our patients has absolutely nothing to wear - her relatives, fearing infection, had burnt all her clothes, shoes, hairbrush, everything. The hospice has a small store of toothbrushes, slippers etc, but the psychological effect of this is worse than the deprivation.

Why the frenzy? We knew the report was due and had agreed that we could manage in two days as long as everything was more or less ready. This is now the third report. I did the first one with Russian support; they took more responsibility the second time, and it was agreed that the Russian team now had sufficient experience to take the lion's share of the third report. We had been in telephone contact: 'How are things? Do you think we'll manage in two days?' 'Oh yes,' they reassured me, 'we've been working on it. We even have a translation. We also have a meeting with a health department official and an invitation to the theatre.'

Why did I not ask what has been translated? Why assume they meant a translation of the report which is now due? Do I not stress the importance of asking the right question in communication workshops? We had to start from scratch, each question leading to a 20-minute discussion. There is no hope for the theatre, but we did meet with the health official who, for the first time ever, came to us instead of expecting us to go to her and wait in an antechamber. As Dr Sergei says: 'First they ignored us, then they began reluctantly to speak to us, and now they use us for their flag waving.' The Yaroslavl Hospice is now mentioned in official documents with pride, and when the team recently won a prize for NGO management, they were congratulated by all and sundry, including the mayor's office.

This is the major triumph: the Yaroslavl health department has agreed to adopt the British model of part funding for the hospice which we have been advocating for about five years. We were asking them to pay 33% of the costs, but no, they refused do that: they will pay 75% of the costs of the Day Care Centre, keeping all the staff; they have also signed an agreement to fund 66% of the inpatient unit, rising to 100% after three years. This is a very rare case of public private partnership in Russia: perhaps it will be an example? It needed the approval of the mayor who has been to see the work of the hospice. He also enjoyed his time in Exeter when we launched the city twinning.

This trip started in Ukraine after a couple of days in Moscow. I flew to Simferopol on a one-way ticket with no instructions as to how to get where I was going and very little money. On entry to Russia, I was warned that without the appropriate stamp in the red channel, my right to export any money would be zero. I negotiated my way through the green, since there would be a minimum of a two-hour wait in the red queue: four minutes at least for each of the 29 people in front of me; some were taking twice as long. I need no money in England - my return bus ticket is safe and the pound in my pocket will buy me a cup of tea - but Ukraine is a different matter. 'Don't be silly! They think up these new rules to keep us on our toes; our job is to think of ways round them.' Sasha, father of my Russian godson, was full of ideas, but to be on the safe side, the usual methods of secretion should not be eschewed: it would be foolish indeed to arrive alone and penniless in Ukraine, now a foreign land.

Simeiz, Crimea

So I was not destitute, but still glad to be met and driven to Simeiz, near Yalta, where it was unseasonably cold, where roads were closed because of snowfall, and where we plan to do the second seven-day training for trainers in human rights, democratic processes and peacebuilding.

Our group of young Chechens, North Ossetians and Ingushetians were a delight to work with. How they threw themselves into their vision of the future! With what verve did they practise listening skills, negotiation and mediation! With what passion did they play the parts of Peace, Truth, Justice and Mercy! And how we danced on the last evening!

Mineralnye Vody

We travelled the 28 hours by train together to Mineralnye Vody and parted at 4am on the platform. Let's hope they get home safely! At least they were together and aware of the need to look after each other. It is not safe for a young Chechen to be on his own, even in Simeiz among Crimean Tatars, who shared the fate of deportation under Stalin.

Stavropol

Erik and I met the dawn sitting behind two characters from central casting who had offered to drive us for an agreed fee to Stavropol. The fee doubled en route, perhaps because they heard us speaking English, but they were good natured enough when we declined to play this game. We had gone to support one of the groups from our October training for trainers as they ran their first workshop in conflict management. Feedback from the participants was very positive, and Inna and Natasha agreed in the end that this had been a good learning experience, though there had been some sticky moments. Erik went home to Norway.

Krasnodar

I took the six-hour bus ride to Krasnodar, where another group was planning their first workshop and waiting for support. During the welcome break, when the bus needed attention, I bought a twist of peanuts, chose a shady bench and listened to the various languages. These southern people can all speak Russian, but many choose not to. There is no sign to the primitive loos, but they are not hard to find. The woman charges me a ruble and makes no apology: why should she? She is not to blame for the conditions.

On the whole we are waved through the checkpoints where armed militiamen stand about in flak jackets. Nobody knew an English person was on board, or if they did, they were not saying. Why create a diversion with police involvement, when the point of a journey is to reach your destination? We are flagged down now and then and counted, but would anybody care if we had lost or gained a passenger in this heat? What about a pig? Nobody minded when the driver stopped the reluctant bus and leapt off to inspect the dead pig on a makeshift gibbet at the side of the road. His finger described the bit including a leg which he fancied taking home, perhaps for a shashlik, but then he changed his mind and leapt back on the bus, which had had enough and refused to start. Subsistence farming is in evidence - beautifully kept kitchen gardens contrast with the rather unkempt fields: there is a woman herding one cow, and a man is being followed by five geese; an aeroplane seems to have taken root in a field, there's a tank at the side of the road and three militiamen with a ladder: all these have their stories, but I must get on.

Krasnodar - what a challenge! We had chosen to work here because of the huge numbers of refugees, the unemployment, extreme poverty and social unrest. FHM has been promoting micro economy projects here, plus a women's club for community building, practical training, and legal advice. There are 120 nationalities here and vast numbers of Russian refugees from various parts of the former Soviet Union, where it is no longer safe for them to live. Nazi demonstrations on Hitler's birthday (banned in Moscow, and other cities) took place in Krasnodar. 'Skinhedy,' as they are called in Russian, arrived by car or train and wrought havoc on the streets and in the Armenian graveyards.

I was not able this time to stay with Marina, an oil engineer refugee from Grozny. She has only one room and a kitchen, and her pregnant daughter plus husband were staying. I was not too sorry, as her fridge is brutish noisy and the trams just outside the window beat any ear plugs. Elena kindly took me in. She too has only one room but she is on her own and there are two sofas. I had noticed the water pump in the street several minutes away, so was somewhat alarmed when she put a huge bucket of water on the stove so that I could have a wash. I too have carried home buckets of water. I know how heavy and precious it is. I have also survived in war zones where there is no water. Yes, a wash would be nice after the bus but... 'Oh don't worry. We have a tap and at the moment I have plenty of water, look!' Yes, the bath is full of bowls and saucepans of water, and to flush the loo (a luxury here, where earth closets are more common), you scoop up the water you have used to wash your hands.

The workshop was a brave attempt to work on communication skills and prejudice reduction. These experiential workshops are extremely satisfying, but also hazardous. Facilitators have to be 100% alert at all times to maintain a safe space and to be sure not to miss opportunities for learning. What to do when the process is derailed? A rather aggressive participant told a story to illustrate the bad behaviour of a Caucasian, locally known as 'black': in essence, a young man had sworn at her, so she slapped him. The other participants supported her action. There were several 'teach them a lesson' remarks. The facilitators did nothing. At the next break, I asked them what plans they had for dealing with this tricky situation. Blank. Well, sometimes it helps to see it as a gift rather than a hazard. While you think how to use it to further the aims of the workshop, you can say: 'Thank you for your story. We will come back to that.' It is essential to break in quickly and move on, giving no space to any kind of prejudice-confirming discussion. If you have another day, you can think overnight, if not, you have to think more quickly. We thought overnight.

Anna and Olga decided to use the conflict elevator: starting with a dot at the bottom left of the flip chart, you draw the first riser and step - the young man drops his cigarette stub; the next riser the woman tells him to pick it up; third riser he swears at her; fourth she slaps him; fifth he pins her against the wall; sixth she calls her husband. The conflict has reached the danger zone. On the steps you write (taking your cue from the participants, who all heard the story) what happened; on the risers you write (again consulting the participants) her feelings and needs on the left, and his feelings and needs on the right. You then tease out the choices. At what point could things have been done differently? If nobody suggests that he perhaps had not understood, or that she could have told him the floor had just been swept, you can prompt. They then worked on communication skills - how to look for common ground, how to reduce tension, how to express your needs. The desired result is not always achieved, but still an atmosphere is created in which a potential conflict can be managed.

Several of the participants came with me to the station. PC: 'Can you tell me when the train arrives in Moscow?' 'Do I look like an inquiry office? I sell tickets; I don't answer questions.' PC: 'Well, I'd be happy to buy a ticket from you, if I could be sure that the train arrives when the metro is open.' 'Ask at the enquiries office.' PC: 'Like you, I'm a busy person. I have already waited 20 minutes in this queue and haven't got time to stand in two more queues. Would you please sell me a ticket on any train which arrives either before midnight or after 5am?' 'Passport!' I handed it through the gap. 'Why didn't you say you were foreign? This train arrives at 11.20pm, or there's another one which arrives at 5.20 the following morning.' 'What difference does it make that I'm foreign?' But Olga wisely pokes me in the back: enough prejudice reduction for today. Any more of this, and there will not be time to see the video of her wedding.

I spent the night with a sex dancer who works at a nightclub in Moscow. Actually, it is more of a restaurant, she tells me. It is well paid, and the men aren't allowed to touch her. She will have to go straight to work when we get to Moscow, but that is 22 hours away. She sleeps a lot, so do I, what else can you do in this airless oven, except lie under a wet towel and close your eyes. We are sharing a compartment with a military man buried in a book. According to the etiquette of Russian rail travel, he should have offered me the bottom bunk, but, well, he didn't, and actually I quite like being on the top, if truth be told - you can create your own reality under the ceiling.

Moscow

What do you need most on arrival? The cold tap releases a thin trickle, the hot just gasps. Yes, Friends House too has a store of water in buckets and bowls in the bath. Things could be worse.

The executive committee meeting finished soon after 11pm. Shortage of money makes things at the same time simpler and more complicated: there is no point in discussing a) or b), on the other hand how to share funds fairly between x) and y)? Should we re-examine priorities? What are today's pressing needs? We continue to concentrate on capacity-building and peace education.

JULY

Orekhovo

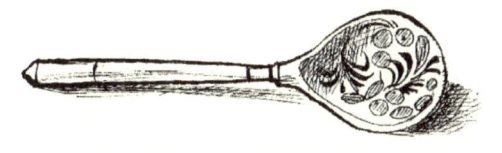

This is a do-it-yourself Chekhov play: the moon, the lake, even a seagull, comings and goings, ancient furniture which once had a use, grandfather's hat, money worries, or rather the decision not to worry about money, hopeless plans and rumours, aimless ramblings, reminiscing and most of all philosophising. Yes, there seems to be an unsuitable love element too, but the rest of us are too busy picking raspberries or chatting with the neighbour about her cow to take much notice. A friend had a spell in hospital this year, so a few of us gathered to help her with her garden. The first person up fetches a bucket of water from the well, fills the samovar and plugs in. But today there is no electricity, so we go for a swim instead. Perhaps it will be on by the time we get back from the river, and so it is.

This is the other Russia; some would say the real Russia. Away from the cities this is how most people live. These are the people who voted communist in their millions. Perestroika has passed them by. What is the good of having the right to go abroad, when these people live nearly an hour's walk from the nearest bus stop? Why do they need flashy advertisements for expensive goods, when their task year after year is to survive the winter? Gardening is for survival. We do an hour or so in the mornings before it gets too hot, but serious gardening takes place at night - we are far enough north to tell weeds from beans at midnight. The mosquitoes are happy.

Krasnodar

It was over 40 degrees in Krasnodar. I had gone to South Russia to support Olga again and also Natasha, a young participant in the previous workshop, who had asked to be trained as a trainer. This was a two-day workshop in human rights for school children. The Amnesty International book which I had given Olga on my last visit inspired her to draft a workshop full of creativity and experiential learning. We had exchanged ideas by email, but there were still gaps, and it was not always clear how she intended to get from a) to b), or what would the desired learning outcomes from c).

We spent a day together working on her material and adding some exercises and games from the new European Commission human rights pack for schools which I had managed to find in Moscow in Russian. The workshop was pitched at brightish 15-year-olds looking at values, the underlying principles of rights and responsibilities, and the identification of human rights in the Russian Constitution. One major exercise was to look through newspapers for examples of infringement or support of your rights in your own society and to compose a group newspaper with the cuttings.

The first two participants to arrive were two very small 11-year-olds. Heavens, how are we going to keep their interest? In fact, they were brilliant – inventive, confident and fun. One took on practically the whole group in her well reasoned argument against capital punishment; and the other, by the end of the second day, could quote several rights, even though learning by heart had not been part of the agenda. They both asked for a full copy of the UN declaration and a copy of the Russian Constitution to take home.

Moscow

By chance, the train I took back to Moscow this time was air conditioned. What a gift! So blissfully cool was it at night, that my fellow travellers and I were glad of the sheets provided. In Moscow, the only way to survive the night was to keep a wet towel by the bed and sponge yourself down every couple of hours. It was far too hot for a sheet, or indeed anything.

At the meeting of the FHM executive committee, we managed to keep hold of our heads, at least until mid-afternoon, when many of us felt the need of a cold shower. We approved a project for a summer camp for children with special needs at the orphanage in Pskov, with which we have had links with for some years; we also supported the ongoing project which encourages people to look for alternatives to violence; two projects in Dzerzhinsk were also approved - one to train volunteers and the other to work with young offenders with the aim of keeping them out of prison; we hope the women's crisis centre will become self-sufficient after just one more FHM grant, and that the children of the Lubertsy orphanage will enjoy their books.

We received reports from some of our projects including a splendid pair of trousers from the refugee project in Penza. We had bought some sewing machines for the group of displaced persons, mainly Russians who, after three generations of settlement, have had to flee from areas such as Kazakhstan, Kyrgyzstan and the Baltic States, where they are no longer welcome. These people had been told to go home to Russia, but most have nowhere to go and no means of making a living. We have found in the past that the weakness in such projects is not the workmanship or the willingness to work, but rather the marketing - a new skill for many. This group has now asked for a loan for a market stall. We felt this was a good risk, as the trousers are certainly of good quality.

Ingushetia

What a pity there were not enough for me to take a rucksackful down to Ingushetia! It is extraordinary that the boys and young men almost all wear uniform to school or college - smart dark trousers and white shirts - even though they have been living in refugee tents for three years. On this occasion my visit coincided with an appalling flood. Two huge downpours on top of a month of rain emptied latrines and turned roads into torrents. Some tents were washed away and hundreds were inundated with a mixture of rainwater, black mud and sewage. The water subsided very quickly but the mess was horrendous. Somehow or other, nearly all the people expected at the refugee school managed to turn up.

Three of us had gone to support the group of young newly trained Chechen, Ingush and North Ossetian trainers as they, in groups of three, prepared for and ran their first two-day workshops in human rights, democratic processes and peacebuilding. All were pleased with the results, although there were some useful learning moments. We are confident that these trainers can now continue to work in the Caucasus with only minimal support. I stayed on to do a workshop on tolerance for the more experienced trainers who are planning a programme of such workshops in schools.

Yaroslavl

The Yaroslavl Hospice marked the imminent end of the TACIS grant by holding a high-level hospice conference. We are hoping to generate a policy on hospice development in Russia and to influence government thinking on standards. About 30 people came from places as far apart as St Petersburg, Astrakhan and Samara. Speeches were made, resolutions passed, toasts proposed and promises made. Meanwhile the work continues.

To celebrate the end of the conference we had a truly Russian shashlik party in the hospice grounds: good company, good food, salad fresh from the garden, songs, stories, laughter, sunset, a swing and a guitar. It was one of those evenings which remind me why I keep coming back.

But it seems to be getting harder to recover from the fatigue. My husband kindly mutters about the stress of travel, the sudden changes in climate, the effort to get things done in impossible circumstances; but there's also anno Domini: I will have completed ten years of this coming and going at the end of 2003; I will also be 60. We have done what we can to train facilitators in peacebuilding, and NGOs in management and fundraising; the future of the Yaroslavl Hospice is now as secure as it can be, and the development of hospice care in Russia is on the right path.

Someone will be found to take over as clerk of the executive committee of FHM. I've been a poor granny to my son's children but at least they have another grandmother; my daughter's children, the first due in August, will not. From January 2004, while continuing to fundraise, I intend to opt for a back seat role, supporting community projects in Russia, with perhaps one or two visits a year.

OCTOBER

Moscow

I cannot get excited about the headlines in the newspapers on the British Airways flight home: Paul Burrell... Estelle Morris, blamed for something or other, resigns. This is a universe away from the reality in Moscow. I was invited to the musical Nordost and was keen to go, as the writers are friends of a friend and I have some of their music and have even learned some of their songs.

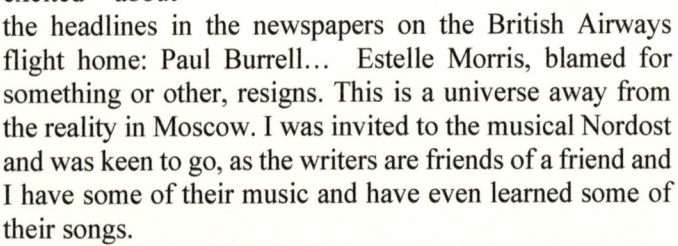

We lived in a state of constant anxiety for two days, not knowing how the theatre siege would end or where it would lead, as demands for an end to the war in Chechnya were ignored. Conditions must be getting worse for the terrified people taken hostage in the theatre and the anxious crowds waiting outside; and then the utter horror of day-long repetitions of TV footage of dead hostage-takers lying in pools of blood, shot while unconscious, and close-ups of their injuries with the commentary: 'There will be no more trouble from that bandit!' The news of the hostages changed constantly: 30 dead, no 60, no 117. It could be more, as 152 are missing: relatives, desperate for news, are locked out of hospitals. It was essential to give everyone an injection, an antidote to the gas, as quickly as possible and to get them out of the theatre, but there were not enough syringes nor people to administer the dose, nor manpower to carry the hostages out: it was the heavier people who died at the scene, mainly men; also, it was not clear to the ambulance crews which unconscious person had been injected and which had not. Violence breeds violence while lives are ruined. So many questions remain unanswered: how did they reach the theatre with so much weaponry at a time when vehicles were being checked? Why were they shot dead when unconscious, rather than put on trial? Who organised this horror? What was the gas? Where are the missing people?

This was the background to the FHM annual board meeting. We had gathered from Germany, Japan, Norway, the United States, and Britain to meet with local board members and staff to discuss policy, personnel, and finance issues. We spent a long time looking at the proposed registration document. Can we accept a revision of our priorities - a sort of spineless version of the mission statement? We cannot register as a religious organisation because much of what we do would not be allowed under the current strict rules: there is little chance that our registration will be accepted if we talk about the spiritual basis of our work, and yet we looked for places to insinuate naughty words like 'love' and 'trust', 'peace' and 'community'.

Twenty project proposals were presented to FHM, but, partly because of a lack of funding, we were able to support only ten. It seems a good idea to help an organisation in Moscow send teenagers with disabilities to Kiev for a festival of street theatre for disabled people a) because they have so few opportunities and it will be fun and b) to help to generate a positive image of difference in a country where even basic needs for disabled people are not met, but we cannot afford this; nor can we afford to buy a karaoke machine to improve speech and social skills for another group of children which we support in Krasnodar, nor unfortunately can we help a project in Dzerzhinsk which seeks to encourage parents not to reject their disabled children by offering training in how to look after them, plus legal and psychological support. Nor were we able at this time to support a major project which seeks to develop tolerance and democratic principles in schools, though we do agree that this is important against a background of increasing xenophobia. We asked for a clearer application from the project for trainings in negotiation skills and will consider this in due course.

We did agree to continue supporting:
- The orphanage in Novgorod, so that they can buy art and craft materials
- AVP which trains trainers in communication skills and conflict management
- The conscientious objection network, by funding an up-to-date manual on how to apply for alternative service
- Mediation training for teenagers to enable them to cope with bullying and other conflict situations in schools, and we hope that this will lead to a network of support for school children
- We also supported a project to set up a structure to defend the rights of people living in care homes.

The evening train journey to Yaroslavl takes 4.5 hours, and in twelve years I have never been more than 15 minutes late. Well, I have had worse nights - at least it was warm enough, and the loos were open. When told of the goods train derailment ahead, several passengers, those without children, rucksacks or other impedimenta, walked to the nearest station. One or two of these, like Noah's doves, came back and tapped on the windows bringing news of the conditions they had found: no café, telephone not working, last bus gone.

'Which would you like - lights or a video? You can't have both.' 'Video!' We all shouted. 'I've got love or heroism,' the conductor offered. 'Love,' we shouted. 'Yes love,' said the military gentleman with the endless supply of beer, 'who needs heroism at midnight?' It was an excellent film - Monsieur Hulot meets Dostoevsky with

Kurt Weil music, plus a dash of Clochemerle and Mary Poppins.

Yaroslavl

I had gone to work with the Yaroslavl Hospice team on the final report to Brussels. Of course, it was not possible to take time to recover, but it did seem unfortunate that a rat or a mouse had chosen this week to die somewhere in the office making it hard to concentrate. We finished the job in spite of the TV cameras and a visit to the director of social services. The health authority has accepted a version of the British model of part financing the 20-bed unit, which means that we have to raise about 1/3 of the costs, but there is still not enough support for the patients while they are at home.

The Yaroslavl Hospice team registered as a nongovernmental organisation when Russian law permitted such things about eight years ago, and they have achieved a great deal even though there is still a vertical structure and a tendency to expect decisions to filter down from the director despite trainings in democratic processes. Not for the first time, we discussed responsibility and job descriptions - how to identify what skills are lacking and how to organise training and skills sharing.

My neighbour on the BA flight was a young Russian returning to boarding school in Kent after the half term holiday. 'My parents think the education is better in England.' Oh dear, back to Estelle Morris, Secretary of State for Education: blame, victims, scapegoating - is this the best we can do?

Please let me know if you can take a box of Russian toys and craft to sell at Christmas. Next year will be the last opportunity as my time at FHM comes to an end.

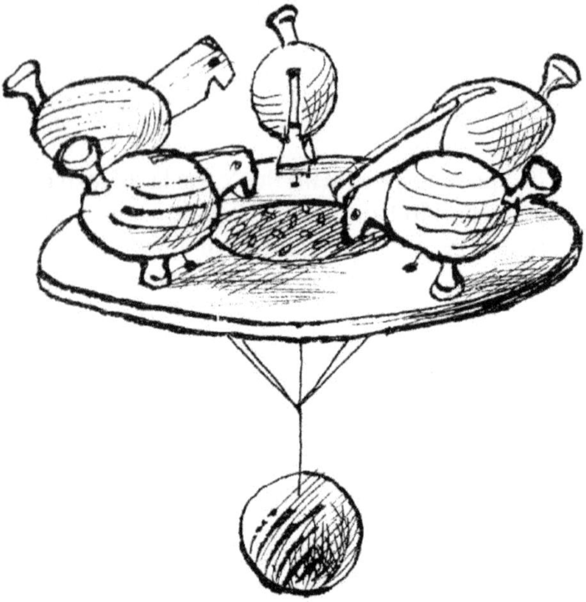

2003

JANUARY

Moscow

So I paid my debt to the fruit lady. Khurma, caught at the right moment, is the nearest thing to heaven your lips will experience this side the grave - too soon and your mouth, deprived of natural lubricant, assumes a rictus ghastly to behold; too late and a sweet putrefaction will have set in. I have learned to ignore the ranks of bright orange taut-skinned beauties and to wait for the wrinkles. Frost damage is the key. In the box, which only that morning had contained a dozen, one perfect fruit remained. Alas, the coins in my pocket did not quite match the price, and I was too ice-weary to hunt for more in secret nooks. The street-trading fruit lady, seeing the look in my eye, agreed to expect the balance in the morning. Khurma is at its best in January.

Ufa, Bashkortostan

After 42 years of living (nearly four years) in Russia or regular visits, I have decided not to come again in January, except in emergency. There are wonderful experiences to be had in deepest winter, apart from the khurma: it was -33 when Zhenia and I were working in Ufa, the capital of Bashkortostan, so cold that the air froze, and tiny rainbow sparkles danced in the sun. Day after day we watched entranced, losing the use of our toes, then ankles, while waiting for the tram, as the cold crept up from the pavement. It was even colder in Kyrgyzstan. The thermometer read -27, but with the wind from the North Pole via China, it felt like -40. We had been invited to work with local groups on communication skills, democratic processes and management.

Based on respect for self and the other, the workshops are constructed to encourage people to believe in their own power. This is experiential learning, not superior knowledge handed down by experts. We have some exercises which demonstrate the adage - two heads, or, in our case, six or so in each subgroup (a good size for NGO management) are better than one if we are prepared to look at each other, listen deeply, choose vocabulary with care, and accept that wisdom may come from any quarter. Analysis of the exercises offers good scope for learning: what happened? Why? Were we held back by the traditional vertical structure of management - dominance and subordination? Could teamwork offer more scope for growth, shared responsibility, creative thinking, and therefore better decision making?

We aimed to train trainers so that ideas could be passed on, and we always shared local conditions rather than emerging from a comfortable hotel having had a good breakfast. Apart from minimising the 'us and them' effect and the costs, it was good to make friends and to share stories sitting over the samovar long into the night. Two-year funding for this local capacity-building work came from Quakers, from government sources and from the European Commission.

Balakchi, Kyrgyzstan

In Kyrgyzstan last week, Zhenia and I thought our doom was writ, when the car which met us at Bishkek airport skidded on ice, hit a mountain in the pitch dark and then refused to start. But no, the engine was repaired with a 1 kopek coin, and we reached Balakchi on Lake Issyk-Kul at about midnight. Tea and pancakes, yes, but first the bania (bath house), wonderful invention: business and gossip club, gym, refuge, life saver, and love nest (too many people in the two roomed house, too cold in the fields in winter), laundry, beauty salon, kitchen: in Chechnya the wood-fired bania was often the only source of heat, and when you haven't eaten all day in -7, eggs scrambled on the brazier are a real treat. The bania is also, so we were told, a good place to give birth.

Yaroslavl

There's also the sport in January – the cross-country skiing or walking on crunchy snow - and the indescribable beauty of sun sparkling on the hoar-frosted trees as you look up from your book on the train to Yaroslavl, not to mention the hours of birch forest which pass by magically lit from below as the sun bounces off the snow on the forest floor. I made a mental note to preserve images of all these, but there is also the slush, the black ice, the very real danger of broken bones as pavements freeze, thaw, freeze again. And in many places there is the chilly privy in the garden and snowdrifts, like the one we fell into on the way to the care home in Yaroslavl while trying to make room on the road for a van. As the near side passenger, I had no choice but to step out into a yard of snow. I took off my socks in the director's office while she summoned up hot borshch and a bottle of traditional Russian prophylactic.

I had come to see Sasha who had spent some weeks at Saint Loyes, the Centre for Rehabilitation in Exeter. Of course we had a party and I look forward to singing with him and his friends again, but he had difficulty adjusting back to life in Russia, and it's hard to know how to support him further. Another challenge for radical thinking: the director sees her job as keeping the residents warm, clean and fed and this she does; it is not for her to question policy, for example why young men who have lost the use of their legs are sent here to live out their years in boredom and frustration. The home is on the very edge of town, a 20-minute walk for a fit person to the nearest bus stop.

A very dear patient at the Yaroslavl Hospice has recently died an unnecessarily tormented death. She became a hospice patient aged 45, having been pronounced 'hopeless' by the oncological hospital. She had been in the hospice for nearly a month, when her students, denying the benefits of palliative care and ignoring the advice of the hospice doctors, took her to a local hospital for an operation to save her life. She died the next day. What should we do to advocate the benefits of palliative care? More publicity leaflets perhaps?

Moscow

At FHM we have lost a Sergei and gained a different Sergei, someone who came to a Quaker gathering about four years ago and has kept in touch. We look forward to working with him. We have also acquired a British student helper until June - Sophie is a student of Russian at St Andrews.

At the quarterly meeting of FHM, while continuing to support the crisis centre in Gatchina and projects promoting alternatives to violence in Moscow and in Ingushetia, we agreed to support another project: Big Change will offer educational opportunities and training in life skills to vulnerable 17-year-olds newly released from orphanages. We will look again at the revised application from the young offenders' project in April.

In 1961 Izvestia showed pictures of a smiling Yuri Gagarin claiming that he had not met God in space, and therefore communism is right – God doesn't exist; headlines today carry icons and quotes from church leaders about the holiness of Christmas, which is celebrated on 7 January. Vysotsky, the famously angry young man of the 60s, was harassed by the authorities in his day and never shown on TV in his lifetime; today on the 65th anniversary of his birth, tributes to his memory were led by Putin. Ever fascinating, what next for Gogol's chariot?

APRIL/MAY

Moscow

Non-toothache, said Thich Nhat Hanh in Moscow last week, is wonderful. We should celebrate each day when we wake up without toothache. A quiet loo is also wonderful. On the third night of persistent intermittent hissing and dripping, I tied some string round the arm of the ballcock and nailed it to the wall. Wonderful! There is no heating and no hot water, and this evening we had to plan the next day's timetable in our heads in the dark, as there was no electricity, but still the silence is wonderful.

I have become something of an expert on Russian loos: one worked perfectly with a champagne cork stuck onto the end of the handle rod so that the loop of the plunger would not fall off after each flush; on another occasion a judiciously placed bath plug allowed the system to fill up without emptying at the same time. Solutions are often easy as long as you can get the lid off, but even though I usually travel with a screwdriver, string, bluetak and a torch, this is not always possible, as here in Novocherkassk, where the lid yielded only a three-finger crack.

Novocherkassk

Erik from Norway and I had come to do a three-day workshop on peacebuilding with local young people plus groups from Rostov-on-Don and Astrakhan. Participants were invited to apply for the next training course while Erik and I kept an eye out for trainer material. We were alarmed to discover that one of the young women we had picked out for her energy, confidence, willingness to listen, and her dedication to the cause of peaceful relationships, plus her skills in argument and negotiation, is not yet 16. In vain did we ask what is the law - to what extent are we responsible for her at a residential workshop? She it was who found the best solution during a listening exercise; she also took central position at the 'press conference' on the last day, when each participant had written down their most pressing social concern. By a process of argument and negotiation, small groups centred around shared interests: one group decided to work on ecological issues, another on interethnic tensions and peacebuilding, the largest group, these being mainly students, were concerned about student issues - grants and living conditions, eg the student hostel has no hot water. They decided they wanted to form a students' union.

Each group had one hour to marshal their arguments and to prepare a presentation to the people they need to convince: the group of peace workers meeting potential funders; the students meeting the university management board; the ecologists - the press. Before each presentation, the rest of the participants became the target group, having found rudimentary props and organised the room - a huge table for the university boardroom with unsmiling bigwigs; serried ranks of sharp journalists facing a top table with microphones (plastic bottles) and glasses of water for the potential funders and also for the press conference; there was even an intrusive TV camera - an upturned chair.

We then had a feedback session: how could they have been more effective? How could Lena have handled the rudeness of the chairman? Could they have worked better as a team?

Learning outcomes included the following:

- It can be helpful to prepare a statement about why the status quo is not satisfactory, but avoid a moaning tone
- Concentrate rather on the purposes and benefits of the change you are proposing, not just to yourselves, but to a wider group if possible – how might this benefit the university/the city?

- Try to make it easy for potentially hostile people to hear what you have to say - see them not as the enemy but as allies in looking for solutions
- Be clear about your vision; try to foresee the likely questions.

Erik and I had not foreseen some of the questions put to us by the militia on the train on the way back to Moscow. For some years now, trains have been guarded by Ministry of Interior police. As they walk up and down the trains in uniform, we had thought they were there to guard us, upstanding citizens, from highwaymen and brigands. In the new era of war on terrorism, Erik had become the threat: he had marked himself out as being 'not one of us', with his beard, his refusal to eat borshch for breakfast and his preference for coffee without sugar.

Of all the stamps and visas in his passport, they chose one with a little aeroplane and last week's date. 'What is this? What does it say here?' 'Copenhagen.' 'This proves he should have left the country. He has no right to be here.' 'It's the day he arrived.' 'What's he doing in Russia?' Oh dear, the long version is a peacebuilding programme - training local people in negotiation, mediation, problem solving; encouraging the voiceless to find a voice, rather than turn to violence, promoting dialogue... But peace is a provocative word. We had to leave the compartment and face more questions in the office, where Erik's visa was examined and his registration found wanting. The irony was that whereas Erik was registered, I was not. They could have arrested me, but at no time did they ask to see my documents. Gratifyingly, they took me for a local and told me to tell Erik that he would be handed over next time he was caught.

St Petersburg

There were questions of a different nature in St Petersburg where I had been asked to investigate the provision of hospice care. What are the prospects for development and funding? What is their vision? Why is it that the two factions cannot work together? The British Embassy doctor who also has an interest in this from the point of view of the care of AIDS patients, put me in touch with the military hospital where the professor in charge of palliative care reckons that the first hospice beds were established in the Soviet Union before the English came bringing their ideas of separate buildings. Professor Novik has recently been appointed adviser to the minister of health on hospice care in Russia, so it is likely his views will prevail, at least as long as the present minister is in place. 'We cannot afford the English way, and besides it's not for us. What we need is a few palliative care beds within the hospitals.' Yes, but what about home care, day care and family support?

Meanwhile, in another part of the city a huge 50-bed inpatient unit is nearing completion. This project which started life as a hotel was rescued after bankruptcy with $1,000,000 injection secured by the widow of Sobchak, the former mayor of St Petersburg, a colleague of Putin's. The originally planned marble slabs have given way to ceramic tiles, but still there are vast halls and corridors while the entrance to the showers and toilets is a tight squeeze. It seems there will be funding to finish the building and to buy equipment. There appears to be no budget for staff training.

I was pleased to visit again the other hospices in St Petersburg, especially Lakhta, which was established with the support of Victor Zorza, the inspiration for Yaroslavl.

Yaroslavl

Of course, I spent some time in Yaroslavl too. It is sad that Galina, who had asked to be admitted with her sewing machine, can no longer sit up for long enough to use it. Sad too that Lisa a 37-year-old musician will never sing again, and that Marusya cannot be fitted with a prosthetic leg because she has lost her pension book. She could go home now if she had some proper crutches, but the hospice has only one pair left. If they give them to Marusya, they might never see them again. These came from England. It is not easy to buy them here. Perhaps a carpenter could make some?

Moscow

At FHM we were pleased to see an application for funding AVP workshops in a troubled area of Russia from one of our recently trained trainers. We considered 12 other projects and approved as many as funding would allow. We wondered whether we could support a nun who has taken 14 homeless people into her flat but are afraid of locking ourselves into an endless commitment. We decided to ask if there was any one finite thing that we could help with and will make a decision in due course.

OCTOBER/ NOVEMBER

Moscow

Time zone travel is OK as long as there is scope for a good wilt at both ends. My first evening at home must be devoted to a simple meal, a hot bath and early bed. Similarly, the first morning in Moscow must allow for a quiet cup of tea in bed while the body catches up with the clock. So, what am I to do with this Victor who has arrived at Friends House at 6.45am after a 30-hour train journey from Simferopol? His needs are a kettle, a bathroom and, unfortunately for me, a listening ear for an exposition of his life, including his excitement about discovering Quakers. Deficient not only in brain activity at this hour but also in the ear department, of which more later, I must have presented a sorry image of what he called a real Quaker.

In order to have a look at Moscow, Victor had come a few days early for the residential gathering of Friends, which was due to take place in a sanatorium outside Moscow, and I had slept on the couch in the office, so as not to confuse my friend Ania with too much coming and going, for today I must go to Yaroslavl where I am to collect a Russian honour from the regional governor.

Yaroslavl

The occasion was a celebration of 250 years of public medical services in Yaroslavl which has a famous and ancient Medical Academy. Official speeches about advances in the region were interrupted now and then for nearly thirty doctors, nurses, midwives and other medical practitioners to receive awards. After a speech about the development of hospice care in Yaroslavl, mine was the last to be given, and, perhaps for this reason, I was allowed to say a few words in response about the importance of teamwork and local support.

Of course, bottles of Sovietskoe Shampanskoe featured in our celebrations afterwards, as did caviar and a good deal of bonhomie, so much so that the organisers forgot to give me the passport for the award, which would allow me to get it through customs. The signed and stamped document reached me by taxi at first light and I was appalled to see the gold and silver content of the gong. It is good to have the work recognised and honoured, but not at this cost: a little medal on a purple ribbon would have sufficed.

Life for small NGOs has been complicated by Putin's determination to impose the dictatorship of law and by the unease generated by the atmosphere of fear which is provoked by the war on terrorism. Whereas the hospice team was able to get on with promoting new standards of care, networking, running workshops and trainings, and publishing materials and booklets to encourage healthy living, self-examination and early diagnosis, they are now being told that the hospice must conform to inappropriate medical norms: peripheral activities, like family support and volunteer training, are suspicious.

Democracy is going into reverse. The needs of the people, expressed by grassroots groups working for change to solve real problems, can now be ignored, more than ignored – closed down. One sad consequence of this is that the hospice, after an official spot-check, has been warned not to accept or harbour any medicines or equipment brought in from the West. As there were no crutches, walking frames or grab sticks on the premises at the time, we are not sure if the ban extends to them. We have only brought into Yaroslavl those things which are not available in Russia, or only available at great cost or in small quantities. We have always tried to respond to requests, including the quite specific needs of one patient.

For the first time ever, I had to leave Yaroslavl without visiting the hospice. Most of the staff had joined the noisy celebration, which we took to be in recognition and appreciation of what has been achieved by the team and the staff, with support from funders and the local authority, but I do like to see the patients too, and the hospice pancakes are to die for! Time is short: my flight to Russia had had to be postponed for a couple of days because of a painful middle ear infection which left me temporarily deaf in one ear then the other, and then for a few days in both. Things gradually improved but it was a nuisance as I tried to chair meetings in Moscow, run workshops in Sochi, and lead a session on the peace testimony at the Quaker gathering, not to mention just talking to people and making arrangements by phone; on the other hand, the lack of ear power was eye opening.

Moscow

Nowadays my temporary accommodation in Moscow is with Ania, a member of the Deaf Association of Russia with which we have a strong link through Exeter University. Armed with information from various sources, including the Exeter School for the Deaf, to which her team was invited from Moscow (including the professor of defectology!), Ania and others have been battling for ten years for recognition of the needs of deaf children in Russia. About two months ago, legislation was passed, but there is no funding for the recommended changes and Ania is not optimistic. Public awareness and acceptance of handicap is another major issue. Parents are still advised to give up their babies at birth if there is clearly something wrong with them. Blind and limbless people beg on the metro. Very few wheelchairs are in evidence, largely because access is so poor. One of the families we support has asked in vain to be rehoused on the ground floor, because their child is now too heavy to be lifted down the seven floors and her wheelchair does not fit in the lift.

About 34 people came to the three-day residential Quaker gathering in the snow. FHM has not embarked on such a thing before, and I saw it as something of a swansong as I worked on the theme, timetable, handouts etc with Galina and Sergei. At the end of this year, I finish my term of service after ten years including the initial two years spent on setting up FHM. I have always seen my time here as temporary – a time to listen, learn, wonder and enjoy; an opportunity to encourage people and maybe to inspire them to believe in themselves and perhaps to take over the work that I have been doing.

Sochi

The FHM board gathered for the annual three-day meeting in Moscow in November, and then Erik and I went to Sochi to run our last training for trainers in human rights and peacebuilding with a group of 20 young people from South Russia including two Chechens, a Crimean Tatar and a Scythian. It was an excellent workshop. We have a lot of faith in these people who have confidence and a thirst for new ideas. They also have no tradition of fear of the authorities having grown up in post-communist society. Let's hope the circumstances allow them to flourish!

Exeter

Travelling with me to Exeter were two men from Glas, the choir with which Roger sang when he was on sabbatical in Yaroslavl. We arrived at 2am, and at 7pm on the same day we were expected as VIPs at the Cathedral for a performance of the Brahms Requiem given by the Exeter Festival Chorus. No time for a wilt. On the other hand, we now have agreement to perform Britten's War Requiem in 2005 to mark the 60th anniversary of the end of World War ll in Exeter, in Yaroslavl and in Hanau (all twinned cities), with a mixed nationality choir and orchestra and a Russian soprano, English tenor and German baritone in each city. This will be a major project involving hundreds of people and hours of bureaucratic negotiation re visas and other hazards.

I will no longer be travelling to Russia four or five times a year, and there will be no more visit reports but please let me know if you would like news from Russia. I intend to make a couple of visits a year to keep in touch with friends and to encourage projects, especially the Yaroslavl Hospice. FHM now has a website: www.friendshousemoscow.org, and information about Quakers in Russian can be found at www.quakers.ru. Thank you for your interest in this work and for your support over the years. And I still have a stock of toys and bowls that can be sold to raise funds for the hospice.

2005

The Ram of Pride: The War Requiem and the Triangle of Hope Project, 2005

In the 60th year since the end of the Second World War, three choirs, three chamber orchestras, three groups of choristers, with three organs, three conductors, three soloists, two symphony orchestras and a handful of organisers working in three languages called upon Wilfred Owen and Benjamin Britten to make a major anti-war statement in three countries. In short, the War Requiem was performed in a spirit of reconciliation and hope to packed audiences with a Russian soprano, a German baritone and an English tenor (in line with Britten's original vision) in Yaroslavl, on the eve of what they call Victory Day, and in her twin cities – Hanau, on the anniversary of the bombing of the city by the RAF, and Exeter, a victim of the Baedeker raids.

The two years of planning threw up many challenges, some of which seemed to us at the time to be insuperable; and there were many more hazards - visa problems, lost luggage, a missed flight, and a dodgy bus - when about 100 musicians crossed frontiers to perform with local choirs; but with a good deal of media and civic interest, the anti-war message was widely broadcast. What a rich experience it was for all of us and what friendships were made as guests enjoyed international hospitality!

Struck by the contrast between the reality of his own experiences on the battlefields of World War 1 and the deception both of heroic war poetry and official propaganda, which tended to portray the enemy as the monster which had to be destroyed at all costs, Wilfred Owen wrote: 'All a poet can do today is warn. That is why true poets must be truthful.' Aged 25, he was killed in battle on November 4th, 1918, one week before the armistice.

After World War II, Benjamin Britten too, in incorporating Owen's poems (not always complete) into his setting of the *Mass for the Dead*, was determined to shock people out of an acceptance of war and to promote the cause of peace.

The Mass, which is sung in Latin by soprano soloist and choir with full orchestra, is punctuated and at times mocked by the poems sung by the tenor and baritone accompanied by chamber orchestra. The comforting Latin words at the beginning of the Mass – praise, everlasting rest, perpetual light - are rudely interrupted by the tenor as he sings the *Anthem of Doomed Youth*: no, this is wrong - death is not like that for 'these who die like cattle':

'No mockeries for them from prayers or bells,
 Nor any voice of mourning save the choirs,
 The shrill demented choirs of wailing shells…'

The storyline of this hugely complex and moving work is simple: the English soldier (tenor) kills the German soldier (baritone) then is himself killed. The angel voices (children) intercede for their souls and the Mass comes to a satisfactory end. The strange thing is that there is no conflict between the two soldiers, the frontline protagonists of war; they have no appetite for this killing business. To a jolly marching tune, they sing together of laughter, chasing girls, taking risks: 'We whistled while he shaved us with his scythe.' These are young men bragging a little: individuals who want to live, not soldiers fighting for flags.

The conflict is between them and the authorities who decreed that they should sleep in the 'shadow of dread by a foreign riverside, while bugles sang', and the governments who caused the 'long black arm' to be raised. Chillingly the baritone declaims this poem just before a reprise at full volume of the threatening Dies Irae (the Day of Wrath) as a warning to all mankind - arrogance is the enemy, not us, the foot soldiers:

> 'Great gun towering toward heaven, about to curse;
> Reach at that arrogance which needs thy harm,
> And beat it down before its sins grow worse;
> But when thy spell be cast complete and whole,
> May God curse thee and cut thee from our soul!'

There is tension too between the Mass (organised religion) - with its strict iambic rhythm and tortured three-line rhyme pattern, its subjunctive mood and passive voice, its talk of vengeance, awe and the desperate hope of salvation on judgement day - and the mild *Recordare Jesu Pie*, the only part of the work song exclusively by women's voices: gentle Jesus who, having pardoned Mary and heeded the thief, *'mihi quoque spem dedisti'*, has given me hope too. This tension is made explicit in the poem *At a Calvary near the Ancre*: in this war, He too lost a limb, while priests 'stroll' on Golgotha, and scribes 'shove' the people,

> '…and bawl allegiance to the state,
> But they who love the greater love
> lay down their life; they do not hate.'

The contrast in attitudes between the ritual of the Mass and the reality of confusion on the battlefield is also disturbing. In the poem *Futility*, torn between love and rage, the tenor hopes that 'the kind old sun' will know how to revive a still warm corpse:

> 'Move him into the sun –
> Gently its touch awoke him once,
> At home, whispering of fields unsown…'

The simple words of this poem, reminding us of homely and wholesome activities and of the waste of young life lost, are repeatedly interrupted by a few staccato Latin words: 'rising from the ashes… guilty man… to be judged.'

The choristers beg for the deliverance of the souls of the faithful departed from the pains of hell, the bottomless pit, the darkness. The choir takes up the theme: 'But let the holy standard bearer Michael lead them into the holy light, as Thou didst promise Abraham and his seed.'

Ah yes, Abraham.

The Parable of the Old Man and the Young is the shocking retelling of the story of Abraham and Isaac. Tenor and baritone sing together the familiar words of Genesis 22 v 7, but verse 9 - 'bound Isaac, his son, and laid him on the altar' (King James) - is embellished here with a sinister warning of what is to come:

'Then Abraham bound the youth (this could be an individual or a generic term in English) with belts and straps (soldiers' uniforms), and builded parapets and trenches there and stretched forth the knife to slay his son...'

At this point, with some relief, we hear the modified words of the angel announced by the harp, and sung as a duet reminiscent of plain chant with minimal accompaniment:

'Lay not thy hand upon the lad, neither do anything to him.
Behold a ram, caught in a thicket by its horns:
Offer the Ram of Pride instead of him.'

Abraham refused to listen.

'But slew his son and half the seed of Europe one by one.'

What now? What about the oft-repeated promise God made to Abraham and his seed that souls would pass from death to life?

The baritone tests this promise by singing with due gravitas a parody of a Victorian poem, all metaphor and drama, but instead of ending with the expected victorious glory, he asks simply:

'Shall life renew these bodies?' 'Not so... mine ancient scars shall not be glorified.'

Libera me, sings the choir: 'Liberate me from eternal death on that dreadful day.'

The tenor is liberated in reverse: death releases him from the horror of life on the battlefield. He goes down into the tunnel where the dead of both sides have gathered. The baritone, recognising him, rises to meet him. In the poem *Strange Meeting* he sings the haunting line which encapsulates the essence of the War Requiem - the pity of war, the senselessness and waste:

'I am the enemy you killed, my friend.'

The two men can think now only of sleep, as the choristers, the choir and the soprano pray for them to be received into paradise and given eternal rest. The themes of the work are reconciled, and the *Amen* ends on a major chord, which many have seen as hope for the future. The conclusion of each performance in all three countries was greeted by a long moment of a respectful, some found it to be a worshipful, silence.

As many of us contemplate the ram of pride - how often have we too refused to offer this as a sacrifice? - the Triangle of Hope project continues. Exeter Festival Chorus was given a grant to work on the Home Front Recall Programme: war survivors in all three countries were interviewed after the concerts, and films of these interviews are being assembled with other material for an educational resource to be distributed free of charge to every secondary school in Devon.

AND FINALLY - THE HOSPICE IN NIZHNY NOVGOROD

AGREEMENT

Document 1

The Victor Zorza Hospice Trust ('the Grantor') in the person of Patricia Cockrell on the one hand and the Department of Health of Nizhny Novgorod ('the Grantee') in the person of the Director Vladimir Nikolaevich Lazarev ('the Project Director') on the other in signing this document have agreed to collaborate on the following project the establishment of the first hospice for oncological patients in Nizhny Novgorod ('the Project') with the aim of providing hospice care for oncological patients. The project shall be co-funded by the City Administration of Nizhny Novgorod on the one part and by a grant (hereinafter 'the Grant') not exceeding £190,000 from the Victor Zorza Hospice Trust on the other part. The Grantee undertakes to use this charitable funding from the Grantor exclusively for the purposes of achieving the goals of the project in accordance with the budget (Document 2 of the contract) and the conditions of this Agreement...

... and so on for five pages, including the transfer of funds in four tranches and the timely receipt of accounts. There were five supplementary documents.

I was chairman of the Victor Zorza Hospice Trust. Our task was to use the money left to us by Victor Zorza, the pioneer of the hospice movement in Russia, to promote the development of palliative care in the countries of the former Soviet Union. Responding to applications from Ukraine and Belarus as well as Russia, modest amounts were disbursed for trainings, publications and conferences, but when Elena Vvedenskaia contacted us from Nizhny Novgorod, I went with two other trustees to meet her and to see what opportunities there might be for a major project. We found her to be a highly skilled and energetic doctor with good networking skills, and the city of Nizhny Novgorod to be welcoming and willing to collaborate on establishing a hospice.

Victor Zorza trustees considered spending our funds and closing the Trust. Was this the right time and place to invest the rest of the money? We had never previously partnered a city administration. I went again two or three times to build confidence, to have more detailed talks with the health department and to check the budget with the mayor's finance officer. Elena would meet me each time off the night train from Moscow at 6.30am and take me home for breakfast.

In 2006 I went with another trustee to look at a building which had been identified as a potential hospice. Hospital No.47 had been largely abandoned for safety reasons. More cobwebs and rot, but I was not dismayed – there were aspects of this building which took me back full circle to the first (much smaller) hospice I had worked on in Kurba near Yaroslavl. Since our normal application form was evidently not up to this task, I told Vladimir Nikolaevich that we would need a letter of application which could be shown, if necessary, to the Charity Commission. This is what he wrote:

Dear Mrs Patricia Cockrell and dear Sirs

We would like to express our sincere gratitude for giving us the opportunity to request support for the establishment of the first hospice for oncological patients in the Nizhny Novgorod Region.

The health department has considered the question concerning the creation of a hospice and has decided that nursing hospital No.47 which the English specialists visited in September 2006 a hospice of 15 beds will be created to provide help and care for patients in the fourth stage of cancer.

The department health has made one of its objectives the creation of excellent conditions for patients in the hospice. In connection with the fact that the hospital building will require major repairs we are looking for the resources to refurbish and equip the hospital.

According to preliminary estimates the total sum required for repair will be 21 million rubles or £430,000. 7,000,000 rubles or £144,000 will be set aside in the city's budget in 2007 for the works involved in replacing the electrical supply, heating, ventilation, sewerage, water supply, roof repairs and other works. Ten million rubles or £208,000 are planned to be set aside from the local budget in 2008 for works to grounds and the building itself.

We will be very grateful if you could give us financial support in carrying out reconstruction and repair work on the ground floor of the building where the patients' wards will be situated together with a treatment room, kitchens, and also to obtain necessary equipment.

According to preliminary estimates the cost of this work together with materials and architect's costs will amount to 7.9 million rubles or £158,000. In addition the acquisition of hospital beds, bedside tables and anti-bedsore mattresses for 15 patients will cost 350,000 rubles or £7000. A detailed list of expenses is attached.

We understand that this is a large sum of money but we would like to create in the city's first hospice excellent conditions to enable us to look after patients to train specialists to give qualified palliative care so that this hospice could become a model and a stimulus for further hospices in our city and region and in other Russian cities.

With sincere respect and gratitude
Director of Nizhny Novgorod Health Department V.N. Lazarev

It took more than three months to agree the contract partly because of cultural differences and the need of both sides to sign an agreement that would be acceptable to our governing bodies – the Charity Commission for us and the government of Nizhny Novgorod Region (population 3.3m) for them. A major stumbling block was the currency to be used for accounts. VZHT agreed that funds would be sent to Russia in euros and that accounts could be submitted in rubles. What to do about the fluctuating rates of exchange? My experience on the receiving end of TACIS grants from Brussels showed me how painful it is to budget for something and then to cut back because of the fall in the international value of the ruble; on the other hand, VZHT had a finite amount of money. For our part, we wanted to include a budget line for staff training but had to admit that this was an unnecessary complication: trainings could be accounted for separately. I went again to sign the contract with the mayor of Nizhny Novgorod, the deputy mayor, the director of the health department and the chief doctor.

The same view before and after. Wide doors, covered balconies and ramps so that patients can be brought outside in their beds, an idea borrowed from the Exeter Hospice.

This project took nearly three years. What a party we had after the TV interviews and the opening ceremony in 2008 – music, dancing, drinking, eating, speeches and a boat trip on the Volga!

When we met in London, the professor of palliative medicine in Moscow told me there are now 50 hospices in Russia. Well, slava Bogu!

Ingram Content Group UK Ltd.
Milton Keynes UK
UKHW041955240523
422293UK00004B/238

9 781800 310285